But I Thought You Meant . . .

But I Thought You Meant...

MISUNDERSTANDINGS IN HUMAN COMMUNICATION

. . .

JULIA T. WOOD

The University of North Carolina at Chapel Hill

Mayfield Publishing Company
Mountain View, California
London • Toronto

Library of Congress Cataloging-in-Publication Data
Wood, Julia T.
     But I thought you meant . . . : misunderstandings in human
communication / Julia T. Wood.
        p.   cm.
     Includes index.
     ISBN 1-55934-968-9
     1. Miscommunication.   I. Title.
P91.W66   1997
302.2—dc21   97-30504
                                                                  CIP

Manufactured in the United States of America
10 9 8 7 6 5 4 3 2 1

Mayfield Publishing Company
1280 Villa Street
Mountain View, California 94041

Sponsoring editor, Holly J. Allen; production editor, April Wells-Hayes;
manuscript editor, Patterson Lamb; art director, Jeanne M. Schreiber;
text designer, Laurie Anderson; cover designer, Joan Greenfield; illus-
trators, Robin Mouat and Angela Ng-Quinn; manufacturing manager,
Randy Hurst. The text was set in 10½/13 Electra by TBH Typecast, Inc.,
and printed on 50# Text White Opaque by The Maple-Vail Book Manufacturing Group.

For Cam

who has taught me a great deal about ways
I misunderstood his generation and who has
helped me gain insight into the issues,
values, and music that frame his life.

CONTENTS

TO THE INSTRUCTOR

I wrote this book to help students become more informed and skillful communicators in a diverse social world. *But I Thought You Meant . . .* focuses on some common misunderstandings that surface in communication among people who have diverse backgrounds, experiences, perspectives, and identities. Students should become more aware of how and why misunderstandings arise in communication among people whose dissimilar backgrounds and identities lead them to have disparate views of what communication means and does. Knowing about sources of human differences should help students reduce misunderstandings in their communication with and about others.

This book is appropriate as a supplement to courses in a variety of areas, including interpersonal communication, culture and communication, gender and communication, social diversity, introduction to communication, and relational communication. The chapters amplify and extend various course emphases by examining particular kinds of misunderstandings (for instance, different interpretations of interrupting or of what family means) and showing how they occur in varied contexts such as the workplace, mass communication, personal relationships, and social situations.

Special Features of This Book

But I Thought You Meant . . .: Misunderstandings in Human Communication differs from many textbooks in three ways that I want to call to your attention.

Goals One distinguishing feature of this book is its purpose. Because my goal is to raise students' awareness of misunderstandings in human communication, I don't attempt to analyze every misunderstanding comprehensively. Instead, each chapter aims to provoke insight into the many forms of and reasons for a particular misunderstanding. Individual instructors may elaborate the specific issues related to misunderstandings that are most relevant to their particular courses and teaching goals.

Because my goal is to explain specific kinds of misunderstandings, chapters are shorter than those in most textbooks. The brevity of each chapter allows me to focus on a distinct type of misunderstanding and to sketch the reasons it occurs, what consequences it may have, and how we may lessen the likelihood that it will occur in our interactions.

For example, Chapter 7, "It's Only Skin Deep," concentrates on misunderstandings that arise when we rely on stereotypes or have a tendency to totalize—to perceive and deal with only one aspect of a person. I show how this kind of misunderstanding surfaces in interpersonal encounters, mass communication, and interaction in the workplace. I also illustrate how this misunderstanding operates in communication between people of different races, social classes, religions, and sexual orientations and how it appears in interaction between able-bodied people and people with disabilities.

The range of issues related to each misunderstanding cannot be examined exhaustively in the space of a single short chapter. Because each chapter surveys many issues related to misunderstandings, instructors can tailor class discussion to highlight the issues and contexts of special concern to them and their courses.

Writing Style   Writing style is a second special feature of *But I Thought You Meant* . . . . I've adopted a very conversational tone because I want to engage the reader personally. Throughout the book I share some of my own experiences, including misunderstandings I've confronted in my personal, social, and professional communication. I want students to know that, like them, I sometimes get tangled up in misunderstandings. I refer to myself as "I" rather than "the author" because use of the third person distances me from students and suggests that I am removed from what I write about. I want students to realize that, as with any author, my values, attitudes, beliefs, thoughts, feelings, and experiences affect what I think and write.

Into the chapters I also weave stories from friends and students who have encountered misunderstandings in their lives. More than 20 years of teaching have taught me that concrete illustrations are among the most effective ways to clarify conceptual points. Thus, I rely heavily on stories to show how and why misunderstandings can happen when people communicate in an era marked by social diversity.

In this book I've also tried to avoid extensive use of technical language. In *But I Thought You Meant . . .* I use few specialized words, preferring instead to explore important ideas and issues using ordinary language. When I think it is necessary to use a specialized term, I explain what it means and show why that term is more useful than a less technical one.

Research and Citations   One of the most frequent and emphatic student complaints about textbooks is that research citations are intrusive. Many students dislike APA citations because parentheses within paragraphs disrupt the flow of ideas. Again and again, students ask me, "Why can't authors just talk about the issues and put the references at the end?" Although it took a while, my students persuaded me that the APA format isn't the only way to acknowledge research. In this book, I use parenthetical citations only to indicate page numbers when I quote a source verbatim. When I discuss specific scholars' work extensively, I identify the writers by name in the text, often mentioning their research programs and disciplinary affiliations.

At the end of each chapter I identify all research that contributes to my discussion. The end-of-chapter references include current as well as classic works. You will also note that I draw on interdisciplinary research, although scholarship in the field of communication is particularly prominent. My experience has shown me that this form of acknowledging research makes the book accessible and engaging to students.

Acknowledgments

To be accurate, the cover and title page of this book should list all the people who contributed to my thinking and writing. Unfortunately, book covers aren't large enough to allow me to do that, so here I want to acknowledge some individuals who have clarified, corrected, and enriched my thinking about misunderstandings in communication. First on that list is Holly Allen, my editor at Mayfield. When I proposed this book to Holly in the autumn of 1996, she immediately grasped what I wanted to do and provided enthusiastic support that has never waned. Holly gave direction to this project, and her thoughtful responses to early drafts encouraged me to make substantive refinements that improved the final book.

Along with Holly, others on the publishing team have made substantial contributions. Patterson Lamb's copyediting is simply superb. More often than I like to admit, she untangled my prose so that the ideas are clearer and more forceful. Others whose talents and dedication were invaluable are April Wells-Hayes, production editor; Vicki Moran of Publishing Support Services; and Pam Lucas, editorial assistant.

I am also indebted to the generous and insightful reviews of early drafts provided by Walid Afifi, University of Delaware; Kathryn Dindia, University of Wisconsin, Milwaukee; Katrina M. Eicher, Elizabethtown Community College; Robert J. Glenn, III, Owensboro Community College; Elizabeth Graham, Ohio University; Laura Guerrero, Arizona State University; and Elizabeth J. Natalle, University of North Carolina at Greensboro.

I also acknowledge Walter Carl, who is the author of Chapter 15, "A Sign of the Times," which focuses on misunderstandings between hearing and Deaf communicators. Walter has generously shared his knowledge of the Deaf culture with me, and he has helped me recognize its distinctive character. I could not have written a chapter on the topic of Deaf communication, but I thought one belonged in this book. Fortunately, Walter had the experience and writing ability to author it.

And, as always, I am grateful to the people at the center of my life. Their presence, ideas, and support make it possible for me to learn ever more about communication and to write about what I learn. Robbie Cox, my partner for 26 years (and, I hope, for many more), is an unfailing source of support and a perceptive and thoughtful critic. Along with Robbie, my life is blessed by close friends who work with me to explore and straighten out the misunderstandings that arise in our relationships. Thank you, Carolyn, Linda, Becker, Shelly, and Nancy.

Julia T. Wood

TO THE READER

In opening this book, you've made a choice to learn more about misunderstandings in communication. The insights you gain into how and why misunderstandings occur will enable you to reduce misunderstandings in your own thinking and interactions. In addition, learning about the sources of misunderstandings will enhance your appreciation of social diversity and the varying communication patterns it fosters.

A Personal Introduction

This book explores a variety of topics, some of which are challenging and controversial. Because dealing with challenges to our values and identities is difficult, you should anticipate some discomfort. I've experienced moments of uneasiness in reflecting on some of the topics in the chapters that follow. The way I was brought up made me resistant even to thinking about some issues that I discuss in this book; yet I don't want to let my background limit my growth, so I struggle to learn about people and communication patterns that are unfamiliar to me.

Perhaps knowing something about me will allow you to understand why I wrote this book and why it's worthwhile for all of us to tolerate the difficulty of thinking about challenging issues. I am a 47-year-old European American woman; I've been in love with the same man for 26 years and married to him for 22 of those years. Along with my partner Robbie, my immediate family consists of my sister Carolyn; my niece Michelle; my nephews Cam, Daniel, and Keenan; Madhi-the-wonder-dog; and two cats who named themselves Sadie Ladie and Wicca. These people, along with friends Nancy, Linda, and Shelley, form the center of my life.

At 24 I earned my Ph.D. and joined the Department of Communication Studies at the University of North Carolina at Chapel Hill, where I have enjoyed and continue to enjoy both teaching and research. Teaching is a passion for me. Introducing students to perspectives and skills that help them communicate better and interpret the communication of others more effectively is one of the most gratifying things I do.

I also conduct research and write, activities that allow me to learn more about human communication and to share what I learn with others. Teaching and research complement each other. What I learn from research enhances what I have to offer students in my classes. At the same time, issues my students raise and questions they pose stimulate my research and writing.

In fact, my students' questions and reflections prompted me to write this book. In my courses, students frequently discuss problems they encounter when they interact with others. Many of the problems that concern them arise from misunderstandings in communication — instances in which they and others don't assign the same meanings to verbal and nonverbal behavior. In other words, many — though not all — misunderstandings in communication arise from discrepant meanings. The chapters in this book address some of the insightful and challenging questions my students have posed to me.

I should also introduce Walter Carl, who is the author of Chapter 15, "A Sign of the Times," which deals with communication by and about Deaf people. As an undergraduate, Walter served as a resident assistant in a residence hall with many Deaf students. He learned ASL (American Sign Language), and he learned about Deaf culture (read his Chapter 15 if you want to know why I'm capitalizing "Deaf"). I didn't have the knowledge or experience to write a chapter on communication by and about members of the Deaf culture, so I felt very fortunate when Walter agreed to do so.

An Introduction to This Book

The purpose of this book is to enhance your understanding of different meanings that people may attribute to what they say and do. Effective communication begins with realizing that words and nonverbal behaviors can mean different things to different people. Diversity in how we communicate reflects individual and cultural contexts in which we learn to communicate. Some differences in meanings reflect our unique experiences in relationships and in life. For example, if members of your family engaged in frequent touching and hugging, then you may consider nonverbal displays of affection to be very natural actions. On the other hand, if there was little or no physical affection displayed in your family, you may be uncomfortable hugging or kissing friends, especially when others are present.

Other differences in meaning arise because people participate in different social communities often defined by ethnic heritage, gender, economic class, (dis)ability, sexual orientation, and age. For example, Hispanic cultures tend to be more communal than European American cultures. Thus, the assertion and individualism that many Westerners admire may be perceived as self-centered behavior by people raised in Hispanic societies.

In the chapters that follow, we'll explore differences that arise from both personal and social influences. A key assumption of this book is that effective communication is based in large measure on our willingness to learn about differences among people and the diverse styles of communicating those differences prompt. When we open our minds and hearts to other ways of living and interacting, we learn much that enriches not only our understanding of others but also our insight into ourselves.

Psychiatrist Robert Coles relates a story that shows what we can learn from people who differ from us. He describes a conversation he had with a 10-year-old Hopi girl. Coles asked her what her religion meant.

"The sky watches us and listens to us. It talks to us, and it hopes we are ready to talk back. . . . Our God is the sky, and lives wherever the sky is. Our God is the sun and the moon, too; and our God is our people [the Hopi], if we remember to stay here [on sacred Hopi lands]. This is where we're supposed to be, and if we leave, we lose God."

Coles asked the young girl if she had explained this to her Anglo teacher.

"No."

"Why?"

"Because—she thinks God is a person. If I'd told her, she'd give us that smile."

"What smile?"

"The smile that says to us, 'You kids are cute, but you're dumb; you're different and you're all wrong.'"

"Perhaps you could have explained to her what you've just explained to me."

"We tried that a long time ago; our people spoke to the Anglos and told them what we think, but they don't listen to us; they listen to hear themselves" (p. 25).

Coles's story illustrates several key principles. First, it shows how often we judge people who differ from us as wrong, inferior, or dumb. Second, the story shows that our preconceptions can prevent us from understanding others on their own terms. Third, the story teaches us that we are the losers when we discount perspectives that differ from ours. We lose the possibility of enlarging our horizons by considering ideas that arise from different circumstances and experiences. Thus, we are diminished.

Learning about and respecting differences in communication is important for all of us, but it isn't a cure-all that will neatly resolve all problems in human relationships. There are circumstances in which people understand each other perfectly well, but they still disagree, perhaps even violently. There are also situations in which our own values may make it difficult or impossible for us to respect what others feel, believe, and do. For example, we may find ourselves unable to respect people who engage in hate speech (discussed in Chapter 2). Even so, we can increase our insight into why they do what they do. That alone is a worthwhile goal. Although understanding differences does not remove them, it is a starting point for competent participation in a diverse social world.

How to Read This Book

The book is organized into four parts. The six chapters in Part 1 introduce you to concepts and principles of communication that are necessary for studying misunderstandings. Part 2 includes four chapters that show how perceptions and misperceptions can lead to misunderstandings between people. In Part 3 we explore misunderstandings that arise because people belong to different social groups that socialize them into distinct ways of communicating. Finally, Part 4 focuses on misunderstandings that are common in families and romantic relationships. Taken together, these four parts offer information that will allow you to reflect on how you communicate and to learn about other ways of communicating. In turn, this enables you to increase your understanding of yourself, others, and our richly pluralistic social world.

But I Thought You Meant . . . differs from many textbooks. One difference is that the chapters are shorter than usual. The brevity of each chapter allows us to focus closely on a specific type of misunderstanding and to sketch what it involves, why it occurs, and what consequences it may have. You may choose to reflect at greater length on some of these topics than others.

Another feature of this book is the conversational writing style. You'll notice that I depart from standard academic writing in favor of a style that is more accessible (after all, this book *is* about understanding!). For example, I use contractions, as we do in normal conversation. I also refer to myself as "I" rather than "the author." To illustrate ideas, I share stories from friends and students, and I describe some of the misunderstandings I've confronted in my own communication. Just like you, I sometimes have misunderstandings in my relationships. Writing in a personal style lets me show you that my values, attitudes, beliefs, thoughts, feelings, and experiences affect what I think and write.

I use nontechnical language whenever possible. My students tell me they have difficulty understanding books that are filled with technical words. Academics—like members of any profession—sometimes need specialized terms to be precise. However, technical terms aren't always necessary, so I use ordinary language as much as is appropriate. When a specialized word is called for, I explain it and give concrete examples so that you understand what I mean.

My students also complain that the conventional way of citing research interrupts the flow of ideas in a book. Perhaps, like you, my students want solid research to support what they read, but they dislike having source citations in the middle of paragraphs. For instance, authors (Wood, 1997) typically discuss an idea (Smartie, 1989) and include citations (Footnote, 1998; Reference, 1996; Bibliography, 1994) within the discussion (Talker, 1990) so that the sentence (Grammar, 1992) is difficult to read.

In this book I use parentheses only to reference direct quotations of others' words. When I highlight a particular individual's work, I mention that person by name and tell you something about him or her. At the end of each chapter, I list the research informing that chapter so you will know where to find more information on topics that interest you.

I hope you find that the writing style of this book allows you to engage the ideas we discuss. If so, then you should gain insight into yourself and the dynamic and sometimes confusing nature of human communication.

Reference

Coles, R. (1990). *The spiritual life of children.* Boston: Houghton Mifflin.

PART 1

Basic Communication

Concepts and Principles

| 1 |

WHAT WE HAVE HERE IS A FAILURE

TO COMMUNICATE*

. . .

A Framework for Studying

Misunderstandings in Communication

A few weeks ago I was trying to write an essay, but I just couldn't get it started. I had writer's block. In frustration, I left my office and went to talk about the problem with my friend Rick.

"I'm stuck," I grumbled.

"Maybe you should make an outline," he suggested.

"I just don't think I can write this paper," I said.

"Why don't you start with a concrete case that's interesting?"

"The problem isn't getting a good case. The problem is that I don't seem to be able to write," I muttered.

"Then why don't you put it aside for now and try to write it later when you're in the mood?" Rick suggested.

"I wish you'd quit telling me what to do and give me some support," I replied in frustration.

He looked perplexed. "I thought I *was* supporting you."

---

*From the film *Cool Hand Luke*, 1967, Warner Brothers.

Was Rick supporting me or not? Why didn't I understand the support he thought he was giving? Why didn't Rick understand what would feel supportive to me? He was trying to help by giving me advice and concrete suggestions for how to combat my writer's block. What I wanted, however, were sympathy and assurance that he understood my frustration at not being able to write. What might we have done to understand better what the other one meant?

Misunderstandings such as the one between Rick and me are common. We communicate with others continuously. We use words and nonverbal behaviors to express ourselves, and we interpret the words and nonverbal behaviors of others to figure out what they are telling us. When everything goes smoothly, we understand what others mean and they understand us.

Yet things don't always go smoothly. Sometimes we say something and another person misunderstands us. Perhaps we intend to joke and a friend thinks we are serious; then, he is hurt. Perhaps we ask a question out of interest and another person feels we are challenging her. In other cases, people say things to us and we're not sure what they mean. We feel frustrated and confused. We don't know exactly what's going wrong, and we're even less sure how to set things right.

This book is about misunderstandings in human communication. In it, we discuss some of the misunderstandings that can plague everyday interactions. We explore some of the reasons for misunderstandings so that we learn how to reduce them in our lives. And we consider what misunderstandings can teach us about how to engage in effective communication and build healthy relationships.

In this chapter, we establish the framework for the book. First, we discuss communication. Next, we define misunderstandings in communication and explore some of the reasons they occur. Third, we consider the value of misunderstandings, discovering that they can lead us to better insight into ourselves and others.

What Is Communication?

Although we communicate all the time, we aren't always effective communicators. Communicating may be natural — after all, we do it continuously. Yet communicating well is neither natural nor simple. That's because effective communication is a very complex process that requires knowledge and skill. This chapter and the others in Part 1 of this book present basic perspectives and ideas important to understanding communication. Let's begin by discussing three concepts that are central to human communication: meanings, dynamism, and systems or contexts.

Meanings

The word *communicate* means *to commune*, or *to make common*. When we communicate with another person, we seek to create common perception of feelings, attitudes, goals, desires, ideas, experiences, and so forth. The heart of human communication is meaning. We need to express ourselves in ways that others will understand. This is true whether our communication is to inform or persuade others or to express our feelings and nurture relationships.

We use verbal and nonverbal communication to share thoughts, feelings, events in our lives, and other information. We cannot give our actual emotions, thoughts, and experiences to someone. There's no way another person can enter our minds or hearts, so we rely on symbols (words and nonverbal behaviors) to express our feelings, ideas, and experiences to people. They, in turn, interpret our symbols in an effort to grasp those feelings, ideas, and experiences. When we and others have similar meanings for symbols, we will probably understand each other. When our meanings differ, however, misunderstandings may arise. So, one key to effective communication is creating shared meanings.

To say that effective communication involves shared meanings is not to suggest that meanings must be identical. Because people are unique, they seldom, if ever, have exactly the same meaning as others for anything. As we communicate with others in our personal and social contexts, however, we learn the general meanings that symbols have in our communities. We may tailor general social meanings to fit our individual experiences, but we still share the broad meanings of our social communities.

Dynamism

Dynamism is another feature of communication. The process of communication is continuously changing, evolving, moving ever onward. Heraclitus, an ancient Greek philosopher, declared that we can never ford the same river twice because new waters flow in, making the river different from the way it was when we first stepped into it.

In much the same way, communication never stays the same. What happened in previous communication encounters and in specific relationships affects what we say now, what we mean, and how others interpret our verbal and nonverbal communication. The meaning of what we said a moment ago changes as we say more to elaborate, explain, correct, or qualify our earlier words. What we plan to say or do in the future affects how we express ourselves in the present moment. For example, if we anticipate a continuing relationship with a particular person, we may communicate with that person differently now from the way we would with someone we think we'll never meet again. Communication, then, is always tied to what came before and it always anticipates what may come later.

The dynamic quality of communication keeps it open to revision. If someone misunderstands our words or nonverbal behavior, we can say or do something to clarify our meaning. If we don't understand another person's communication, we can look puzzled to show our confusion or ask questions to discover what the other person meant. Communication is dynamic, so when misunderstandings arise, we can continue to interact to increase our mutual understanding.

Systems

Finally, communication occurs within systems, or contexts, that affect meanings. We do not communicate in a vacuum. We speak our words and use our nonverbal behaviors in particular cultures, situations, times, and relationships, all of which affect how we communicate and interpret the communication of others.

In many Asian and Native American cultures, for example, looking directly at another person is considered rude. Within mainstream culture in the United States, however, eye contact is a sign of respect and honesty. The meaning of looking directly at another person depends on cultural context. Formal greetings are appropriate in business situations, but they are not customary in close friendships or romantic relationships. The relationship within which we communicate affects how we express ourselves and what is considered normal and acceptable.

John Muir, founder of the Sierra Club, once observed that when you touch anything you find it is "hitched to the universe." By this, Muir meant that nature is a whole in which all parts are interconnected and interacting. The same is true of communication. All facets of communica-

tion are connected to one another. If we change the setting from an office to an intimate dinner, our communication will change. If communicators alter their nonverbal behaviors, the feelings between them may change as may their verbal behaviors.

The same words and actions mean different things in various contexts, cultures, and relationships. Because all parts of communication are connected, we cannot understand communication simply by looking at verbal and nonverbal behaviors. Instead, we must examine influences such as cultural context, social group, relationship, time of day, and setting. Each of these factors influences both how we communicate and how we interpret the communication of others.

In the chapters that follow, we explore communication as a dynamic process that occurs within systems and that involves efforts to create understandings by sharing meanings; but first, we need to consider misunderstandings that can undermine our efforts to communicate effectively.

What Are Misunderstandings in Communication?

We frequently hear people refer to *miscommunication, failures to communicate,* and *communication breakdowns.* Despite the widespread use of such terms, they are imprecise and even misleading. After all, communication doesn't break down simply because people don't understand each other. It continues—though perhaps not as effectively as we would like. As a foundation for our discussion, we need a clear perspective on misunderstandings in communication.

Not All Problems Are Communication Problems

At the outset, we should realize that not all human problems are the result of misunderstandings in communication. Too often we hear the naive claim that communication can solve all problems or that what is needed is better communication. In reality, however, not all problems are communication problems. Some of the tensions that plague human interaction do not result from lack of understanding in communication.

In many situations, people understand each other perfectly well, but they disagree on values, goals, or courses of action. In such cases, misunderstanding isn't the problem. A good example of problems that aren't caused by misunderstandings in communication comes from the film *Cool Hand Luke*. Since its 1967 release, this film has achieved status as a classic.

In an early scene, the supervisor of a prison chain gang is irritated by a sassy remark made by an inmate named Luke. The supervisor strikes Luke hard enough that Luke falls to the ground. Looking at Luke's prostrate body, the supervisor says, "What we've got here is failure to communicate." The supervisor means, of course, that what Luke said didn't please him. The communication between them is crystal clear. There is no misunderstanding.

In perhaps the most memorable scene from the film, Luke has escaped for a third time and is cornered in a church, surrounded by law officers who are poised to shoot him. An officer orders Luke to surrender. Luke smiles devilishly, then repeats the supervisor's words in a mocking tone: "What we got here is a failure to communicate." Again, the communication is clear. Luke and the officer understand each other perfectly well. Both the supervisor in the earlier scene and Luke in the climax are speaking ironically. They know misunderstanding isn't the problem.

In this book, we don't explore problems such as the one between Luke and his supervisor or between him and the officer. We aren't concerned with the many problems in human life that neither reflect nor result from misunderstandings. Instead, we focus on genuine misunderstandings — instances in which people who are communicating don't share meanings.

Sources of Misunderstanding in Communication

We've seen that understanding involves shared (though not identical) meanings. It follows that misunderstandings in communication occur when people don't share meanings. When we and others do not understand communication in the same ways, we are likely to be confused, hurt, offended, or otherwise unsatisfied. Misunderstandings can arise because of personal differences between communicators and differences in social and cultural groups.

Personal Sources of Misunderstanding   Many misunderstandings in communication arise from individual differences in backgrounds, experiences, values, and beliefs. Because we are unique, inevitably we will sometimes communicate in ways that others misunderstand and we will sometimes misunderstand others' communication. My mother grew up during the Great Depression and she learned to conserve whenever possible. She used the back of every piece of paper and often scolded me if I threw away a sheet of paper that was "only half used." (When recycling became popular late in mother's life, she reminded me that her generation had started it.) Her personal experience of living through the Depression affected her perceptions and her communication. Because I didn't have her experience or perceptions, we sometimes had different meanings.

In my family, friendly bantering and jesting insults were a standard form of communication. To us, verbal jabs were a sign of affection and connection, and they were a game of wits we enjoyed. In my partner Robbie's family, however, bantering was not commonplace. When he and I first began seeing each other, he was sometimes hurt by my playful insults, and I was often disappointed that he wouldn't reciprocate and "play the game." Eventually we learned to interpret each other's reactions and to adjust our styles of communicating with each other. The misunderstanding between us arose from differences in personal backgrounds.

Misunderstandings that arise from personal differences are especially significant in close friendships and committed romantic relationships because we expect those who love us to understand our idiosyncratic meanings, needs, and motives. If we are to develop and sustain healthy intimacy, we must understand personal differences. People who care about each other should invest the time and energy to explain their own personal meaning systems and to accommodate their partners'.

In this book, we consider some misunderstandings that reflect personal differences—our unique individual experiences, relationships, and ways of perceiving. Part 3 consists of chapters that examine misunderstandings in romantic and family relationships. Exploring these should help us appreciate many of the subjective influences on communication.

Social Sources of Misunderstanding   As important as they are, individual differences are not the only sources of misunderstandings in communication. A great many misunderstandings arise from and reflect communicators' membership in different social groups. It is in social groups, such as ones defined by gender, ethnicity, religion, sexual orientation, and economic class, that we learn how to communicate and interpret others' communication.

Each of us belongs to a number of social groups that affect how we perceive ourselves, others, and the world, and influence how we communicate. Misunderstandings often emerge because individuals belong to distinct social groups that teach different ways of communicating and interpreting the communication of others.

For example, masculine and feminine socializations tend to emphasize different ways of telling stories. In general, men are socialized to tell stories in a relatively linear manner and to focus only or primarily on major events. Women typically are socialized to tell stories in a less straightforward fashion and to include many details in addition to major events. Thus, it is not an individual misunderstanding but a gender-based misunderstanding when Jake is frustrated that Sally doesn't tell him about her day in a concise manner (Chapter 14 elaborates this misunderstanding).

Emily, a white woman, may misunderstand and be hurt when her African American friend Shenetta breaks a movie date so she can go home for her grandmother's 70th birthday party. If Emily is like many white people, she may not regard grandparents as part of the immediate family. If Shenetta is like many African Americans, her grandparents are almost as close as her parents (Chapter 16 discusses these differing perceptions). The misunderstanding between Shenetta and Emily arises from differences that are not personal, but that reflect teachings typical of their distinct ethnic groups.

For many years, scholars have studied misunderstandings that result from people's membership in different social groups. Research on this kind of misunderstanding is generally based on standpoint theory—a commonsense explanation of differences that result from belonging to discrete groups. According to standpoint theory, a society consists of many social groups that distinctively shape members' ways of communicating and understanding themselves, others, and the world.

Probably the earliest standpoint theorist was German philosopher Georg Wilhelm Friedrich Hegel. Hegel explained standpoint with the example of a slave and a master. Both the slave and master participated in the slave-master relationship and were members of a common overall society. Yet, noted Hegel, their membership in separate social groups (slaves as an indentured working class and masters as a privileged class) led them to perceive the relationship quite differently. Masters could not appreciate the conditions of slaves' lives or how slaves perceived members of privileged classes. Masters had no comprehension of being hungry, cold, or forcibly wrenched from their children. Masters had a vested interest in not seeing the inhumanity of slavery, as that system was essential to sustaining the privileges the masters enjoyed. Slaves, on the other hand, were likely to view masters and the system of slavery as inhumane and exploitive. Slaves also might have been unable to comprehend a life of luxury, economic security, and property ownership.

Insight from Hegel's example of slaves and masters can be generalized to other social groups. How we understand ourselves, others, and society reflects the groups we belong to or have belonged to for significant periods of time. These groups shape how, when, and why we communicate. They also influence the meaning that different kinds of communication have for us. Because people are socialized in different groups, they have different understandings about communication. Thus, we should not be surprised when people from different social groups communicate and misunderstandings occur.

Linguists Jennifer Coates and Deborah Cameron have identified specifically feminine rules of communication — ones that women routinely (though not universally) learn and that men just as routinely do not learn. For example, Coates and Cameron pointed out that women typically use more standard pronunciation and grammar than men do. Women's greater attention to proper speech may reflect efforts to increase their status. Educator Scott Swain has reported patterns of expressing affection that are common among men but are less typical of women. He noted, for instance, that men tend to show care by doing material favors for friends, rather than talking about feelings which is more common between women friends. Sociologist Patricia Hill Collins has shown that black feminist scholars notice academic practices that white scholars may not perceive because those practices are routine in white but not black communities. For example, Collins pointed out that white sociologists focus on middle-class white contexts, which do not provide information about the sociological behaviors of many working-class and minority Americans.

Qualified Generalizations

We need to be careful not to overgeneralize about the impact of a person's membership in particular social groups. Although our social groups affect how we communicate and what the communication of others means to us, we should not assume that every member of a social group reflects all the communication practices generally typical of that group. The three conditions discussed next can explain why such assumptions could be misleading.

Multiple Group Memberships   First, our communication reflects the influence of more than one social group. All of us belong to multiple groups, so we learn a variety of communication styles and meanings for them. Emily is white and female; therefore, gender and ethnic groups may influence her verbal and nonverbal behaviors. Her identity and communication are also influenced by economic class, sexual orientation, religion, age, and other factors. Shenetta is African American and female, yet membership in those two groups is only part of who she is and how she communicates. We get into trouble when we fail to consider the multiplicity of influences a person may be reflecting.

The word *totalizing* refers to the practice of defining someone or something by a single factor. When we totalize, we act as if a particular aspect of a person is the totality of that individual. For example, if we refer to someone as gay and think only of his being gay, we totalize the individual on the basis of his sexual orientation. As a result, we are less likely to perceive the many other aspects of that individual that are beyond the totalizing label we have imposed. Chapter 7 discusses totalizing in more detail.

Differences Within Groups   Second, social groups are not homogeneous; everyone in them is not identical. There are many variations among people we lump together under the label of Native Americans. This label includes Lumbee, Cherokee, Iroquois, Cree, Apache, and other distinct Native American tribes. Not only are there differences among tribes, but there are also differences within each specific tribe. Elders in many Native American tribes have different values, experiences, and perspectives from those of younger members of the tribe. Men and women in a single tribe may have different status, roles, and experiences.

The same kind of differentiation characterizes members of other social groups. A 1997 cover story in *Newsweek* highlighted differences among African Americans. Authors John Leland and Allison Samuels documented a generation gap that differentiates older and younger African Americans. According to Leland and Samuels, many young African Americans identify with hip-hop and rap culture and their parents despise it. The African American community is further divided by economics. Civil rights legislation and increased opportunities for education have allowed many African Americans to live well: Today there are four times as many black families with annual incomes over $50,000 as there were in 1967. At the same time, other African Americans have not shared in this prosperity. The benefits of increased opportunities have been unequally experienced by this ethnic group.

Group labels are useful, perhaps even necessary, as they allow us to recognize commonalities among members of groups. Such recognition is essential for political alliances and arguments, which use labels to speak of groups and issues — "the working poor," "women's interests," and "discrimination against minorities." Group labels do have practical value, but they can also limit our ability to perceive differences among members of a group. A good general principle is to remember that a group label describes a range of individuals who have both commonalities and differences.

Essentialist Thinking   A third reason to qualify generalizations about social groups is what scholars call the danger of essentializing. We essentialize when we assume some characteristic or set of characteristics is the essence, or essential nature, of all members of a group. For example, to presume that loving children is the essence of being a woman is to essentialize all women by that single quality. Many women (and men) do love children, but this is not true of all members of either sex. A very important element of understanding is realizing that not every member of a social group follows all the communication practices generally associated with that group. Some men communicate in ways that are often considered feminine, and some women communicate in ways generally associated with men. Many Asians, Latinos and Latinas, and members of other groups do not use exclusively the communication styles of their social groups. Within any group, there will be differences that reflect personal experiences as well as members' participation in other groups.

The extent to which a particular group shapes an individual's communication may also vary over time. For example, a person who lived the first six years of life in Senegal might learn many communication practices common to certain African groups. If that person moves to the United States at the age of 5, he or she may learn many Western perspectives and ways of interacting and may rely less on traditionally African forms of communication. We can summarize our discussion by emphasizing that membership in a group (or groups) affects communication, but it is not the only and not necessarily a permanent influence on how any individual communicates.

Despite the variations we have noted, social groups affect who we are and how we communicate. Thus, we need to understand how different social groups communicate if we want to be effective in our increasingly pluralistic world. Part 2 of this book focuses on misunderstandings that arise from our ways of perceiving and interpreting others, and Part 3 includes chapters that analyze misunderstandings reflecting membership in and identification with different social groups. If we learn about meanings of diverse social groups and learn to respect the legitimacy of alternative communication styles, differences need not condemn us to misunderstandings.

What Can Misunderstandings Teach Us?

Many people think misunderstandings are undesirable. True, they can make us uncomfortable and we try to resolve them. But misunderstandings can also enrich our insight into ourselves, others, and the rich diversity of social life.

Insight into Ourselves

In the example that opened this chapter, I talked with Rick and he didn't support me in the way I wanted. I felt frustrated, but I didn't realize why. I couldn't articulate what was wrong, and I fussed at him for not supporting me. But our conversation didn't end there. I continued to think about what had happened between us. My reflections led me to a clearer understanding of what I had wanted from Rick. Later, I went back to his office.

"I hope you're not having another writing block," Rick said with a smile.

"No; I wanted to talk about what happened this morning. I was upset that you weren't supporting me—or that I didn't feel you were," I corrected myself. "So I tried to figure out what I wanted from you."

"And," he prompted.

"I think I wanted sympathy more than solutions."

The misunderstanding Rick and I experienced enriched my knowledge of my needs and motives. As a result, I have more insight into myself—insight that can help me communicate more clearly with Rick and other people in my life. I learned something about what I want from others when I am frustrated, so now I can express my needs with greater precision.

Misunderstanding also occurred between Emily and Shenetta. If they talk about the misunderstanding, Emily is likely to gain insight into how she views family. As long as she does not encounter someone with a different view of family, Emily will regard her own view as normal and perhaps as the only perspective. By exploring differences in how she and Shenetta define family, Emily can learn about herself. When misunderstandings crop up in communication, they are opportunities to learn about ourselves.

Insight into Others

Misunderstandings also invite us to learn about other people. When we don't understand others' communication, this failing is a clue that we don't understand something about them as people. And that is an invitation, an opportunity, to find out more about them. As my second conversation with Rick continued, we each discovered more about the other.

"Why would you tell me about your problem if you didn't want advice on how to fix it?" He was clearly puzzled.

"I might like advice later, but first I wanted to ventilate my frustration and have you understand how I felt," I explained.

"How would that help you overcome your writer's block?" he asked, still trying to figure out my needs.

"I'm not sure it would, but it would have made me feel connected to you. Because you're my friend, I wanted to know that you understood what I was feeling."

He nodded. "I think I get it now. So if you come into my office frustrated, the first thing you want is to know that I hear your frustration and care that you are upset?"

"Exactly."

"Okay; in the future, I'll try to show that I'm sympathetic," he promised. "But it's important to me that you understand I was trying to support you by offering advice."

"How is that supporting me? It made me feel you didn't think I could solve the problem myself."

"That isn't how I saw it. I saw my friend upset and all I wanted to do was solve your problem," he explained. "I wanted to make it better for you. That's why I was making suggestions and giving you advice."

"So you did understand that I was upset?"

"Of course. That's why I tried to help."

"Okay. Now I see that you did understand how I felt, but you express sympathy differently from the way I do."

In this conversation, I learned that Rick indeed understood that I was frustrated and he did care about me. I also learned something about how he expresses caring and support. Although his way of communicating support differs from mine, I now understand it and can appreciate his advice in the way he intends it. Because Rick and I were willing to explore the misunderstanding in our earlier conversation, we gained insight into each other's meanings and needs. Our increased appreciation of each other enriches our relationship and the communication in it.

Misunderstandings, however uncomfortable, are opportunities to learn and grow. They invite us to explore differences, and doing that can lead to improved awareness of ourselves, others, and the rich diversity in our world.

This book offers you the chance to reflect on the meanings of your communication as well as the meanings of others' communication. Equally important, it invites you to enlarge your understanding of the range of meanings that can be present in human interaction. This point is important because the first step in effective communication is understanding ourselves and others — both how we are alike and how we differ. Each chapter that follows explores a particular kind of misunderstanding and helps you see how it is rooted in personal or social differences between communicators.

Key Words

- communication
- dynamism
- essentializing
- meaning(s)
- misunderstanding
- personal differences
- social groups
- standpoint
- systems
- totalizing

Reflecting on This Chapter

1. Identify the social groups within which you have been socialized. What gender, religious, racial, and other groups have influenced your ways of communicating and your ways of interpreting how others communicate?

2. One of the limitations of standpoint theory (as it has been developed so far) is its tendency to focus attention on a specific group to which people belong. All of us belong to multiple social groups, however, and

each of them influences our communication. Can standpoint logic be used to provide us with insight into how multiple groups shape individuals' communication?

3. How accurate and useful is thinking about distinct social groups within a single society? Does attention to group differences fuel divisions among people? Or does it recognize legitimate differences that need not divide us or create hostilities? Are there ways our actions can help determine which outcome is more likely?

4. In the dialogue that opened this chapter, did you identify with me or Rick? Have you engaged in interactions such as the one I recounted? What did you feel—frustration, anger, confusion? How did you handle the misunderstanding?

5. In this chapter, I claim that not all problems are communication problems. Think about your interactions in personal, social, and business situations. Can you identify tensions that are not rooted in misunderstanding of communication? Can you identify other tensions that arise from misunderstandings of communication? How do the two groups of tensions differ?

6. Because communication is dynamic, we can add to what we say to clarify our meaning and transcend misunderstanding. Can you identify communication encounters in your life in which an initial misunderstanding was resolved by further communication?

References

Burke, K. (1966). *Language as symbolic action*. Berkeley: University of California Press.

Coates, J., & Cameron, D. (1989). *Women in their speech communities: New perspectives on language and sex*. London: Longman.

Collins, P. H. (1986). Learning from the outsider within: The sociological significance of black feminist thought. *Social Problems, 33*, 514–532.

Cool Hand Luke. (1967). Warner Brothers.

Cose, E. (1997, March 17). The Black gen X nobody knows. *Newsweek*, p. 62.

Haraway, D. (1988). Situated knowledges: The science question in feminism and the privilege of partial perspective. *Signs, 14*, 575–599.

Harding, S. (1991). *Whose science? Whose knowledge? Thinking from women's lives*. Ithaca, NY: Cornell University Press.

Hartsock, N. C. (1983). The feminist standpoint: Developing the ground for a specifically feminist historical materialism. In S. Harding & M. Hintikka (Eds.), *Discovering reality* (pp. 283–310). Boston: Reidel.

Hegel, G. W. F. (1807). *Phenomenology of mind* (J. B. Baillie, Trans.). Germany: Wurzburg & Bamburg.

Janeway, E. (1971). *Man's world, woman's place: A study in social mythology.* New York: Dell.

Labov, W. (1972). *Sociolinguistic patterns.* Philadelphia: University of Pennsylvania Press.

Leland, J., & Samuels, A. (1997, March 17). The new generation gap. *Newsweek,* pp. 52–57, 59.

Ruddick, S. (1989). *Maternal thinking: Toward a politics of peace.* Boston, MA: Beacon.

Smith, D. (1987). *The everyday world as problematic.* Boston, MA: Northeastern University Press.

Swain, S. (1989). Covert intimacy: Closeness in men's friendships. In B. Risman & P. Schwartz (Eds.), *Gender and intimate relationships* (pp. 71–86). Belmont, CA: Wadsworth.

Williams, H. (1989). *Hegel, Heraclitus and Marx's dialectic.* New York: Harvester Wheatsheaf.

Wood, J. T. (1993a). Gender, communication, and culture. In L. Samovar & R. Porter (Eds.), *Intercultural communication: A reader* (7th ed., pp. 155–164). Belmont, CA: Wadsworth.

Wood, J. T. (1993b). Gender and moral voice: From "woman's nature" to standpoint epistemology. *Women's Studies in Communication, 15,* 1–24.

Wood, J. T. (In press). Different views of different cultures: Clarifying the issues. *Journal of Personal Communication.*

Wood, J. T., & Cox, J. R. (1993). Rethinking critical voice: Materiality and situated knowledges. *Western Journal of Communication, 57,* 278–287.

| 2 |

BUT WORDS WILL NEVER HURT ME

* * *

The Power of Communication

While he was an undergraduate student at Brown University in Providence, Rhode Island, Douglas Hann* turned 21. To celebrate arriving at the age of legal adulthood, Hann drank heavily and then entered the campus quad where he began cursing loudly, insulting certain groups with epithets such as "niggers," "Jews," and "faggots." This was the second time in as many years that Hann had combined too much alcohol with inflammatory language.

The school responded by permanently expelling Hann. The formal charge was that he had violated Brown's code prohibiting inappropriate, demeaning, or abusive actions based on race, religion, gender, ethnicity, handicap, sexual orientation, or national origin. The key word is *actions*. In announcing the expulsion, Brown president Vartan Gregorian asserted that the decision was not an infringement on free speech because Hann was being expelled for how he acted, not what he said.

---

*Because this incident was widely publicized, I have not disguised identities or facts. Douglas Hann is the real name of the student. Other names and facts are also real.

Gregorian's distinction between actions and speech is debatable, however. As *Boston Globe* columnist Ellen Goodman noted, Hann's "outrageous behavior was accomplished with his mouth" (p. 96). The action that was judged offensive was his speech — what he said.

Hann's case is dramatic, but it is not an isolated example of the power of communication. Daily in our ordinary lives we are the beneficiaries and the victims of communication that has impact. Around the country, what is often called hate speech erupts both on and off campuses, as do actions that denigrate or otherwise harm people. Students at a number of schools drape Confederate flags on porches and mount replicas of them on their cars as license tags. A group of Emory students exercised their entrepreneurial ambitions by printing T-shirts emblazoned with women's backsides. Threatening and derogatory messages are scrawled on car windshields and house doors of African Americans and other minority groups. Graffiti in bathrooms and on public buildings routinely include demeaning comments to and about a variety of groups. Swastikas are painted on the homes of Jewish citizens, and anyone who is thought to be gay or lesbian is frequently assaulted with malicious slurs.

According to David Morris, vice president of the Institute for Local Self-Reliance, 9 of 10 Americans in a 1996 poll said they thought incivility is a serious problem in the United States. Conservative William Bennett claims that America has become vulgar and coarse, a state of affairs reflected in and encouraged by crude language. In *Miss Manners Rescues Civilization*, Judith Martin pleads for the return of common courtesy. Meanwhile, Dennis Rodman achieves best-seller status with *Bad as I Wanna Be*, in which he mocks moral sensibilities while simultaneously offending them.

Whether we regard behaviors such as Douglas Hann's outburst as speech or other types of action, they are powerful to both those who engage in them and those who are their targets. They also affect the overall society by challenging our ideas about what is and is not acceptable conduct. Whether or not you believe freedom of expression should be protected by the First Amendment, the impact of expression can be profound.

In this chapter, we focus on the power of communication. We explore the ability of communication to affect how we think, feel, and act as well as how we perceive ourselves and others. In our discussion, we focus on both verbal and nonverbal communication for two reasons. Because both are kinds of communication, similar principles apply to them. Also, as

Douglas Hann's case demonstrates, the line between speech and other kinds of action is often blurred.

Realizing the Power of Communication

Remember the childhood saying, "Sticks and stones may break my bones, but words will never hurt me"? Words may not break our bones, but they can definitely hurt us—sometimes more than physical assaults. Perhaps that is why some people have revised the childhood saying to this: "Sticks and stones may break my bones, but words can really hurt me." Children learn early that words can wound. The label "sissy" may invite open warfare. When I was growing up, the ultimate insult was to say "you have cooties." None of us knew what a cootie was (and I still don't), but we knew the accusation was menacing. It had impact.

Just as words can hurt, so can they warm and enchant us. Certain phrases and song lyrics can summon up fond memories of special times, places, and people. Just hearing the words has a magic effect on us. Reciting the Pledge of Allegiance or hearing the stirring "I Have a Dream" speech by the Reverend Martin Luther King, Jr., moves some people to tears. Hearing hymns or saying prayers can calm us when we're upset or grieving. Other music can arouse energy and compel us to dance. Words even have the power to hypnotize us—to transport us to another state of being.

The ability to affect our perceptions, thoughts, and feelings is not restricted to verbal communication. Nonverbal communication also packs power. As the adage reminds us, in some cases "actions speak louder than words." There are gestures that convey scalding disdain and derogation. Baseball stars spit in umpires' faces. Drivers routinely aim the insulting third finger at strangers in traffic. If you've ever felt withered by another person's glare or appalled that someone would burn a flag, you know how effectively nonverbal communication can express contempt for people and values.

Also, like words, nonverbal communication can convey extremely positive messages. Sometimes a hug can express affection, sympathy, or forgiveness more eloquently than any words. A friend's spontaneous smile when you meet says "Welcome! I'm so glad to see you." Eyes can convey love and longing, and touching can express closeness. A handshake can seal a job offer or agreement.

Nonverbal communication also symbolizes identity. We may wear a ring to communicate that we are engaged or married or that we belong to the Promise Keepers. Expensive jewelry and clothing can proclaim wealth and status. Furniture in offices as well as the location of offices may announce power. White coats and stethoscopes proclaim membership in the medical profession, whereas military uniforms announce rank and branch of service. And moving the tassel on a mortarboard cap from one side to the other announces that an individual has changed his or her status from student to graduate. As these examples show, both verbal and nonverbal communication are powerful in expressing thoughts, feelings, and identities.

Understanding How Communication Works

How does communication manage to charm, anger, delight, insult, energize, and disturb us? What makes communication so powerful? To answer that question, we need to examine what communication does. Specifically, we explore how it defines, evaluates, and classifies our experiences and perceptions. Understanding these functions of communication sheds light on its extraordinary power in our lives.

Communication Defines

The most fundamental power of communication is naming—and by that, defining. In her landmark essay, "Defining Reality—A Powerful Tool," Australian scholar Dale Spender highlighted the power to name. As she noted, we name what we consider important and we do not name other phenomena. Extending this point, Spender argued that we are unlikely to perceive what we don't name. In other words, communication is directly related to perception. On the one hand, language reflects our perceptions by naming what we consider important. On the other hand, language guides our perceptions by calling some things and not others to our attention.

The reciprocal relationship between communication and perception is illustrated by the specialized language that is used in most professions. You may be satisfied to speak about your leg, but orthopedists would refer to particular bones, tendons, and muscles in the leg. You or I might say we wanted a purple vase whereas a decorator would be more likely to specify a vase that is amethyst, mauve, violet, lavender, lilac, or plum. You probably use the words *nonverbal communication,* but communication scholars often use more precise and technical terms such as *kinesics* (face and body motion), *proxemics* (use of space), *haptics* (touch), and *chronemics* (use and perception of time). For specialists, it's important to make distinctions that may not be noticeable or useful to laypersons.

The connection between communication and perception is pertinent not only to individuals but also to cultural life. The verbal and nonverbal symbols that have prominence in a culture reflect the priorities, values, and perceptions of that culture — or at least the mainstream of the culture. The link between culture and communication was the focus of theorizing by Benjamin Whorf and Edwin Sapir. Based on their collaboration, Whorf wrote *Language, Thought, and Reality.* The title expresses the fundamental point of the book: that language shapes our thinking about reality. This observation has become known as the Sapir-Whorf hypothesis. As an example, in the United States we use the word *snow* to refer to frozen white precipitation that sometimes falls during winter. The single word is all we need. In some arctic cultures, however, there are multiple words to name what we call snow. Among the people of these cultures, it's important — sometimes a matter of life and death — to distinguish among different kinds of snow that have distinct implications for travel, hunting, and other activities.

Inspecting verbal and nonverbal communication gives us keen insight into those things a culture values. Western cultures prize individualism, a value that is reflected in recurrent images of lone individuals standing on top of a mountain, walking on a beach, or driving in a car. Individualism is also evident in our language. We speak of "my home," "my father," "my school," "my class," and "my teacher." Other cultures value community and group above the individual and this cultural priority is reflected in language. Koreans, for instance, do not emphasize the individual; they speak of "our home," "our father," "our school," "our class," and "our teacher." The Korean culture, as well as a number of other Asian cultures, esteems age, so elders are routinely addressed with a reverential title and language that is not part of Western language.

One illustration of how language reflects cultural values is the historical use of male generic terms. These are terms that literally refer only to men but are claimed to include both sexes — for example, chairman, mailman, foreman, and policeman. Male generic language reflects the historical position of white men as the members of society who had the property, status, and education to coin language, name what existed, and write the laws of the land. The masculine emphasis that characterized

English for many centuries is not universal. In some cultures, both masculine and feminine inflections are used. Similarly some cultures, notably Hispanic ones, have a tradition of double last names that preserve both the mother's and father's family names.

In the 1970s, the use of male generic terms came under fire. Scholars documented the tendencies of such use to foster thoughts and images of men and not women. In one study, researchers asked grade school students to draw pictures for chapters in a sociology text. Half the students were asked to draw pictures for chapters with titles such as "Urban Man" and "Man in Politics." The other half of the students were asked to draw pictures for chapters with titles such as "Urban Life" and "Political Behavior." The first group of students drew pictures that featured only men; the other students drew pictures that included both women and men. From this exercise the researchers concluded that male generic terms are not routinely perceived as referring to women. As a result of many studies that reached similar conclusions, linguistic reform evolved. Today, most publishers and dictionaries do not allow male generic terms.

Male generic terms are not the only ones that can exclude some members of a culture. Communication can be exclusive in many ways. For example, referring to the December break in the school year as the "Christmas break" ignores the reality that many people don't celebrate Christmas, instead observing Kwanzaa, Hanukkah, and other non-Christian traditions and holidays. The ubiquitous images of Santa and the reindeer and of the nativity scene are nonverbal recognitions of Christmas but not of holidays and holy days for non-Christians. Similarly, calling January 1 "New Year's Day" ignores the existence of Rosh Hashanah, the Jewish New Year. The terms *spouse, wife,* and *husband* apply only to heterosexuals; our language doesn't include terms that designate committed relationships between gays and between lesbians. The exclusions in language reflect the culture's historical values and the citizens who historically have held power and status. Those may or may not be values and power relations we wish to continue reflecting and reproducing in our language.

Communication Evaluates

We've noted that communication has the power to define people, experiences, and other phenomena, but the definitions that communication advances are not objective. Rather, they are laden with values—the values of individuals and the groups to which they belong—so, as communication is defining, it is also evaluating. Perhaps you've encountered humorous conjugations such as these:

I am colorful.	I am assertive.	I am casual.
You are flamboyant.	You are aggressive.	You are messy.
They are garish.	They are belligerent.	They are slobs.

Although we laugh when we see these conjugations, we may also recognize the truth beneath the humor. We tend to be generous in describing ourselves, and we're likely to describe people we like with language that highlights their virtues and deemphasizes their flaws. The reverse is often true of our descriptions of people we don't like.

The evaluative character of communication is evident in different words that can be used to describe the same phenomena. Consider the different connotations reflected in the following words and phrases.

Kike	Hebrew	Jew	Jewish person
Nigger	Negro	Black	African American
Retard Goon Dummy		Retarded person	Retarded citizen
Bimbo	Chick	Girl	Woman
Fag Dyke Fairy	Queer	Homosexual	Gay Lesbian
Fuck	Screw	Have sex Engage in intercourse	Make love
Drunk	Alcoholic		Person with drinking problem
Cripple Amputee	Handicapped Physically challenged	Disabled	Person with disability
Feminazi Bra-burner	Believer in equal rights		Feminist

Honkey	Whitey	Caucasian	European American
Redman Savage Injun	Indian	Native American	Cherokee Apache Lumbee
		First Nation American	Crow etc.
Geezer Has-been	Oldster	Elderly person	Senior citizen Mature person
Slant-eye Gook, Jap Chink	Oriental	Asian	Taiwanese Japanese Nepalese
Welfare queen			Person on welfare

Less than a decade ago, one contingent of politicians proposed a bill designed to increase the hiring of minorities. Another group of politicians who opposed the bill dubbed it "the quota bill." The legislators who wanted to defeat the bill were savvy about the power of language. They realized that labeling it a "quota bill" would ensure its defeat, and they were right: The bill was killed. An interesting note is that the bill did *not* propose quotas; in fact, the language in the bill specifically *rejected* using quotas in hiring. In this case, the truth was less powerful than the language.

Very similar language was used to derail the appointment of Lani Guinier, whom President Bill Clinton proposed for the position of Assistant Attorney General for Civil Rights during his first term in office. By her opponents she was tagged "the quota queen," a label that stuck and contributed to her withdrawal from consideration for the post. George McGovern lost the Senate seat he had held for many terms when his challenger labeled McGovern "antifamily." McGovern had been married to the same woman all his adult life and they had five children; his contender was single. The evaluations that inhere in communication can affect our perceptions and actions.

Communication Classifies

A third quality of communication is its ability to organize and classify phenomena. We couldn't function if we had to think of everything and everyone as a totally specific, unique phenomenon. We have to order our perceptions, and we do so by grouping them in ways we find meaningful — by classifying. For example, in planning meals and diets, we think in terms of food groups (such as proteins, fats, carbohydrates, and fiber) rather than individual items of food. In fulfilling graduation requirements, we think of types of classes (humanities, social sciences, physical sciences, fine arts). Serious backpackers — at least those who survive — classify plants and snakes into poisonous and nonpoisonous groups.

To organize our perceptions we rely on what scholars of communication and psychology call cognitive schemata (mental structures). One schema, called a prototype, defines what we consider to be the model of a category. For example, you have a prototype, or model, of a good friend — the person who exemplifies what a good friend is and does. The prototype defines the whole category of good friends by identifying the ideal case or exemplar. You define others as friends if they approximate your prototype for a good friend.

We use a second type of schema to measure people and situations. Called personal constructs, these are measuring sticks of judgment. We perceive people in terms of where they fit on measuring sticks such as honest or dishonest, intelligent or unintelligent, and selfish or unselfish. Notice that judgments are based only on the personal constructs, or measuring sticks of judgment, we choose to use. We might assess people and situations on many qualities other than those on which we selectively rely.

The third schema is stereotypes, or the predictive generalizations we make. We anticipate what a person will do or what will happen in a situation based on the group into which we place a person or situation (using prototypes) and where we perceive a person or situation as fitting on our measuring sticks of judgment (personal constructs).

All of us have stereotypes about various groups. You may have such predictive generalizations about liberals, conservatives, rural people, professors, and politicians. Stereotypes reflect our perceptions and beliefs, which may be more or less accurate. Stereotypes also encourage us to think in terms of groups, not individuals. Once we place someone in a group (notice how actively we're involved in structuring our perceptions), we tend to see him or her in terms of the characteristics we associate with the group as a whole.

The final kind of schema is called a script. As the name suggests, scripts are guides to action. Based on our experiences and observations, we develop scripts that tell us what we should do and what others are likely to do, what sequence of activities is appropriate, and how particular interactions will unfold. For example, you use a script when you meet a new person. Probably you introduce yourself, engage in small talk about majors, hometowns, or things going on in your immediate context (music, food, other people). If you and the other person enjoy the conversation, you may move out of the script for first meeting and into a different script — perhaps exploring friendship or romance. Then you'll follow the sequence of actions you have learned are appropriate to the new script.

Our ability to organize perceptions is essential to daily living. We couldn't function without using schemata to order perceptions and actions; however, the capacity to organize perceptions is not without dangers. When we stereotype people and other phenomena, we place them in broad groups. The danger is that we can lose sight of individuals and their unique qualities. Once we label someone as belonging to a particular group, we may respond more to the label (and what it means to us) than to the individual. A related concern is that we may see only how the individual is like other members of the group and not notice how she or he is different from others whom we place in the group.

Let's consider a few common examples to see how stereotyping people by membership in groups can diminish our awareness of differences among individuals in the group. Several of my students have told me they resent the term *Asian American* because it lumps together people from dramatically different cultures including those of Nepal, China, Taiwan, Korea, Japan, and Malaysia. "Asians aren't interchangeable," they protest. I hear similar complaints from students who belong to fraternities and sororities. Many of them are serious students and not heavy drinkers, and they resent being stereotyped as Greeks who party. Athletes too often feel unfairly judged by stereotypes of "dumb jocks." In each of these cases, the individuals feel that they do not fit some of the qualities associated with a group. They dislike being seen only in terms of what they have in common with others in the group (Asian heritage, membership in a fraternity or sorority, being an athlete); they resent the failure of others to perceive how they differ from some members of the group (specific ethnic heritage; studiousness and moderation with alcohol; intelligence and attention to academics). Chapter 7 provides further discussion of stereotyping.

Have you ever felt that others placed you in a group that described only one part of you and ignored other aspects of who you were? If so, you know how frustrating or hurtful it can be to have important facets of your

KUDZU. By permission of Doug Marlette and Creators Syndicate.

identity ignored or erased. And if you've ever been assaulted by a racial or ethnic slur or by a sign or image that demeans your identity, you know how deeply that behavior offends.

Improving Communication

We opened this chapter with the dramatic case of Douglas Hann who screamed insulting language in the quad at Brown University, but we didn't restrict our discussion to extreme cases like his. Instead, we surveyed the ordinary, everyday ways in which communication shapes our feelings, thoughts, perceptions, and actions. In the course of our discussion, we saw that communication has the power to affect not only what we think and do but also how we see ourselves and others.

How do we become more competent communicators? How do we become more responsible in harnessing the power of human communication? Although there aren't any quick and sure formulas for achieving competence, there are three guidelines that can help us.

First, we can make a conscious choice to become aware of the power of communication. Most of us use language and nonverbal behavior without giving much thought to its impact on ourselves and others. Swearing, slurs, and expletives have become commonplace in everyday interaction. As a result, few of us are surprised if we hear fuck, shit, or other words that would have shocked our parents. The ordinariness of vulgar language and gestures today lessens our sensitivity to the impact of communication. However, we don't have to participate in the coarse communication that has become commonplace. We can choose not to use strong words carelessly and not to adopt demeaning terms. This is an important choice for each of us as an individual.

A second way we can be more responsible individually is to monitor the ways we organize and interpret other people and situations. Monitoring is noticing and regulating how we act. Remember that perception is selective as are the schemata by which we organize and evaluate our perceptions. Realizing this allows us to be mindful of the ways we create order and meaning in our lives. For example, do you use group labels such as *Asians* or *Native Americans*? If so, do the labels encourage you to perceive similarities among Asians and Native Americans of different heritages but not to perceive differences among them? Would other, more specific labels encourage you to perceive both differences and similarities among people? Reflecting on your own ways of classifying experiences and people allows you to become a more competent, thoughtful communicator.

A third step each of us can take is to assume some responsibility for the collective life of our society. One way to do that is to remind ourselves of a theme in this chapter: The language and nonverbal behaviors that circulate in a culture both reflect and shape the values of members of that culture. The implication of this point is that we can make a difference in the kinds of communication that are regarded as normal in our society. A society, after all, is made up of individuals—people like you and me. Current social codes of communication can be altered if we choose to challenge uncivil communication by others and to refrain from engaging in it ourselves.

If a friend of yours utters an ethnic slur or disparages a gay person or has a Confederate flag, what do you do? To do nothing is to offer tacit approval of the actions. To speak up and question the actions is to invite change. It may seem that you personally can't really make significant changes in the overall life of our culture, but it would be a mistake to underestimate the impact of any individual, including yourself. Through our choices of how to think and act, each of us affects the collective society. What it is and can be depends on our courage, creativity, and thoughtfulness.

Communication is powerful; it has the capacity to harm and heal, to elevate and lower, to calm and anger, to connect and separate. Understanding the power of communication is a critical step in learning to use communication wisely, carefully, and respectfully.

Key Words

- classifying
- cognitive schemata [prototype, personal constructs, stereotype, scripts]
- defining
- evaluating

- hate speech
- incivility
- language
- male generic terms
- monitoring
- nonverbal communication
- Sapir-Whorf hypothesis

Reflecting on This Chapter

1. What labels have been applied to you that you dislike? Explain why they annoy or anger you. Do you perceive them as devaluing you or misrepresenting you? Do they affect you in other ways?

2. Do you think institutions (schools, government) should protect individuals and groups against hurtful speech? What responsibility, if any, do individuals have to fight their own battles? Can individuals or groups that are frequently targets of hate speech defend themselves effectively? Can policies, laws, or codes effectively enforce limitations on speech and other behavior?

3. Do you think Brown University acted appropriately when it permanently expelled Douglas Hann? Did the punishment infringe on Hann's right to free speech? If you think it did, was the infringement warranted?

4. What limits, if any, would you attach to the right to freedom of expression? Current laws recognize certain qualifications on freedom of speech, such as fighting words and slander. Should freedom of expression be qualified in additional ways?

5. Does your school have a code or policy that places limits on the speech of students, faculty, and others associated with the institution? If so, what are the limits? Do you agree with the regulation?

6. Do you agree with the president of Brown University that Hann's offense was what he did, not what he said? Where do you draw the line between speech and other kinds of action?

7. Think about the tension between freedom of speech and freedom from discrimination. Does one person have a right to say something

even if another person perceives what is said as harassing? Where do one person's rights end and another person's begin?

8. Should intent be considered in the decision of whether a person engages in hate speech or other actions that are offensive to some people? On some campuses, students have defended displays of the Confederate flag by saying that they don't see it or intend it as a symbol of slavery but rather as a symbol of Southern heritage. Many African Americans and some European Americans argue that, regardless of the intent of those who display the flag, it is irrevocably associated with the system of slavery.

9. In recent years there has been controversy — among both laypersons and judges — about the lawfulness of burning the U.S. flag. Once universally regarded as both illegal and blatantly unpatriotic, flag burning is now considered by some as a form of nonverbal speech that is entitled to First Amendment protection. What is your opinion? Is it a form of expression? Should it be punished or be protected?

10. Do you think swearing, identity slurs, and crude communication are commonplace today? How often do you curse or use sexual terms as expletives? How common are these behaviors among people in your circle of friends and acquaintances? How do you think common use and acceptance of crude communication affects our sensitivity to the power of communication?

References

Applegate, J. (1990). Constructs and communication: A pragmatic integration. In R. Neimeyer & G. Neimeyer (Eds.), *Advances in personal construct psychology, 1* (pp. 203–230). Greenwich, CT: JAI Press.

Beck, E. T. (1992). From "kike" to "JAP": How misogyny, anti-Semitism, and racism construct the "Jewish American princess." In M. Andersen & P. H. Collins (Eds.), *Race, class and gender: An anthology* (pp. 88–95). Belmont, CA: Wadsworth.

Burleson, B., & Waltman, M. (1988). Cognitive complexity: Using the role category questionnaire measure. In C. Tardy (Ed.), *A handbook for the study of human communication* (pp. 1–35). Norwood, NJ: Ablex.

Folb, E. (1994). Who's got the room at the top? Issues of dominance and nondominance in intracultural communication. In L. Samovar & R. Porter (Eds.), *Intercultural communication: A reader* (7th ed., pp. 131–139). Belmont, CA: Wadsworth.

Goodman, E. (1993). When names hurt. *Value judgments* (pp. 95–97). New York: Farrar Straus Giroux.

Hamilton, M. C. (1991). Masculine bias in the attributions of personhood: People = male, male = people. *Psychology of Women Quarterly, 15,* 393–402.

Hoijer, H. (1994). The Sapir-Whorf hypothesis. In L. Samovar & R. Porter (Eds.), *Intercultural communication: A reader* (7th ed., pp. 194– 200). Belmont, CA: Wadsworth.

Houston, M. (1997). When black women talk with white women: Why dialogues are difficult. In A. González, M. Houston, & V. Chen (Eds.), *Our voices: Essays in culture, ethnicity, and communication* (2nd ed., pp. 187–194). Los Angeles: Roxbury.

Kelly, G. (1955). *The psychology of personal constructs.* New York: W. W. Norton.

Kramarae, C. (1996). Classified information: Race, class, and (always) gender. In J. T. Wood (Ed.), *Gendered relationships* (pp. 20–38). Mountain View, CA: Mayfield.

Martin, J. (1996). *Miss Manners rescues civilization.* New York: Crown.

Morris, D. (1997, March–April). The civility wars: Is poverty more vulgar than profanity? *Utne Reader,* pp. 15–16.

Penelope, J. (1990). *Speaking freely: Unlearning the lies of the fathers' tongues.* New York: Pergamon Press.

Rodman, D. (1996). *Bad as I wanna be.* New York: Delacorte.

Schneider, J., & Hacker, S. (1973). Sex role imagery and use of the generic "man" in introductory texts: A case in the sociology of sociology. *American Sociologist, 8,* 12–18.

Spender, D. (1984a). Defining reality: A powerful tool. In C. Kramarae, M. Schultz, & W. O'Barr (Eds.), *Language and power* (pp. 195–205). Beverly Hills, CA: Sage.

Spender, D. (1984b). *Man made language.* London: Routledge and Kegan Paul.

Weber, S. N. (1994). The need to be: The socio-cultural significance of black language. In L. Samovar & R. Porter (Eds.), *Intercultural communication: A reader* (7th ed., pp. 221–226). Belmont, CA: Wadsworth.

Zorn, T. E. (1991). Construct system development, transformational leadership, and leadership messages. *Southern Communication Journal, 56,* 178–193.

| 3 |

OBVIOUSLY, YOU'RE NOT COMMITTED
TO THE FIRM

. . .

Understanding Constitutive Rules

of Communication

Last year, my friend Mark completed law school and joined a prominent firm located in my town. In December, the firm sponsored its annual holiday banquet, complete with live entertainment and spectacular food and drinks. Mark didn't attend because his son was appearing in the school holiday program the night of the banquet. A few days later, John Holloway, a senior partner in the firm, said to Mark, "We were disappointed you weren't at the banquet."

"Me, too," Mark replied, "but Danny's school pageant was on the same night and I felt I had to be there."

"Bad choice," John said curtly. "Obviously, you're not committed to the firm."

"How can you say that?" Mark protested. "I work late most nights and nearly every weekend."

"But you didn't think the banquet was important enough to attend." John turned and walked away.

When Mark told me about the exchange, he growled, "I give them nearly 80 hours a week. Isn't that commitment? What the devil do they want?"

"Perhaps John thinks the banquet is an important sign of commitment to the firm," I suggested.

"The only reasonable sign of commitment is the work I do," Mark snapped. "And I do a helluva lot!"

"Did all the other junior associates attend?"

"I think so, but they didn't have a son whose school pageant was the same night." Mark thought for a moment, then continued. "It would be different if there was a trial strategy meeting or work that had to be done that night. But I couldn't disappoint Danny just to go to the banquet. That would be putting partying ahead of family."

Was the banquet "partying" or a "sign of commitment to the firm" or both? Was Mark's absence from the banquet a sign of disrespect or lack of identification with the firm, or was it a sign that he places family above socializing?

In this chapter we'll explore a common type of misunderstanding—one that occurs because people have different ideas about what particular verbal or nonverbal behaviors mean. When communicators attach different meanings to the same words and actions, they are likely to misread each other's behaviors and sometimes each other's motives.

Understanding the Misunderstanding

Communication scholars Barnett Pearce and Vern Cronen observe that when we communicate with others, we are trying to coordinate our meanings and theirs. To do so, we rely on communication rules, or guidelines, about how to interact. Although usually we aren't aware of rules, they structure our understandings—and our misunderstandings.

Communication specialists emphasize two kinds of communication rules that guide human interaction. One type is regulative rules, which govern, or regulate, when we communicate. Regulative rules specify when it's appropriate to talk, gossip, show affection, interrupt, argue, and so forth. We discuss regulative rules in Chapter 4.

Our interest now lies with the second type. Scholars call these constitutive rules because they constitute the meaning of communication. Constitutive rules define what counts as what in communication. Put another way, constitutive rules specify, or construct, meaning. You have constitutive rules for what counts as affection (hugs, thoughtful gifts), respect (attention, looking at someone when he or she is speaking), imposition (the expectation that you will do someone else's work), challenge (disobedience, questioning authority), and so forth.

In Mark's case, he and John had different constitutive rules for the meaning of attending the firm's holiday banquet. They attached disparate meanings to attendance.

JOHN: Attending the banquet = a sign of commitment to the firm

MARK: Attending the banquet = partying (or socializing)
         Attending the banquet = neglecting family

Something even more important than different constitutive rules is afoot in the misunderstanding between Mark and John: Neither man realizes that he is operating from constitutive rules, much less that the two of them have *different* constitutive rules. As long as Mark and John remain unaware of their own constitutive rules, they are unlikely to recognize the reason for their misunderstanding. Instead, each man may presume that his understanding of what attendance at the banquet means is the only legitimate understanding, and each will then regard the other as unreasonable or foolhardy.

Some years ago, a philosopher named John Searle distinguished between concrete actions, which he called "brute facts," and the meanings we have for those actions. To dramatize the difference between brute facts (or actions) and the meanings we attach to them, Searle asked us to imagine a naive observer of a football game:

> Our observer would discover the law of periodical clustering: at statistically regular intervals organisms in like colored shirts cluster together in a roughly circular fashion (the huddle). Furthermore, at equally regular intervals, the circular clustering is followed by linear clustering (the teams line up for the play). . . . (p. 52)

The observer's description specifies behaviors that occur during football games. It does not, however, capture the meaning of the behaviors. Searle's point was that meaning does not inhere in behaviors. We attach meanings to behaviors when we stipulate what counts as what. In football, circular clustering counts as huddling, lining up counts as getting ready for a play.

Just as in football, in communication we attach meanings to behaviors to define what counts as what. Some of our constitutive rules are

learned in our families, especially families of origin. During the early years, families teach us what counts as affection (in some families, members kiss and hug; in other families, affection is not displayed overtly), how to deal with conflict (families differ in how openly and civilly they manage differences), and what dinnertime means (the one time of day that all the family members come together to share their lives versus a battlefield where arguments erupt versus a time to eat and watch television without conversation). We also learn constitutive rules in our social communities. Race and ethnicity, social class, and gender are three of the social groups that seem most influential in forming our constitutive rules.

Race and Ethnicity and Constitutive Rules

Several years ago, I spoke to an African American organization on my campus. While I was speaking, several of the students interjected comments such as "Tell it," "Go on now," and "I'm hearing you." At the time, I thought they were being rude to interrupt while I was speaking, even though I also sensed they were appreciating my remarks. After my speech,

I asked Cornell, a student whom I knew well, why people had talked during my presentation. "Because they were in it with you, that's why," Cornell explained.

MY RULE: Talking during a speech = rudeness

LISTENERS' RULE: Talking during a speech = involvement

Cornell suggested that I might understand what happened during my speech if I attended church with him. I did so the next week, and throughout the sermon the congregation repeated aloud the minister's words and interjected comments: "That's right, now," "Preach it, preach it."

Scholars have labeled this form of communication the call-out, or call and response, pattern. Shirley Weber teaches African American studies at San Diego State University. She explains that African Americans generally communicate more interactively than do European Americans. Within their speech communities, calling out responses counts as a compliment to the speaker. It means listeners are involved, interested in what the speaker is saying, and eager to participate in the communication event.

Weber explains that black preachers call out to the congregation and expect the congregation to respond. Through call and response, the preacher and members of the congregation become one. If members of the congregation (or listeners at a speech) don't respond, the preacher will scold them and spur them to speak back to him or her. Members of the congregation take their responsibilities seriously because they know that a preacher alone can't control the effectiveness of a sermon. The preacher needs their support and guidance ("Amen," "That's the story") and, occasionally, their corrections ("Better check that out with the Lord").

As a footnote to this experience, Cornell admitted to me that he had been amazed by how unresponsive the congregation seemed when he attended church with some of his white friends. I explained to him that the white congregation's silence counted as expressing respect for the preacher and his sermon.

CORNELL'S RULE: Not responding = apathy

WHITE CONGREGATION'S RULE: Not responding = respect

Racial and ethnic groups differ in a number of their constitutive rules. For example, many U.S. natives, especially men, are taught that assertiveness counts as standing up for your individual rights. In many Asian and Native American cultures, however, individuality is admired less than group harmony and concern for collective interests. Thus, people socialized in Asian and Native American societies are often less assertive than U.S. natives and they are more likely to defer to others and help others save face in embarrassing situations. It would be a mistake to interpret their behaviors as indicating a lack of self-confidence.

People who grow up in Jewish communities learn many constitutive rules that may not be learned by non-Jewish people. A good example is *kvetching*, which is ritual griping, or complaining, to air frustrations. The point of kvetching is not to solve problems. Instead, the whole purpose is to bemoan how terrible something is. The first time I encountered kvetching, I misunderstood what it meant, so I communicated ineffectively.

Jerry Phillips, who directed my doctoral studies, was Jewish and he was a champion kvetcher. One day early in our acquaintance I stopped by Jerry's office and he was complaining loudly and dramatically about the painters who were working on his home. I tried to show empathy by sharing problems I'd had with people who had worked on my home, but Jerry was uninterested in my experiences. Next, I tried to suggest ways he could persuade the painters to do better work, but my suggestions only annoyed Jerry. After about five minutes of miscues between us, Jerry finally exclaimed, "Quit trying to help. I don't want help. I want to kvetch!" And then he explained to me what kvetching was.

Social Class and Constitutive Rules

Social class also sculpts constitutive rules. My friend Louise confronted this issue with her in-laws. The first year of her marriage, Louise and her husband, Jack, spent Christmas with Jack's family. When they returned home, Louise wrote a gracious thank you note to her in-laws to express her appreciation for their hospitality and gifts. Having been raised in an upper-class family, Louise had been taught to write "bread and butter" notes of thanks on a routine basis. In fact, to this day she sends notes to her own parents to thank them for gifts. When Jack's parents didn't send a thank you note, Louise was hurt. Didn't they like their gifts? Had she offended them during the visit?

When Jack called his parents a few weeks after the visit, his mother remarked that she was sad that Louise didn't accept them as her family. Jack asked his mother why she thought that, and she said she had gotten Louise's thank you note and that families aren't so formal.

LOUISE'S RULE:	Thank you note = politeness
JACK'S MOTHER'S RULE:	Thank you note = formality
	Formal = not familylike

Gender and Constitutive Rules

Gender groups also tend to cultivate some distinct constitutive rules; as a result, women and men often misunderstand what counts as what to each other. Ellen considers asking Milton about his day a sign of interest in him and his life. He defines asking about his day as "pumping him." When Milton doesn't ask Ellen about her day, she views that as meaning he's not interested in her. Milton, on the other hand, counts it as respecting her independence and her ability to initiate discussion of her day by herself. In Chapter 11, we discuss the misunderstanding between Milton and Ellen in more detail.

Other misunderstandings based on gender-related constitutive rules routinely emerge in interaction. One of the more common misunderstandings occurs because women and men tend to have different constitutive rules for what counts as support. Socialized to share their feelings, women learn to express their emotions and to offer sensitive verbal responses when others talk to them about problems. Masculine socialization, on the other hand, encourages men not to reveal their emotions, so they are less likely to share their feelings openly. They may be uncomfortable offering emotional, verbal responses when others disclose feelings. Further, men are usually socialized to try to solve problems, give advice, or otherwise provide instrumental help rather than affective sympathy. These differences in constitutive rules can complicate interaction between women and men.

MASCULINE RULES:	Showing emotions = weakness
	Responding emotionally = not helping
FEMININE RULES:	Showing emotions = being intimate
	Responding emotionally = helping

What counts as love also seems to differ somewhat between women and men. Counselor Catherine Riessman talked with spouses to find out what they counted as a good marriage. She discovered that most women feel their marriages are gratifying as long as they and their husbands routinely talk about the marriage and their feelings. The men told a different story. For them, marriage is good as long as they and their wives regularly do things together.

Riessman also noted that men and women don't always agree on constitutive rules for talk about marriage. Most men see talk about the relationship as useful only if there is some problem, whereas women see talk as a way to sustain intimacy. Supporting Riessman's findings is linguist

Deborah Tannen, who says men tend to think a relationship is fine as long as they don't have to talk about it, whereas women tend to feel a relationship is working well as long as they *are* talking about it. In Chapter 6, we focus on misunderstandings that arise from disparate constitutive rules for talking about relationships.

HUSBANDS' RULES: Doing things = healthy marriage, intimacy
                    Talking about relationship = problem

WIVES' RULE: Talking = healthy marriage, intimacy
                    Not talking about relationship = problem

Improving Communication

Differences in constitutive rules are to be expected because people are socialized in different groups that teach distinct rules for what counts as what. Even so, normal, predictable differences in constitutive rules need not doom us to misunderstanding others and to being misunderstood by them. There are ways to reduce the chance of misunderstandings such as the one between Mark and John in the example that opened this chapter.

Use Metacommunication to Explain Your Rules

Years ago, the ever-sassy Aretha Franklin dominated the airwaves with her song "R-E-S-P-E-C-T" in which she sang, "R,e,s,p,e,c,t—find out what it means to me." We could all take a lesson from Aretha. Telling others what we mean is one of the best ways of reducing misunderstandings that arise from dissimilar constitutive rules. In other words, we should explain what counts as what to us so that others can understand our meanings. Translating our constitutive rules provides others with insight into how we think and how we interpret them and their communication. When Jerry explained kvetching to me, I could understand what it meant to him and respond appropriately.

Scholars use the term *metacommunication* to refer to communication about communication. When we metacommunicate, we comment on our communication. For example, Jerry metacommunicated when he explained kvetching to me. Couples may comment on patterns in their communication: "We seem to be interrupting each other a lot"; "your tone sounds really hostile"; "have you noticed that we almost never talk about anything except logistics any more?" Each of these metacommunications states an observation about the process of communication. Metacommunicating allows us to notice patterns in communication and to call them to our attention so that we can correct them, if appropriate.

In Mark's case, he would have been wise to talk with some of the senior partners in his firm before the banquet. Using metacommunication, Mark could have explained to senior partners how to interpret his absence from the banquet. He could have told them that his son's pageant was also scheduled on the night of the banquet and he felt that attending the pageant was part of being a good father. If the partners had understood this, they might have been less critical of Mark's failure to appear at the banquet. Even if they had been disappointed that he couldn't attend, Mark's advance explanation would have reduced the likelihood that they would perceive his absence as a lack of commitment.

Mark is not the only one who could have lessened the possibility of misunderstanding. The senior partners might also have foreseen the value of explaining to a new member that the annual banquet was considered a celebration of solidarity among members of the firm. If Mark had known that the banquet meant this (versus partying) to the senior partners, he might have joined the banquet after his son's pageant. Alternatively, he might have explained why he couldn't come and found other ways of demonstrating his commitment to the firm.

Discover Others' Constitutive Rules

When my cat, Sadie, first came to live with us, she and I had some confrontations over house rules. She quickly learned where the litter box and food and water dishes were. But she didn't understand why it was okay to walk and perch on the counters in bathrooms but not in the kitchen. For the first month she was in our home, I regularly scolded her when she jumped up on the kitchen counter: "No, Sadie, no. It's unsanitary for you to walk where we fix food." Just as regularly she flicked her tail at me as if to say, "What a foolish restriction; a counter is a counter."

MY RULE: Cats on kitchen counter = unsanitary

SADIE'S RULE: All counters = places to walk

Unlike Sadie, we humans can understand that rules vary according to context. We realize that we and others have rules for what counts as what.

And if the rules are explained to us, we can learn them, even the complicated ones. We can use metacommunication to ask others what their communication means to them.

Unlike Sadie, we can ask others what things mean to them. For example, Mark might have asked John or one of the other long-time members of the firm about the banquet. Over coffee one day he might have said to John, "So, I got the invitation to the banquet. Is this a big deal?" Had he asked this, John probably would have replied, "Yes, it's an occasion when we take time to celebrate the firm's success and to appreciate how we work as a family." Knowing this, Mark might have changed his plans or explained his conflict to his partners. As a result, misunderstanding would have been less likely or less serious.

Be Aware That You and Others Have Constitutive Rules

A third guideline is to remind ourselves that we and others *have* and *use* constitutive rules. This reminder discourages us from dismissing others as unreasonable, misinformed, insensitive, or otherwise inept. I learned this after delivering a speech to members of an African American organization. During the speech, I realized that something was amiss when I perceived them as both interested *and* rude (by my constitutive rules). Because I couldn't reconcile these two perceptions, I talked with Cornell who helped me understand how to interpret the call-out style of communication.

If my friend, Louise, had given herself this reminder, she might not have been so quick to assume that the lack of a thank you letter from her parents-in-law was rudeness. By the same reasoning, had her mother-in-law realized that she and Louise each have constitutive rules, she might not have been so hasty to judge Louise as formal and unfriendly.

A bottom line for reducing misunderstandings based on different constitutive rules is to recognize that there are not absolute, correct meanings for what we say and do. People have different meanings for what counts as what, and we cannot safely assume that our meanings match those of others. What we can do is engage in metacommunication to explain our constitutive rules and ask others what their communication means. We all have constitutive rules. Metacommunicating about them may not eliminate all the misunderstandings that arise from differences among our rules, but talking about them will reduce the frequency and seriousness of mixed meanings in our interactions with others.

Key Words

- brute facts
- call and response
- communication rules
- constitutive rules
- gender
- metacommunication
- racial and ethnic groups
- social class

Reflecting on This Chapter

1. What are your constitutive rules for showing love, respect, interest, and support? To what extent do your rules reflect your membership in particular social groups, such as race-ethnicity, gender, and social class?

2. This chapter focuses on misunderstandings that arise from membership in different social groups; however, misunderstandings of constitutive rules also occur because of personal differences in communicators' backgrounds. Can you identify constitutive rules you learned in your family or other important relationships in your life? When, if ever, have those rules caused misunderstandings in your interactions with close friends, romantic partners, and their families?

3. Attend a religious service in a church, synagogue, or temple other than the one you usually attend. If you are white, you might attend a service in which the congregation is primarily black or Asian. If you are Christian, you might attend a Buddhist sitting or Jewish synagogue. Notice how members of the congregation do or do not interact with each other and the preacher, minister, priest, or other spiritual leader.

4. Think about the last time you were a newcomer to some organization or in some context. Perhaps it was when you took a new job or enrolled in school. How did you learn what counts as what in the new context? Can you identify constitutive rules in the context that were or are unique to it?

5. Young children provide us with clear examples of how people learn constitutive rules. If you interact with young children (perhaps you baby-sit or have young siblings, nieces, or nephews), observe them in the process of figuring out what counts as what. What is "being bad" and "being good"? What is "sassing" and what is "being respectful"? What is "playing nicely" and "playing too rough"?

6. Write out your constitutive rules for the following:

   A. What is conflict?

   B. What is dinnertime?

   C. What counts as showing affection?

   D. What counts as disrespect?

   E. What is a nice party? (Describe the food and beverages, lighting, number of people, dress, and so forth.)

   F. What counts as showing interest in what another person says?

Compare your answers with those of others in your class. Discuss both similarities and differences among you. Can you explain why you share constitutive rules with some people and not with others?

References

Houston, M. (1997). When black women talk with white women: Why dialogues are difficult. In A. González, M. Houston, & V. Chen (Eds.), *Our voices: Essays in culture, ethnicity, and communication* (2nd ed., pp. 187–194). Los Angeles: Roxbury.

Katriel, T. (1990). Griping as a verbal ritual in some Israeli discourse. In D. Carbaugh (Ed.), *Cultural communication and intercultural contact* (pp. 99–114). Hillsdale, NJ: Lawrence Erlbaum.

Maltz, D., & Borker, R. (1982). A cultural approach to male-female miscommunication. In J. J. Gumpertz (Ed.), *Language and social identity* (pp. 196–216). London: Cambridge University Press.

Park, M. (1979). *Communication styles in two different cultures: Korean and American.* Seoul: Han Shin Press.

Pearce, B., & Cronen, V. (1980). *Communication, action, and meaning: The creation of social realities.* New York: Praeger.

Ribeau, S., Baldwin, J., & Hecht, M. (1994). An African American communication perspective. In L. Samovar & R. Porter (Eds.), *Intercultural communication: A reader* (7th ed., pp. 140–147). Belmont, CA: Wadsworth.

Riessman, C. K. (1990). *Divorce talk: Women and men make sense of personal relationships.* New Brunswick, NJ: Rutgers University Press.

Searle, J. (1976). *Speech acts: An essay in the philosophy.* London: Cambridge University Press.

Smitherman, G. (1977). *Talkin' and testifyin': The language of black America.* Boston: Houghton Mifflin.

Tannen, D. (1990). *You just don't understand: Women and men in conversation.* New York: William Morrow.

Watzlawick, P., Beavin, J., & Jackson, D. (1967). *Pragmatics of human communication*. New York: W. W. Norton.

Weber, S. N. (1994). The need to be: The socio-cultural significance of black language. In L. Samovar & R. Porter (Eds.), *Intercultural communication: A reader* (7th ed., pp. 221–226). Belmont, CA: Wadsworth.

Wood, J. T. (1997). *Gendered lives: Communication, gender, and culture* (2nd ed.). Belmont, CA: Wadsworth.

| 4 |

IT'S RUDE TO INTERRUPT WHEN
I'M SPEAKING

. . .

Understanding Regulative Rules

of Communication

You won't believe what happened on campus today," Bess exclaims as she slips into the booth where Duane is sitting.

Duane looks up and folds the paper he was reading.

"A group of students held a rally to protest the university's new foreign language requirements. They were upset that . . . "

"What's so big about a student protest?" he asks. "They happen all the time."

"Not like this one," Bess replies. "The students marched into the General Administration Building and staged a sit-in right in the president's office. Not only that . . . "

"That's no big deal. But I have some real news," Duane says. "Today I registered to take the MCAT."

"Wow." Bess looks at him and smiles warmly. "I was hoping you'd decide to go for the MBA."

"Well, I did. I signed up to take the exam in January."

"That's great, Duane," Bess says, nodding enthusiastically. "In just two years you'll have the degree and you can get a job and we can start our life for real. I'll have been working for a year by then so . . . "

Duane interrupts to tell Bess how he plans the next two years. "I figure I'll do better if I focus on school and don't work. So I'll get a loan for the first year. Then, you'll graduate and you can put me through the second year of the program. Then we can move to wherever I find a good job."

"But I might have a good job already so you might need to move where I am," Bess points out.

"Where we locate isn't the immediate issue. For now, the priority is for me to take the MCAT and get into a good school and do well."

"Right. That's the first priority," Bess agrees. "But I thought you said the business school here was excellent. I mean, I just assumed you would go here because that would mean we could stay together while I finish school and . . ."

"We'll have to see where I get in and then decide. But right now I'm hungry. Let's order lunch."

"Okay," she agrees, nodding. "But isn't this school your first choice? I mean, you said . . ."

"Everything depends on how I score on the MCAT and which schools accept me, so there's no point in talking about preferences right now," Duane says to put an end to the topic. Bess nods reluctantly to signal she is willing to leave the subject.

"Let's get lunch and then I want to go check out the sale on tennis racquets," Duane says. "Mine is so old it's totally worthless."

How would you describe this conversation? How do you perceive the flow of conversation? What happens to topics that Bess initiates? What happens to topics that Duane initiates? If you're observant, you noticed that subjects Bess introduced were not developed. More than once, Duane didn't even respond to issues Bess put on the talk table. Instead, he tended to interrupt Bess and reroute the conversation to topics that interested him. You may also have noticed that the subjects Duane initiated were developed more fully than Bess's topics and that Bess responded to the ideas he put forth for discussion.

Is Duane self-centered? Is he rude to ignore Bess's concerns and interrupt them to put forward his own? Does he want to dominate the conversation? Although it would be easy to jump to the conclusion that Duane is an insensitive communicator, that may not be an insightful interpretation of what's happening between him and Bess. More is at work here than how polite and responsive Duane is.

In this chapter we focus on how we regulate communication. We discover that people have different perspectives on how to coordinate interaction and find that these differences sometimes lead to misunderstandings. We also learn that personal and social factors influence individuals' views of how to structure communication.

Understanding the Misunderstanding

In Chapter 3 we learned that communication is guided by two kinds of rules. Constitutive rules, which were the focus of that chapter, deal with *what* communication means and does. They assign meaning to verbal and nonverbal communication by defining what the communication means. For example, constitutive rules specify what is considered an insult, a compliment, an invitation, a reprimand, and so forth.

The second type of communication rule is the regulative rule. These rules regulate interaction by specifying *how* communication operates. Regulative rules tell us when it is and is not appropriate to speak; when interruptions are acceptable, when responses are called for and what kinds of responses are suitable; where we can interact in various ways; and with whom we can communicate about particular topics. Generally we're not conscious of regulative rules; we don't realize we're organizing communication in patterned ways. Nonetheless, we tend to rely on recurrent routines to structure our interactions.

A good example of regulative rules in operation is turn-taking in conversation. We know we're not supposed to interrupt if a person is speaking rapidly and without pauses or if a person doesn't meet our eyes. We figure out that we can take a turn speaking when a person who has been talking stops and looks at us. We realize we've been monopolizing conversation if others look bored and restless or if they keep trying to speak over us. Verbal and nonverbal communication gives us cues that tell us when to speak, when we've talked too much, and when to let others speak. The following chart illustrates regulative rules.

Examples of Regulative Rules

Never talk back to your elders.

Be quiet and bow your head during prayers.

Do not fight during meals.

Do not talk loud in the library.

Answer when a professor calls on you.

Help others enter conversations.

Take turns in communication.

Don't kiss or hug in public places.

In business negotiations, assert your interests.

Do not interrupt when others are speaking.

How many of the rules in the chart do you follow in your communication? Probably you follow some and not others. It's also likely that if you present the rules to a dozen people, you'll find differences in how much they agree with and use them. The reason is that we do not all learn the same regulative rules, and that can be a source of misunderstanding between people. Let's look at alternative rules for each of the examples in the chart.

Alternative Regulative Rules

Correct elders if they are wrong.

Participate actively and vocally in prayers.

Engage in vigorous conversation, even disagreement, during meals. Often such activity enhances your enjoyment of the meal.

You may call out to greet a friend in the library.

If you don't know how to answer a professor's question, you may look down and remain silent when a professor calls on you.

If you want to speak, you should assert yourself and not expect others to make room for you in the conversation.

If someone wants to monopolize communication and if others allow it, that's permissible.

Do kiss and hug in public places.

In business negotiations, you should honor others' interests.

Interrupt conversations when you have something to say.

Although the two sets of rules are conflicting, you probably know some people who would agree with each rule in the two charts. That's because regulative rules, just like constitutive ones, are not absolute and not universal. We learn regulative rules in the process of interacting with others throughout our lives. Because different people interact with different individuals and groups, they learn various and sometimes contradictory rules for how to organize communication. Differences in our regulative rules can be traced to both personal and social factors.

Personal Influences on Regulative Rules

As in all aspects of communication, regulative rules are shaped by personal experiences with family, friends, work associates, and romantic partners. Many parents teach children that *please* and *thank you* are "magic words" to be used to request things and to express appreciation for what they receive. If your parents stressed saying *please* and *thank you*, you probably have a regulative rule that tells you to say those words when you ask for and get things. Did your parents argue in front of you? If so, you may have a regulative rule that defines public argument as acceptable. On the other hand, if you never saw your parents arguing, you may have a regulative rule stipulating that arguments should be conducted in private.

What have you learned from interactions with friends? Have you learned, as Bess has, that you should respond to topics others initiate to show that you are polite and supportive? Or have you learned that you need to respond only to topics that interest you? Through interacting with friends, you've probably developed regulative rules that tell you whether discussing fears, personal issues, sports events, feelings, and relationships is appropriate.

We also generate regulative rules in romantic relationships. For an intimate relationship to be comfortable for both partners, the two individuals must coordinate their regulative rules for communication. Otherwise, their communication will be full of miscues and bumbling. As partners interact, they develop shared understandings of how to organize communication, how to signal attentiveness, when to talk about serious matters, how to respond to each other, which topics are off limits, and so forth. The shared regulative rules that partners develop help them coordinate communication relatively smoothly.

Each of us has a range of individual experiences that influence the regulative rules we use to guide the way we communicate with others. Thus, there is an idiosyncratic or unique character to regulative rules. Even so, individual experiences are not the only influence on regulative rules. Social factors also shape the way individuals organize communication.

Social Influences on Regulative Rules

As we've noted in previous chapters, individuals exist in contexts or systems that influence who they are and how they communicate. Each of us was socialized in multiple social groups that taught us how to communicate and how to interpret the communication of others. Of the many

Calvin and Hobbes   by Bill Watterson

social groups that influence our regulative rules for interacting, gender and ethnic groups are especially important.

Gender   Gender is a significant influence on regulative rules. Gender seems to affect how, when, where, with whom, and about what many people communicate. Although not all men follow typically masculine regulative rules and not all women adhere to conventionally feminine ones, pronounced gender patterns occur in regulative rules.

One of the gender patterns that researchers have identified is the use of interruptions. Both men and women interrupt others at times, but they tend to do so in different ways and for different reasons. Daniel Maltz and Ruth Borker's studies of early childhood games revealed that boys generally learn to interrupt others so they can grab the talk stage. Thus, they interrupt to reroute conversations and to assert their own agenda. A boy might ignore what another boy said and start a completely distinct topic in the hope of commanding the situation. Maltz and Borker found that girls less often interrupted others; when they did, the girls tended to interrupt to encourage or support others. A girl might interrupt a friend's story by saying, "That's interesting" or "Wow, and then what did you do? I mean how did you feel when that happened?" These interruptions signal interest and keep attention focused on the person who is telling the story.

Gendered tendencies to interrupt showed up in Victoria DeFrancisco's research on communication in marriages. From her study, she reports a clear pattern in some marriages in which husbands don't respond to topics their wives initiate. The husbands also tended to interrupt their wives and to reroute conversations to topics they wanted to discuss. Neither husbands nor wives in DeFrancisco's study were aware of this pattern! Nonetheless, it occurred again and again in their interaction, suggesting that consistent regulative rules were at work.

Gender differences in regulative rules were evident in the dialogue that opened this chapter. Like the husbands in DeFrancisco's study, Duane was unresponsive to topics Bess initiated and he interrupted her to put forward his own ideas. Was Duane being rude? Perhaps he was if we use Bess's regulative rules as the standard for judging his communication. If we use Duane's regulative rules, however, he wasn't being rude; he was only following masculine rules that a person should assert himself in conversation and attempt to get and hold attention.

Gender also seems to influence how we respond to others when they tell us about troubles or problems. Socialized to be empathic and to discuss feelings, women often respond to others' problems by expressing understanding and inviting others to talk about how they feel. Communication scholar Fern Johnson says that women typically focus on dialogue, especially personal dialogue, when responding to friends. When a woman hears about a friend's problem, she is likely to respond by saying, "I know how you feel. I was in a similar situation last year" or "You must feel really sad. Tell me what's going on in you." The first response displays empathy (I've been there too; I can understand); the second response encourages open discussion of emotions.

Because masculine socialization emphasizes maintaining emotional control and independence, many men are reluctant to talk openly about their feelings, especially with other men. Educator Scott Swain reports that men typically rely on more covert displays of concern and support. After hearing about a friend's problem, a man might suggest, "Let's go out and catch a movie." By feminine communication rules, this suggestion might be interpreted as demonstrating a lack of involvement and dismissing the friend's problems. By masculine communication rules, however, the suggestion is an appropriate response: It offers company and a diversion from the problem, both of which are supportive.

Gender differences also affect regulative rules governing listening styles. Feminine socialization emphasizes giving verbal and nonverbal signs of listening and interest. Read again the opening of this chapter and notice how Bess signals that she is listening to and interested in what Duane says. Like many women, Bess gives nonverbal cues (head nods, smiles) and verbal displays of interest (repeating what Duane says, saying "right" and "that's great") to let others know she is involved in a conversation.

Masculine socialization places less emphasis on giving overt responses to others. Some researchers think this stems from traditional masculine concerns with control. Revealing feelings or responses to others could diminish control in a situation. Other researchers think control is less the issue than learned, arbitrary patterns. According to this line of thinking, people who interrupt and don't respond overtly to others are not conversational bullies but are simply acting according to the scripts they learned for normal conversation. Regardless of the reason for interruptions and overt responsiveness, misunderstandings and frustration are likely when people operate from disparate regulative rules for how to listen. We explore this topic in greater detail in Chapter 5, which focuses on different styles of listening.

Ethnicity   Along with gender, ethnicity influences regulative rules for communicating. The ethnic groups in which we interact teach us particular regulative rules — ones that are not always shared by people outside our groups. Knowing this can help us recognize one source of misunderstanding between people of different racial and ethnic origins. Consider the differences in the rules of Westerners and the Japanese; and African Americans and European Americans.

Here is one scenario: Takeyo Hayashi owns a successful independent bank in Tokyo. New York financier Maynard Sanger wants to acquire Mr. Hayashi's bank. After Mr. Sanger has explained his proposal for the acquisition, Mr. Hayashi, who finds the proposal unacceptable, says, "This is a very important proposal you have offered." Encouraged by what he sees as a positive response, Mr. Sanger asks, "Then shall I have the papers drawn up for us to sign?" Mr. Hayashi looks down and says, "It is good that you want to come to terms that favor us both." Confused, Mr. Sanger asks, "Does that mean we have an agreement?" Still looking down, Mr. Hayashi replies, "I think we have much to discuss on this worthwhile proposal."

How would you interpret Mr. Hayashi's communication? If you are not Japanese, you may misunderstand his responses to Mr. Sanger's proposal. Knowing that he does not like Mr. Sanger's proposal, you may think that his responses are evasive or even deceitful. Your perceptions might be changed if you knew that Japanese culture places a high premium on not causing another person to lose face. Thus, Mr. Hayashi's regulative rules tell him it is inappropriate to reject directly another person's proposal. He responds in ways his culture has taught him are polite.

Traditional Japanese also have distinctive regulative rules for decision-making — rules that are not shared by and often are not understood by people outside the Japanese culture. In the United States and other Western societies, deadlines are very important. The emphasis on deadlines explains the importance attached to efficiency, directness, delegation of responsibility, and task orientation in decision-making situations. This worldview contrasts sharply with that of Japanese who value thoroughness, harmony, including everyone, and indirectness. When making decisions with Japanese people, many Americans are exasperated by the time and number of meetings the Japanese want in order to involve everyone who could be affected by a decision. Americans may also be vexed by the indirectness characteristic of the traditional Japanese. Like Mr. Hayashi, many Japanese will not state disagreement directly because to them that would be an insult to the other person.

Japanese people sometimes find American decision making at least as frustrating and misdirected as Americans find the Japanese style. Japanese individuals are often disturbed by Americans' lack of attention to group harmony and by what they perceive as excessive directness and insensitivity to others' feelings and inadequate effort to preserve others' standing in a group. Interpersonal respect and sensitivity are central values in many Asian societies, and they may clash with more Western values of task orientation and straightforwardness. Writing for the *Bangkok Post*, Jennifer Sharples pointed out that Thais emphasize showing consideration for others (*kreng jai*) and are often offended by American businesspeople's lack of attention to others' feelings and concerns.

Distinctive regulative rules have also been identified in African American communities. Molefi Asante, a scholar of African American communication, coined the term *Afrocentricity* to refer to the set of beliefs and values of African Americans. According to Asante, African Americans' communication reflects their unique heritage and can be understood only with reference to that underlying heritage.

Especially strong in traditional African American communities is a communal orientation in which each person perceives himself or herself not just as an individual but also as part of a family, a community, and a culture. The individual is part of and responsible to the larger community. The emphasis on communalism helps us understand the highly participative character of preaching in African American groups. In call-response communication pattern, members of congregations respond vocally to the call of the preacher. According to Janice Hamlet, a scholar of intercultural communication, this practice is common in African American groups and rare in European American ones.

The call-response also appears in secular contexts in African American culture. For example, public speaking is a collaborative endeavor in which speaker and audience call back and forth to each other. Similarly, rappers don't give solo performances. Instead, members of the audience call back to the rappers, commenting on the quality of lyrics and the story being shared by the rapper. The communal values of traditional African American culture explain why African Americans regard themselves and the speaker or preacher as part of a whole and why everyone should participate.

Another central value in African American culture is oral skill—finesse in using language for a variety of purposes. Whereas European Americans tend to judge people's communication competence by the directness and clarity of their speech, having those qualities is not sufficient for someone to be considered skillful in African American communities. Also needed are rhythmical speaking, improvisation, drama, playfulness, and subtlety. These communicative qualities show up in African American communication practices such as playing the dozens (engaging in verbal aggressiveness), rapping (speaking in rhyme and/or rhythm), and signifying (criticizing others jokingly and/or indirectly). These forms of African American communication involve regulative rules that differ from those generally used by European Americans, as shown in the following chart.

Ethnic Shaping of Regulative Rules

WHEN	AFRICAN AMERICAN RESPONSE	EUROPEAN AMERICAN RESPONSE
someone insults you verbally	try to outdo the person with a stronger verbal insult	defend yourself verbally or fight physically
someone preaches	participate with verbal and nonverbal responses	listen quietly
someone does something you dislike	signify by jokingly or indirectly showing disapproval	directly state disapproval or say nothing
you feel something strongly	be expressive and display emotions with drama and force	keep your cool and maintain emotional control

Regulative rules are not simply superficial aspects of communication. Instead, they are mirrors of cultural heritage. The patterns we've discussed to illustrate intercultural differences in regulative rules do not begin to exhaust the ones practiced by distinct cultures. You can learn more about

African American culture and the communication it fosters in Chapter 12, which describes interactive patterns of many African Americans that are seldom practiced by European Americans.

Improving Communication

Differences in regulative rules can promote misunderstandings. They may lead us to misinterpret others' motives (she wants to dominate) or feelings for us (he doesn't care enough about me to listen). Differences can also foster misjudgments of others' manners (it's rude to interrupt) and social competence (how could they talk so loudly during the sermon?). Effective communicators strive to avoid such misinterpretations of others and their communication. Three guidelines help us minimize misunderstandings that often accompany differences in regulative rules.

Resist Imposing Standards of Your Groups on Others

In this chapter, we've noted that there is no absolute standard for judging regulative rules. There is no single, universal benchmark that decrees whether interruptions are rude or part of normal conversation, whether it is complimentary or insulting to speak out during a sermon, and whether we should state disagreements directly in business negotiations. What we consider appropriate ways to respond to others and to sequence communication depends on what we were socialized to regard as normal, right, and polite.

The word *ethnocentric* comes from two root terms: *ethno*, which means one's own group or culture, and *centric*, which means centered. Being ethnocentric, then, is being centered on your own group and using your own group as the standard for perceiving and judging everyone else. Effective and ethical communication requires us to realize that the patterns and standards for communication in our own social groups may not be appropriate for interpreting other social groups. We should resist the tendency to be ethnocentric in our judgments of regulative rules used by diverse people. It is more productive to assume that others' regulative rules, like our own, reflect personal experiences and their membership in specific social groups.

Respect Differences and Their Origins

The second guideline extends the first one. In addition to resisting ethnocentrism, we should strive to respect and appreciate regulative rules that differ from our own. In other words, effective communicators attempt to move beyond mere toleration of differences. They see differences among people as opportunities to learn about others as well as themselves. We can learn about others by inquiring into the connection between particular regulative rules and cultural heritage. For example, the call-response pattern we have discussed reflects traditional African values of communalism. Appreciating the origin of the communication practice enriches our understanding of others and of diverse human values and beliefs.

When we are open to learning from differences in communication, we also enlarge our insight into ourselves. When we encounter a worldview that differs from our own, we gain a new lens through which to look at our own culture and our own communication practices. Intercultural communication scholars Judith Martin and Tom Nakayama point out that just as fish are unaware of water, humans tend to be unaware of their cultural background and assumptions. We are most likely to become conscious of our cultural perspective and customs when we encounter assumptions and ways of behaving that differ from our own.

In the United States, the media and history establish whiteness as the norm. It is the standard against which other racial groups are compared. With this viewpoint, for whites to see their whiteness and how it structures their beliefs and behaviors is very difficult. Many people assume that race refers to races other than European Americans, so whites may think they don't have a race and may view racial issues as irrelevant to them. To make whiteness more visible, I sometimes encourage white students to attend a black church. Invariably, a number of those who do so will comment on how formal and stuffy their own religious services seem in comparison to those in black churches. In opening themselves to learn about others, these students also learn about themselves.

Communicate to Clarify Regulative Rules

A final guideline is to communicate about differences in regulative rules. When someone organizes communication in a manner we don't like or understand, we should ask the person to explain what she or he is doing and what it means. Bess might have said to Duane, "Do you mean to interrupt me?" Duane might have been unaware that he was interrupting, in which case Bess's metacommunication would alert him. Alternatively, Duane might see interruptions as part of the normal flow of conversation, in which case he might reply to Bess, "I'm just jumping in the conversation because I'm involved. It's not like I'm trying to cut you off." This comment informs Bess that Duane sees interruptions differently from the way she sees them. At the very least, understanding that Duane's view is different would allow Bess not to misinterpret his motives.

We can also reduce misunderstandings about regulative rules by translating our own rules to others who operate by dissimilar ones. Bess could have said to Duane, "When I bring up a topic, I'd like for you to respond to it before jumping to another topic." This comment gives Duane a clear explanation of how Bess likes to sequence communication. Without Bess's translation, Duane may never realize that she wants a response to her ideas or that she feels he is being rude when he reroutes the conversation.

Clarifying regulative rules will not resolve all problems in interaction. A real possibility is that Duane *does* intend to dominate the conversation and doesn't care whether Bess thinks he's being rude. If that's the case, then Duane and Bess have a problem, but it is not a communication problem. A greater likelihood, however, is that they are operating by different regulative rules and that neither of them realizes this is happening. That problem is rooted in communication, and it can be addressed with more communication.

Key Words

- Afrocentricity
- ethnicity
- ethnocentrism
- gender
- interruptions
- listening styles
- regulative rules

Reflecting on This Chapter

1. Have you ever been in a conversation similar to the one between Duane and Bess? If so, with which of them did you identify? After reading this chapter, can you understand why Duane might think it is acceptable to interrupt and be unresponsive as well as why Bess might think he was being rude?

2. Refer to the two sets of regulative rules on pages 49 and 50. Which of the rules do you follow in your communication? Can you identify when and with whom you learned each rule?

3. Venture into an unfamiliar social context. You might attend a campus gathering of an ethnic group other than your own. Focus on regulative

rules that govern how, when, and with whom people interact. What regulative rules can you infer from the group's patterns of communication? How are they similar to and different from your own?

4. Think about a current or past romantic relationship in which you were involved for a significant time. Identify regulative rules that you and your partner used in your communication. How do the joint rules you and your partner developed vary from those you personally used prior to entering the relationship?

5. Review this chapter's discussion of regulative rules that tend to be followed by European Americans, Japanese, and African Americans. Can you identify how the rules of each group reflect distinct cultural heritages? (You may want to return to this question after reading Chapter 12, which focuses on African American communication.)

6. Read a book on etiquette — anything from Amy Vanderbilt's classic volume to one of Miss Manners's books is appropriate. Notice the regulative rules given for verbal and nonverbal communication. Do these rules reflect the ones used by all members of U.S. society or only people in the mainstream?

7. Select a popular magazine that includes advice on romance or social interaction. Typical article titles are "How to Win the Man/Woman of Your Dreams," "Does She/He Really Care About You?" "How to Be a Sizzling Conversationalist," and "Ten Rules for Making Friends." What do the articles recommend as regulative rules to show interest, caring, commitment, intelligence, and so forth? Can you identify gender scripts in the advice given?

8. Think about the word *whiteness*. What is the meaning of being white in the United States? Why is it difficult to recognize whiteness and all that it implies for thought, feeling, and action?

References

Asante, M. (1987). *The Afrocentric idea*. Philadelphia, PA: Temple University Press.

Carbaugh, D. (1990). Communication rules in Donahue discourse. In D. Carbaugh (Ed.), *Cultural communication and intercultural contact* (pp. 119–149). Hillsdale, NJ: Lawrence Erlbaum.

Cathcart, D., & Cathcart, R. (1997). The group: A Japanese context. In L. Samovar & R. Porter (Eds.), *Intercultural communication: A reader* (8th ed., pp. 329–339). Belmont, CA: Wadsworth.

Daniel, J., & Smitherman, G. (1990). How I got over: Communication dynamics in the black community. In D. Carbaugh (Ed.), *Cultural communication and intercultural contact* (pp. 17–40). Hillsdale, NJ: Lawrence Erlbaum.

DeFrancisco, V. (1991). The sounds of silence: How men silence women in marital relations. *Discourse and Society, 2*, 413–423.

Dolan, R. E., & Worden, R. L. (Eds.). (1992). *Japan: A country study*. Washington, DC: Library of Congress.

Ferguson, R. (1990). Introduction: Invisible center. In R. Ferguson, M. Gever, T. Trinh, & C. West (Eds.), *Out there: Marginalization and contemporary cultures* (pp. 9–14). New York: New Museum of Contemporary Art and MIT Press.

Frankenburg, R. (1993). *White women, race matters: The social construction of whiteness*. Minneapolis: University of Minnesota Press.

Garner, T. (1994). Oral rhetorical practice in African American culture. In A. Gonzalez, M. Houston, & V. Chen (Eds.), *Our voices: Essays in culture, ethnicity, and communication* (pp. 81–91). Los Angeles: Roxbury.

Grice, H. (1975). Logic and conversation. In P. Cole & J. Morgan (Eds.), *Syntax and semantics: Vol. 3. Speech acts*. New York: Academic Press.

Gudykunst, W., & Ting-Toomey, S. (1988). *Culture and interpersonal communication*. Newbury Park, CA: Sage.

Hamlet, J. (1994). Understanding traditional African American preaching. In A. González, M. Houston, & V. Chen (Eds.), *Our voices: Essays in culture, ethnicity, and communication* (pp. 100–103). Los Angeles: Roxbury.

Helms, J. (1994). *A race is a nice thing to have: A guide to being a white person*. Topeka, KS: Content Communication.

Honeycutt, J., Woods, B., & Fontenot, K. (1993). The endorsement of communication conflict rules as a function of engagement, marriage, and marital ideology. *Journal of Social and Personal Relationships, 10*, 285–304.

Johnson, F. (1996). Women's friendships: Closeness in dialogue. In J. T. Wood (Ed.), *Gendered relationships* (pp. 79–94). Mountain View, CA: Mayfield.

Jones, E., & Gallois, C. (1989). Spouses' impressions of rules for communication in public and private marital conflicts. *Journal of Marriage and the Family, 51*, 957–967.

Maltz, D., & Borker, R. (1982). A cultural approach to male-female miscommunication. In J. J. Gumpertz (Ed.), *Language and social identity* (pp. 196–216). Cambridge: Cambridge University Press.

Martin, J., & Nakayama, T. (1997). *Intercultural communication in contexts*. Mountain View, CA: Mayfield.

Nakane, C. (1977). *About Japan*. Tokyo: Kinji Kawamura.

Philipsen, G. (1990). Speaking "like a man" in Teamsterville. In D. Carbaugh (Ed.), *Cultural communication and intercultural contact* (pp. 11–20). Hillsdale, NJ: Lawrence Erlbaum.

Sharples, J. (1995, May 28–June 3). A cross cultural conundrum. *Bangkok Post Sunday Magazine*, pp. 10–11.

Swain, S. (1989). Covert intimacy: Closeness in men's friendships. In B. Risman & P. Schwartz (Eds.), *Gender and intimate relationships* (pp. 71–86). Belmont, CA: Wadsworth.

Terasawa, Y. (1974, May 12). Japanese style in decision-making. *The New York Times*, pp. C-1, C-8.

Ueda, K. (1974). Sixteen ways to avoid saying "no" in Japan. In J. C. Condon & M. Saito (Eds.), *Intercultural encounters with Japan* (pp. 185–192). Tokyo: Simul Press.

Yerby, J., Buerkel-Rothfuss, N., & Bochner, A. (1990). *Family systems reconsidered: Integrating social construction theory and dialectical process into a systems perspective of family communication*. Paper presented at the Speech Communication Association Convention, Chicago, IL.

| 5 |

YOU'RE NOT LISTENING TO ME

. . .

Understanding Different Styles

of Listening

Maureen Evans and Paul McDonald are meeting to develop trial strategy for a product liability case they will try jointly. He is a senior partner in the firm of Williams, Whitfield, and Carlson; Maureen is a junior associate who has been with the firm for three years. Their client is Sure-Seat, manufacturer of child safety seats for automobiles. Bringing the case against Sure-Seat are Reginald and Betsy Bradley, whose 3-year-old son Tommy suffered a head injury when their car was hit five months ago.

Paul opens the conversation. "Frankly, I'm surprised this case is going to trial." Maureen interjects "Um, hm" to signal she too is surprised. Paul continues, "I expected the Bradleys to withdraw the claim when we offered the minimum settlement we always offer for nuisance cases."

"Me, too," Maureen agrees and nods her head to reinforce her words. "But since they didn't accept the settlement, we need to develop our defense strategy."

"Agreed," he says, not looking up.

Maureen looks at Paul as she speaks. "The way I see it our best defense strategy is to emphasize the Bradley's record of carelessness with their children. And I don't mean just Tommy."

Paul glances at the clock on his desk, then makes a note on his legal pad.

Maureen waits for a response—a head nod, a request for her to explain what she means, a look that indicates Paul is interested in hearing more. When he offers no visible or audible response, Maureen continues, eager to demonstrate to the senior partner that she's really done her research. "I've checked hospital records and insurance claims and it turns out the Bradleys have quite a record of being careless, to put it gently, with their children. When Tommy was 1, he fell out of a swing while his mother was at the playground, but she was talking to another mother, not watching Tommy."

"Can you document that?"

"Yep; I've got one witness who was on the scene and a hospital admission statement in which Mrs. Bradley stated that he'd fallen when she was looking away." Maureen is pleased that her research unearthed information Paul didn't discover. "Then, when Tommy was 2½, he suffered a mild concussion when Mr. Bradley was driving and swerved to avoid a dog. Mr. Bradley had Tommy in the front seat without a child safety seat or even a seat belt.

Paul says nothing, and doodles on his legal pad.

"And their daughter Sara has also had some accidents that could have been avoided with normal prudence," Maureen continues. "She was bitten by a snake while playing outdoors without supervision, and just last year she got into some cleaning fluid; it was stored under the kitchen sink and had no child-proof locks on it. Fortunately, neither the snakebite nor the cleaning fluid was lethal; they only caused pain and an overnight stay in the hospital in each case. How do you think jurors would perceive such a string of avoidable accidents?"

Without answering her question, Paul observes, "This is the first time Sure-Seat has been sued for anything."

Maureen nods and says, "That's true."

"It seems to me that a squeaky clean safety record would be persuasive to a jury."

"That's a good point," Maureen agrees and nods. "It's worth calling to the jury's attention, but I don't think it should be the center of our defense."

Paul waits for her to continue.

"No; juries today routinely assume companies are irresponsible and have an endless supply of money, so they're inclined to side against a company when any plausible claim is made. That's why I think our case should pivot on showing that this claim isn't plausible. To do that we need to demonstrate that the Bradleys have a history of being less than responsible parents when it comes to ensuring their children's safety."

"I don't know," Paul equivocates. "The company's record is very impressive."

"I agree," Maureen responds with a nod.

"That should score points with a jury."

"You're right," Maureen agrees looking directly at Paul and nodding. "I think we should definitely make the jury aware of Sure-Seat's perfect record."

Paul nods, satisfied by her response.

"We can note Sure-Seat's record, and still make the Bradleys' neglect the focus of our defense," Maureen continues. She holds up her fingers to tick off points. "Look, here's what we have: One, the Bradleys allege that Tommy was in his Sure-Seat and that they had locked the safety catch. There is no evidence corroborating that claim, so there is some doubt as to whether Tommy was in the seat and, even if he was, whether they had secured the safety lock. Two, the Bradleys have a history of being less than safety conscious with both Sara and Tommy, so there is reason to believe that they could have either forgotten to put Tommy in his Sure-Seat or forgotten to lock the safety catch. Three, there was no mark on Tommy consistent with what would be expected from the strap on the Sure-Seat if he had been locked in it at the time of the wreck. Don't you think those points would be persuasive to a jury?"

Paul's face doesn't reveal what he's thinking.

"And we can bolster that defense with your point about Sure-Seat's spotless safety record. I don't see how any jury could find against the company once we prove both those points. What do you think?"

"Okay, this has been a productive first session. We'll talk again tomorrow. Between now and then why don't you work up a list of people we'd call to testify to document the accidents and an outline of questions for each of them." Paul rises, indicating that the meeting is over. "Right now I've got to meet with Chris on the Berkshire case."

Later, talking with another junior associate in the firm, Maureen says, "I can't believe he wasn't impressed by what I found out about all the accidents the Bradley children have had. It was like I was talking to a stone wall—no response, no interest, no recognition of resourceful research on the case. I'm not even sure whether he was really listening to me. The most I got out of him was an 'umm.'"

When Paul is talking with another senior partner later the same day, he remarks, "That Evans is really on the ball. She did first-rate research on *Bradley vs. Sure-Seat*, and she's mapped out a very strong trial strategy.

When I suggested a less compelling trial tactic, she would have none of it. We may want to consider bringing her up for partner a bit ahead of the normal schedule."

Obviously Paul McDonald was listening and listening closely to Maureen Evans. Just as obviously, he was impressed with her research and her ideas for trial strategy. Maureen, however, didn't feel at all sure that Paul was listening to her, much less that he was impressed by her work and her thinking. The reason Maureen could not see that Paul was attentive and pleased with her work is that she and he have different listening styles.

In this chapter, we discuss listening and some of the factors that influence distinct ways of listening. After reading the chapter you should understand that people listen in different ways. Knowing this will help you avoid Maureen's mistake of using her rules of listening to interpret Paul's style of listening. You may also identify how you listen and consider whether it is always the most appropriate style for different people and contexts.

Understanding the Listening Process

Many people think that listening and hearing are synonyms. They're not. Hearing is a physiological process that occurs when sound waves hit eardrums. Hearing doesn't require effort on our parts. If we are in the vicinity of sound waves and if we have average hearing ability, we will hear sounds. People with hearing impairments receive sound messages by lip reading, by using American Sign Language, or by relying on a dog trained to alert its owner to specific sounds.

According to listening scholar Robert Bolton, listening involves a lot more than merely hearing. Listening is more complex and active than hearing. It involves more activities than simply physically receiving sound. It is more active because when we listen we make choices about what to attend to and what meanings to assign to what we perceive. Although we're not usually conscious of our influence on listening, we nonetheless shape how we listen to and make sense of communication.

Communication researchers agree that listening involves a minimum of five activities that overlap one another. Some communication scholars include as many as seven activities. Listening begins with an attitude of mindfulness—a decision to attend to what is happening in the present moment. When we are mindful, we don't think about what happened the night before or what we plan to do after the present interaction. Instead, we choose to be fully present and involved in the present. We give our full attention to the person or people we are with, the music that is playing, or the experience of the moment.

The second step in listening is to hear or physically receive audio signals; these might be music, traffic noise, or words. Third, listeners select the aspects of noise and messages to perceive. We can't tune into everything around us, so we select only certain stimuli for our attention. Having done that, we engage in a fourth activity: organizing the sounds we have perceived. Although we're not usually aware of it, we order what we selectively perceive, deciding what goes with what and how to classify stimuli. Using her or his trained ear, a skilled mechanic can distinguish normal engine sounds and not attend to them in order to focus on the pings and vibrations that are not normal. The mechanic might then classify some sounds as related to the carburetor and others as related to the exhaust system.

The fifth listening activity is interpreting. After we selectively perceive and organize what we hear, we interpret it. This step involves assigning meaning—again a process that usually we're not conscious of. When we interpret sounds or a message, we make sense of what we have perceived and organized. The mechanic might interpret the various noises from the car as meaning the car needs a tune-up, the master cylinder is bad, or the transmission is slipping. In the example with Paul and Maureen, he interpreted all that she said to conclude that she had done good research and had sound ideas about trial strategy. Maureen, on the other hand, interpreted what she perceived and organized as meaning that Paul was not attentive to or impressed with her. Interpretations are subjective, so we can seldom prove that the meanings we assign are correct. Rather, interpretation is what sounds or messages mean to us in the context of our experiences and our styles of communicating. (Chapter 1 provides a fuller discussion of the subjective nature of perception and interpretation.)

To the activities we've discussed, some communication scholars add two other aspects of listening. One is responding, which is communicating attention and interest. Often we rely on nonverbal behaviors to show that we are attending to others—a head nod to show agreement, a smile to demonstrate approval, a wrinkled brow to signal we're puzzled. Sometimes we also make sounds or inject a few words to show we're involved— "I see what you mean," "Go on," "And then what happened?" These verbal and nonverbal responses signal that we are attentive, interested, and involved in communication.

The Chinese Character for the Word "Listening"

Finally, a number of scholars assert that effective listening includes remembering. If we don't retain others' communication, obviously our listening is less than competent. Communication specialists Ron Adler and Neil Towne note that the average person remembers only about half of a message immediately after hearing it, and only about one-third of a message eight hours after listening to it. Because we don't—and probably can't—remember everything we hear, we should focus on retaining what we perceive as most important in communication.

Differences in Styles of Listening

Let's return to Paul and Maureen. Was he listening effectively to her? Your answer depends on what you consider effective listening. In turn, what you consider effective listening may depend on the social groups with which you identify. Research shows that how we listen and respond —or fail to respond—to others is influenced by gender and power dynamics, both of which were present in the interaction between Paul and Maureen.

Gendered Patterns of Listening

There are general (though not universal) gender differences in how we listen. The differences were first noticed by Daniel Maltz and Ruth Borker who studied young children at play. These authors concluded that boys and girls seem to operate by different rules about how to use communication. The boys they observed tended to communicate to achieve results— clear-cut goals. They also used communication to establish individual status and to maintain control and attention. Thus, the boys might work

ROSE IS ROSE ® by Pat Brady

Rose is Rose is preprinted by permission of United Features Syndicate, Inc.

together in teams, but they also vied for who was the most valuable player on the team.

The girls observed by Maltz and Borker relied on different rules for how to communicate. For them, the primary goal of communication was to build connections with others by including them in conversations and responding to what they said. The girls also used communication cooperatively rather than competitively. They saw conversations as joint enterprises in which everyone participated. No one person dominated.

Linguist Deborah Tannen claims that the gendered patterns many of us learn early in life follow us into our communication as adults. Women are more likely than men to demonstrate expressiveness and responsiveness to others and to invite others into conversations. Women also tend to give obvious visual and vocal clues to signal they are following what others say and are interested in it. For example, women are more likely than men to nod their heads, smile, establish eye contact, and offer responsive gestures (shrugging shoulders) when they are listening to others.

In general, women also encourage others to continue talking with what are called listening noises— "um, hmm," "yes," "that's interesting," "so," "and," and so forth. These listening noises prompt others to keep talking and to elaborate their ideas. If you review the interaction between Paul and Maureen, you'll see that she sought eye contact, engaged in head nodding, invited his opinions, and made listening noises in response to what he said.

Because masculine socialization emphasizes controlling emotional expressiveness, many men listen without showing their feelings and without giving another person the power of obvious attention. They tend to keep their responses and feelings to themselves—close to the vest. When men don't give obvious signs of attentiveness, women may mistakenly think the men aren't listening or aren't interested. Many men, like Paul, however, listen intently but give no obvious signs of doing so.

The workplace is not the only place where differences in listening styles can lead to misunderstandings. In fact, personal relationships are the context in which many people are frustrated by dissimilar ways of listening. Counselor Aaron Beck says that gendered patterns of listening are a recurrent source of misunderstanding between many husbands and wives. According to Beck, a typical scenario is this:

> A wife tells her husband about something that happened at work or when she was with friends or family. The husband listens but gives no verbal or nonverbal signs that he is following his wife's conversation. He just sits silently until she quits talking. She feels frustrated that he's not showing any involvement. Eventually, she exclaims, "I don't know why I talk to you. You never listen." At that point, the husband recites verbatim what she has told him, proving he has listened carefully.

Probably most of us—men and women—can relate to this scenario. At times, we've all felt that others weren't listening to us because they gave no signs of doing so. Also, others have probably accused us of not paying attention when we were listening. It's equally frustrating to feel that others aren't interested in what we say and to sense that other people doubt that we are listening to them.

Although the individuals in the scenario follow patterns typical for their genders, that isn't always the case. Some women are not overtly responsive listeners; some men are. Some women don't invite others into conversations; some men do. What matters is that when any two people have different styles of listening, they are likely to misunderstand each other and perhaps to feel frustrated or hurt.

Power Dynamics in Listening

Power—and different levels of power—is another influence on listening style. Perhaps you have noticed these power dynamics: People in subordinate positions are attentive and responsive to people in superior positions whereas the reverse isn't as often true. For example, secretaries and administrative assistants are usually more attentive and responsive to

CEOs than CEOs are to them. And junior partners in law firms are likely to be more attentive to senior partners than the other way around.

Nancy Henley studied how nonverbal communication reflects and reinforces power differences among people. She found that people with power and status often keep people with less power waiting, but people with little or no power tend not to keep superiors waiting. Henley also reported that people with low power give overt signs of attention and involvement (for example, eye contact and head nods) to people with greater power. Again, the reverse was not common. Finally, Henley noted that people with power are more prone to interrupt, invade others' space, and not respond to others' questions than are people with less power. Each of these power-related tendencies is evident in the communication between Paul and Maureen. The different levels of professional status and power they have account, in part, for their different styles of listening.

Improving Communication

The ways that people listen are not innate; we aren't born with a particular style of listening. Instead, we learn how to listen by interacting with others who are part of our social communities. This implies two ways we can be more effective when we listen and more sensitive when we interpret the listening of others.

First, we can recognize that there are different ways to listen and no one style is inherently superior. When counseling couples who have communication problems, Aaron Beck cautions each person not to assume that her or his style of listening is the only "right" style. As we have seen in this chapter and throughout the book, people have diverse communication styles. The ways we talk and listen and the nonverbal behaviors we use are no more or less natural than alternative ways that other people use. Remembering this can keep us from jumping to erroneous conclusions about whether others are listening.

A second way to improve our listening is to recognize that we can learn new behaviors. Just as we learned our current style of listening, so can we learn alternative styles if we commit to doing so. Beck advises couples that he counsels to learn what each of them considers good listening. (The discussion of constitutive rules in Chapter 3 pertains to this point.)

He says that effective couple communication requires that both understand what each member of the dyad needs to feel confirmed and valued in a relationship. Let's apply this advice to the couple in the foregoing scenario. The husband may have listened well but his wife did not *feel* listened to. If he wants to communicate to his wife that he is listening and interested, he'll learn to give outward signs of his involvement.

The wife too could increase understanding in the marriage. For starters, she might stop assuming that she can tell whether her husband is or isn't listening to her. Rather than criticizing her husband for not listening (when actually he is), she might tell him what kinds of responses she would value from him.

The discussion of communication rules in Chapters 3 and 4 pertains to our thinking about listening. Through our experiences as individuals and members of social groups we learn diverse constitutive rules for what counts as listening and equally diverse regulative rules for whether and how to respond when we are listening. There is no reason for any of us to presume that others listen as we do or know what we want when we are talking with them. Because we listen differently, it's wise not to impose our listening rules on the behaviors of others. It's also wise to explain our rules by metacommunicating. When we metacommunicate about listening, we can clarify our own patterns and gain insight into the meaning of the listening patterns of others.

Key Words

- gendered patterns
- hearing
- interpreting
- listening
- listening noises
- metacommunicating
- mindfulness
- power dynamics
- remembering
- responding

Reflecting on This Chapter

1. Did you identify personally with the typical feminine or masculine patterns discussed in this chapter? Do you rely primarily on one or the other or do you sometimes use each style of listening?

2. Think about people with whom you interact. Can you identify one person who is an especially effective listener? Describe what that person does that you perceive as showing that she or he is a good listener.

3. Reflect on your childhood interactions. Did you interact primarily with members of your own sex, the other sex, or both sexes? Were the rules of communication that you learned consistent with Daniel Maltz's and Ruth Borker's observations of children in their study?

4. Identify three men and three women with whom you regularly communicate. Are their styles of listening consistent with the gender patterns discussed in this chapter?

5. Observe communication between people who have different degrees of status and power. You might watch managers and clerks in stores, faculty and students on campus, or secretaries and administrators in businesses. Are the power dynamics we noted in this chapter evident in the speaking and listening of the people you observe?

6. Should we accept differences in listening as normal and not try to change them? Are there reasons to regard certain styles of listening as more effective than others?

7. Why do you think there are so many courses and books on how to speak (get your message across, make your point, impress others) and so few on listening? Should listening be part of formal education?

8. This chapter focused on the idea that listening style reflects our membership in particular social groups, such as groups defined by gender and professional status. Do you think that listening style can also affect how others perceive our levels of power? Would Maureen be perceived as having greater power and status if she were less overtly responsive and attentive to Paul?

9. Try an experiment. For the next 12 hours follow the listening style that is generally associated with the other sex. If you are male, focus on nodding your head, smiling, keeping eye contact, inviting speakers to elaborate and continue, and making listening noises. If you are female, avoid overt displays of attention and interest; don't show how you feel about what speakers are saying; don't encourage others to elaborate or continue. How do others react to your listening behavior? How do you feel using this style?

References

Adler, R., & Towne, N. (1996). *Looking out, looking in* (8th ed.). Fort Worth, TX: Harcourt Brace Jovanovich.

Beck, A. (1988). *Love is never enough*. New York: Harper and Row.

Bolton, R. (1986). Listening is more than hearing. In J. Stewart (Ed.), *Bridges, not walls* (4th ed., pp. 159–179). New York: Random House.

DeFrancisco, V. (1991). The sounds of silence: How men silence women in marital relations. *Discourse and Society, 2,* 413–423.

Ernst, F., Jr. (1973). *Who's listening? A handbook of the transactional analysis of the listening function.* Vallejo, CA: Addresso'set.

Fishman, P. (1978). Interaction: The work women do. *Social Problems, 25,* 397–406.

Hall, J. (1987). On explaining gender differences: The case of nonverbal communication. In P. Shaver & C. Hendrick (Eds.), *Sex and gender* (pp. 177–200). Newbury Park, CA: Sage.

Henley, N. (1977). *Body politics: Power, sex, and nonverbal communication.* Englewood Cliffs, NJ: Prentice-Hall.

Maltz, D., & Borker, R. (1982). A cultural approach to male-female miscommunication. In J. J. Gumpertz (Ed.), *Language and social identity* (pp. 196–216). Cambridge: Cambridge University Press.

Montgomery, B. (1988). Quality communication in personal relationships. In S. W. Duck (Ed.), *Handbook of personal relationships* (pp. 343–366). New York: John Wiley.

Noller, P. (1980). Misunderstandings in marital communication: A study of couples' nonverbal communication. *Journal of Personality and Social Psychology, 39,* 1135–1148.

Tannen, D. (1990). *You just don't understand: Men and women in conversation.* New York: William Morrow.

Ueland, B. (1992, November/December). Tell me more: On the fine art of listening. *Utne Reader,* pp. 104–109.

Wood, J. T. (1993). Engendered relations: Interaction, caring, power and responsibility in intimacy. In S. Duck (Ed.), *Understanding relationship processes, 3: Social context and relationships* (pp. 26–54). Newbury Park, CA: Sage.

Wood, J. T. (1997). *Gendered lives: Communication, gender, and culture* (2nd ed.). Belmont, CA: Wadsworth.

Wood, J. T. (1998). *Communication mosaics: A new introduction to human communication.* Belmont, CA: Wadsworth.

| 6 |

CAN WE TALK ABOUT US?

. . .

Understanding Sources and Levels

of Meaning

Theresa and Walker stroll along the beach in front of the cottage they rented for a long weekend—the first warm weekend this season. Walker savors his temporary escape from the pressures of school and work and his sense of feeling that he is one with the rugged landscape of the coastline. He can't imagine anything better than walking hand-in-hand in silent companionship with Theresa.

Theresa too basks in this moment. She and Walker started seeing each other nearly two years ago and by now she feels totally comfortable with him. Theresa squeezes his hand and asks, "Can we talk about us?"

Walker flinches inwardly but tries not to show it. "Is there a problem?" he asks.

"No, I just feel really close right now and want to talk about how good it feels to be together."

"But this is such a perfect moment—the sun, the surf, the seagulls. Let's not spoil it with talk."

"Spoil it? I didn't know talking about us would spoil anything. I thought it would *add* to the moment." There is an edge to her voice as she speaks. 'Why does Walker always do this?' she wonders. 'If he cares as much as he says, why doesn't he ever want to talk about the relationship and how we feel about each other?'

Walker resigns himself. This isn't the first time she's wanted to talk about the relationship when he saw no point in doing so. It seems to be a recurrent difference between them. "Okay, so what do you want to talk about?"

"Just how nice it feels to be here together — walking, enjoying the surf, just the two of us away from everything."

"Yep," he agrees. "It's great."

"Do you ever feel like a moment is just perfect and things couldn't be better?"

"I was just feeling that a few minutes ago."

"Why didn't you say so?" she asks.

"It's evident that both of us feel good. There isn't any need to state the obvious."

"But sometimes it's nice to state it anyway."

"It was nice to have the feeling and not need to put it in words."

"But I like to know what you're feeling — especially what you're feeling about us," Theresa says, squeezing his hand. "I feel closer when we talk."

Walker shrugs. To him, talk sometimes takes away from the moment. It forces him to put words on something that is beyond words. When he feels something basic, he likes just to experience the feeling and not try to come up with words that describe it.

After a few moments of silent walking, Theresa says, "Have you noticed that our gait matches now and it didn't when we first got together? Remember how I used to fuss at you for walking too fast?"

"Umm," he replies. 'Why do we have to talk about our walking pace?' he wonders.

"It's like we've synchronized ourselves to each other."

"Yeah, I guess."

"Do you think you slowed down or I speeded up?"

"Beats me," he replies. 'Where is this conversation going? What's the point?' he wonders.

Walker and Theresa are experiencing an age-old friction. "Can we talk about us?" is perhaps the question that most frequently provokes misunderstanding in relationships, particularly ones between women and men. In general — but not always — women enjoy talking about relation-

Drawing by Leo Cullum; © 1996 The New Yorker *Magazine, Inc.*

ships more than men do. Our goals in this chapter are to explore reasons for dissimilar inclinations to talk about feelings and relationships and to unravel what talking about relationships means to different people. In addition, we probe beneath the surface of human communication to explore the levels of meaning, to discover less-than-obvious messages in our verbal and nonverbal interaction. Our discussion should shed light on misunderstandings that may arise because of two distinct levels of meaning that operate in communication.

Understanding the Misunderstanding

What's going on between Walker and Theresa? Clearly, they don't agree on the value of talking about feelings and their relationship. Theresa says commenting on how nice it is to be walking on the beach makes her feel closer; to Walker, it's stating the obvious. Walker finds pleasure in silent companionship; Theresa likes to express her pleasure in being together.

Theresa enjoys talking about small matters such as their synchronized gait; Walker finds such talk pointless.

The differences between Walker and Theresa are not unusual and not strictly personal. Many couples have unmatched desires to talk about feelings and their relationships. Two of the major sources of this difference are gender and constitutive rules of communication, which we first discussed in Chapter 3.

Gendered Patterns

Couples counselor Aaron Beck, noting the influence of gendered patterns, says that women are generally more inclined than men to want to talk about relationships and to gain pleasure from doing so. The men with whom he has worked have less interest in talking about relationships unless there is some problem to be solved or some issue to be addressed. Beck clarifies this difference neatly by stating that many women feel a relationship is working well as long as they are talking about it, whereas many men think a relationship is working well as long as they don't have to talk about it.

Beck's insights are confirmed by communication scholar Linda Acitelli who studies how and why couples talk about their relationships and how individuals perceive the process of talking about relationships. According to her research, women generally derive satisfaction from talking about personal relationships both when they are working smoothly and when there are problems. Men, on the other hand, tend to perceive value in talking about relationships if there is a problem or a specific topic that needs exploring, but they are less likely to enjoy talking about a relationship when there is no concrete issue that requires attention.

Gender socialization sheds light on why men and women, in general, might have different perceptions of talking about relationships. The childhood games that many young girls play, such as house and school, depend on relationships among players. Unlike soccer and football, the games typically played by many young girls aren't structured by formal rules. Instead, the structure develops and is refined as players communicate. Through childhood games and parental teaching, young girls are typically socialized to use communication to build connections with others. They learn to express feelings, comment on relationships, share details of experiences, and engage in small talk. Each of these communication activities allows girls (and, later, women) to share the rhythms of their individual lives with others and to weave relationships.

From her study of women's friendships, communication specialist Fern Johnson concludes that women tend to perceive ongoing dialogue as the essence of intimacy. Catherine Riessman's study of marriages reached a similar conclusion: Wives, more than husbands, regard regular communication as a key measure of the health of a marriage. For many women, communication is not just a means to specific concrete goals. Instead, they learn to view it as a goal in and of itself—the process of communicating is a cornerstone of closeness.

Masculine socialization teaches males a different view of communication. The games that many young boys play emphasize concrete goals —scoring a touchdown, sinking a basket, defeating the other side in war. Because the games are structured by external rules (what is a touchdown, what is a foul), communication isn't needed to work out personal relationships and express feelings. Instead, communication is used to advance instrumental goals—deciding which starting formation to use in football, developing a strategy for a sneak attack in war. The lesson is that communication is not an end in itself but a means to achieving other ends. In other words, talk is used to do things.

The different orientations toward communication that are emphasized in feminine and masculine socialization help us understand what is happening between Theresa and Walker. Like many (but not all) men, Walker views communication as an instrumental process that is used to accomplish specific goals, ranging from deciding on a starting formation to solving a problem in a relationship. As a result, Walker, like many men, is prompted to communicate when he perceives something that needs to be addressed or when he has information to share. He's unlikely to relate the details of his activities and feelings because he doesn't see the point of doing so. To him, major events, topics, and issues are important enough to merit conversation. From Walker's perspective, communication is not an end in itself but a means to other ends.

Socialized like many women, Theresa regards the process of communication as having value in its own right. She likes to express feelings, share small thoughts, and talk about how relationships have changed over time. Like many women, Theresa also enjoys sharing the details of daily life—the mundane stuff of everyday activities. She finds as much pleasure in small talk as in relating big events. For her, communication is a primary way to create and enhance closeness. In other words, intimacy is realized in communication. *What* is talked about often is less important than the process of communicating.

What is the meaning of "Can we talk about us?" That seems to depend in large measure on how we value talking about a relationship. If you think discussing a relationship is important only when there is some problem, "Can we talk about us?" may mean trouble. You may perceive the request as an announcement that something is wrong. On the other hand, if ongoing dialogue about a relationship enhances intimacy for you, "Can we talk about us?" may be a welcome invitation to be closer.

Beyond Gender—Constitutive Rules of Communication

Theresa and Walker fit the patterns typical of women and men in their respective interests in talking about feelings and relationships. It's important, however, to remember that gendered patterns are only generalizations. Some men find it very satisfying to talk about relationships and to share details of everyday life. Some women find doing so pointless. Although gender differences sometimes shed light on misunderstandings in communication, they aren't the whole picture.

Constitutive rules, which we discussed in Chapter 3, are also relevant to understanding differences in preferences for talking about relationships. Recall that constitutive rules tell us how to evaluate particular communication practices. They specify what counts as what. Our constitutive rules are shaped by the social groups to which we belong. If Theresa socialized primarily with other girls when she was learning how to interact, she may have learned constitutive rules such as "talking creates closeness," "expressing feelings is good," and "small talk enhances intimacy."

Social groups are not the only influence on the constitutive rules we develop and use in communication. Our constitutive rules are also shaped by individual experiences, including family dynamics and participation in other relationships. If Walker's parents and friends didn't express their feelings or engage in small talk, he may have learned constitutive rules such as "there's no need to state feelings" and "small talk is pointless."

Couples frequently misunderstand each other because they operate from different constitutive rules about communication. That is the case with Walker and Theresa. Below is a table showing the constitutive rules that each of them has. When we state their rules explicitly, it's easy to see why they might misunderstand each other.

Communication	*Walker's Constitutive Rules*	*Theresa's Constitutive Rules*
Talk about relationship when there aren't specific problems	There's no need to talk.	Discussing the relationship enhances intimacy.
Small talk (e.g., pace of walking)	It is boring. There's no purpose.	It weaves lives together.
Expressing feelings that are fairly self-evident.	It disrupts comfortable silence. It relies on words to express what is beyond words.	It's a way to share feelings. It increases feelings of closeness.

Constitutive rules not only define what particular kinds of communication mean. They also show the meaning of not engaging in specific forms of communication. Theresa and Walker may have unmatched constitutive rules for the meaning of *not* talking about feelings and relationships.

Communication	*Walker's Constitutive Rules*	*Theresa's Constitutive Rules*
Not engaging in small talk	It's normal, natural. Everyday stuff isn't worth sharing.	A person does not want to share feelings, perceptions, thoughts, etc.
Not talking about the relationship	It's normal unless there is a problem or issue to be addressed.	A person is demonstrating low interest in or commitment to a relationship.

If Theresa and Walker realize that they have different constitutive rules for relational communication, they may be able to metacommunicate about them. Doing so would allow them to gain better understandings of each other and to work out more harmonious communication patterns for their relationship.

In addition to the influences on what relational communication means, we should consider another factor—one that is fundamental to human communication. This is the two kinds of meaning that occur in communication.

Levels of Meaning in Communication

People often speak of the *meaning* of communication. It would actually be more accurate for us to think about the *meanings* of communication, because human communication involves more than one kind of meaning.

In 1967, psychiatrists Paul Watzlawick, Janet Beavin, and Don Jackson advanced a groundbreaking idea about human communication. Their experiences as counselors led them to the insight that all communication has two levels of meaning. They also observed that communication problems often result when people notice and respond to only one of the levels of meaning in interaction.

Content Level of Meaning

The first level of meaning is what comes to mind when we think about the meaning of communication. Called the content level of meaning, it is the literal or denotative significance of communication. The content level of meaning is the actual content or data in a message. In the interaction that opened this chapter, Theresa said, "Have you noticed that our gait matches now and it didn't when we first got together? Remember how I used to fuss at you for walking too fast?" The content level of her communication is that she and Walker move at the same pace now whereas he used to walk faster than she did. Also, on the content level of meaning, Theresa is asking whether Walker has noticed that they've synchronized their gaits.

Relationship Level of Meaning

Most people are less aware of a second kind of meaning, which is called the relationship level of meaning. It conveys meanings about a relationship and how communicators feel about each other. Theresa's comment expresses her feeling that she and Walker are harmonized, or coordinated. If she smiles while making her observation, the nonverbal relationship level message is that she is pleased.

Albert Mehrabian focused on relationship levels of meaning, particularly those expressed through nonverbal communication. According to Mehrabian and communication scholars who have followed his lead, three dimensions of relationship-level meaning can be identified. These are responsiveness, liking, and power or control.

Dimensions of Relationship Level Meaning

RESPONSIVENESS	LIKING	POWER (CONTROL)
I'm paying attention to what you say.	I like you. / You matter to me.	We're equal. / I respect the desires of each of us.
I'm involved in this conversation.	I trust you. / I enjoy being with you.	I want us to share responsibility for this decision.
I'm ignoring you.	I don't like you.	My preferences should prevail.
I don't care what you're talking about.	I don't trust you.	I am smarter than you.
You bore me; this conversation bores me.	I don't want to be around you.	I defer to you. / You're in charge.

The first dimension is responsiveness, which refers to how aware of and involved with others we seem to be. If you are talking to someone and she or he looks at the clock, shuffles papers, and gazes out the window, you might perceive the person as unresponsive to you. On the other hand, if you are talking with someone who looks at you, nods while you are speaking, and smiles, you are likely to perceive her or him as responsive and attentive. If Walker makes no reply to Theresa, she may think he is unresponsive, aloof, or distant. She could infer that he is uninterested in their relationship.

The second dimension of the relationship level of meaning is liking or affection. This dimension concerns communication of positive or negative feelings between communicators. We convey positive feelings toward others through verbal communication ("I'm glad to see you," "You're such a great friend," "I really like being with you") and through nonverbal behaviors (giving a smile, hug, or kiss; squeezing a hand; moving closer). Conversely, we can signal we dislike people both verbally ("You're out of line," "I don't want to see you any more," "I don't trust you") and nonverbally (scowling or making an offensive gesture; moving away; physically assaulting). Theresa expressed her affection for Walker by squeezing his hand and by saying she liked being together; he expressed his affection for her by holding hands as they walked.

Power, or control, is the third dimension of the relationship level of meaning. This dimension expresses the power balance between communicators. If a boss says brusquely to an assistant, "Get me the files on the applicants for our opening," the imperative tone and fact that the statement is an order, not a request, reflects the boss's greater power. If the assistant wanted the files from the boss, however, she or he would be more likely to say, "Could I see the files, please?" The use of a request and the word *please* reflect the assistant's lesser power relative to the boss.

Sometimes power messages are more subtle than those between boss and assistant. Friends and romantic partners sometimes engage in covert power struggles on the relational level of meaning. They may argue about where to go for a vacation or lunch, with each person pushing her or his preference. The issue on the content level is whether to spend the weekend at the beach or the mountains or which restaurant to go to for lunch. On the relationship level of meaning, however, the issue may be whose preferences will prevail. In our example, Theresa tries to persuade Walker to talk about feelings and the relationship and she initiates several topics in these areas. Initially Walker resists her attempts to engage in conversation, but he finally accedes to her preferences.

Walker and Theresa have different perceptions of the meaning in their conversation. Walker tends to focus on the content level of meaning. As a result, he wonders to himself why they are talking about her observation that their walking rhythms are matched. He doesn't see any significance to the content of that message. Walker doesn't perceive Theresa's relationship-level message, which is "I care about us. It makes me feel close to talk about our feelings." As long as he perceives and responds to only the content level of meaning, he and Theresa will be involved in different conversations and they will misunderstand each other.

Theresa also contributes to the misunderstanding. She assumes that she and Walker share the same constitutive rules for what it means to talk about their feelings and their relationship and that Walker understands the relationship level of meaning in her communication. There lies the problem. There is no reason to presume that we and others share constitutive rules or perceptions of relationship-level meanings. The ways we interpret communication vary because we have different personal experiences and have participated in different social groups. This is natural, but it means the potential for misunderstandings is great.

Increasing Understanding

To expect Walker and Theresa to have identical constitutive rules or to interpret the relationship level of communication in exactly the same way is not realistic. Because we differ, misunderstandings are inevitable. What may not be inevitable, however, is for us to remain stuck in misunderstandings. Theresa, Walker, and the rest of us can use several ways to increase our understanding of each other.

Better communication begins with the realization that people have legitimate reasons to differ in how they perceive communication and what it means to them. The key word is *legitimate*. This means that different perceptions and meanings can be reasonable. Walker is not dense because he doesn't have Theresa's constitutive rules or understand the relationship level of meaning she intends to communicate. Theresa isn't stubborn or tedious because she perceives small talk as important.

Relationships prosper when each person begins with the assumption that the other has good reasons for the ways she or he communicates. If we assume this, we are likely to ask the other person to explain things that seem odd or uninteresting to us. For example, Walker might ask Theresa, "Why do you want to talk about how fast we walk?" She might reply, "It just seems to me that our synchronized pace is symbolic of how well we've come together overall." Her response gives him insight into the relationship level of meaning in a comment that initially he heard only on the content level.

By extension, we can reduce misunderstandings by remembering that communication has two levels of meaning. If Theresa understands that there are two levels of meaning and that Walker is responding only to the content level, she might metacommunicate to explain her relationship-level meaning. She might say to Walker, "When you don't talk, I don't know what you're feeling and that makes me feel distance between us. I ask what you're feeling because I want to be close." If Walker recognized this, he might also realize that he is perceiving only the content level of Theresa's communication and that he doesn't understand the other level of meaning that is operating in their exchanges. If he had that insight, he might want to explore what she is saying about the relationship between them.

Finally, misunderstandings may be reduced by awareness of general patterns related to gender. When Walker resists talking about the relationship, Theresa might say, "I know you don't feel any need to talk about us when everything is going so well, but it makes me feel closer to you. Okay?" Walker too could be a more effective communicator if he acted from an awareness of gendered tendencies in interaction. He might say, "I don't talk about every feeling I have because I feel close to you without talking. It doesn't mean I'm distant or uninvolved." By offering this explanation, Walker lessens the likelihood that Theresa will misinterpret his silence.

Differences in constitutive rules and perceptions of meaning in communication need not create tensions. They tend to foster misunderstandings and frustration only if we don't recognize and address them. The information we've covered in this chapter should help you recognize the situation when you and a conversational partner are operating from dissimilar constitutive rules or mismatched interpretations of meaning. When you know what's going on, you can alter how you communicate to improve your understanding of one another.

Key Words

- constitutive rules
- content level of meaning
- gendered patterns
- levels of meaning
- relationship level of meaning
- responsiveness
- liking
- power or control
- talk about relationships

Reflecting on This Chapter

1. To what extent do you initiate and enjoy talking about relationships when there is no problem or issue? Do your experiences parallel or dif-

fer from the gendered patterns discussed in this chapter? Do you feel, like Walker in the example that opened this chapter, that talking sometimes diminishes feelings of closeness?

2. Think of two relationships (friendship or romantic relationships) in your life—one in which you and the other person regularly talked about the relationship and one in which you talked about the relationship only if there was some specific issue or problem to be addressed. How did the difference in relationship talk affect the degree of closeness and comfort you felt in the two relationships?

3. Think about your constitutive rules for communicating about relationships. According to your rules, what is the importance of small talk? What is the meaning of talking about a relationship when there is no specific problem or issue requiring attention? What does it mean to express feelings that are probably obvious?

4. Is "small talk" really small? Or is it important to you? Explain why you enjoy engaging in small talk (what do you get from it?) or do not enjoy it (why does it annoy, bore, or not interest you?).

5. Have you ever felt that a person with whom you were interacting responded only to the content level of meaning and not to the relationship level of meaning in your communication? If so, describe both levels of meaning in that interaction. What response did you want to the relationship level of meaning?

6. Identify specific verbal and nonverbal behaviors that you interpret as expressing each dimension of the relationship level of meaning. Specify the kinds of communication that fit your constitutive rules for responsiveness (or unresponsiveness), liking (or disliking), and power (equal, superior, and subordinate). Compare your perceptions with those of others. Are there differences in your constitutive rules for what counts as each dimension of the relationship level of meaning?

References

Acitelli, L. (1988). When spouses talk to each other about their relationships. *Journal of Social and Personal Relationships, 5*, 185–199.

Acitelli, L. (1992). Gender differences in relationship awareness and marital satisfaction. *Personality and Social Psychology, 18*, 102–110.

Aries, E. (1987). Gender and communication. In P. Shaver & C. Henrick (Eds.), *Sex and gender* (pp. 149–176). Newbury Park, CA: Sage.

Beck, A. (1988). *Love is never enough*. New York: Harper and Row.

Brehm, S. (1995). *Intimate relationships* (2nd ed.). New York: McGraw-Hill.

Cancian, F. (1988). *Love in America*. Cambridge, MA: Cambridge University Press.

Christiansen, A., & Heavy, C. (1990). Gender and social structure in the demand/withdraw pattern in marital conflict. *Journal of Personality and Social Psychology, 59*, 73–81.

DeFrancisco, V. (1991). The sounds of silence: How men silence women in marital relations. *Discourse and Society, 2*, 413–423.

Gottman, J. (1993). The roles of conflict engagement, escalation, or avoidance in marital interaction: A longitudinal view of five types of couples. *Journal of Consulting and Clinical Psychology, 61*, 6–15.

Inman, C. (1996). Friendships among men: Closeness in the doing. In J. T. Wood (Ed.), *Gendered relationships* (pp. 95–110). Mountain View, CA: Mayfield.

Johnson, F. (1996). Friendships among women: Closeness in dialogue. In J. T. Wood (Ed.), *Gendered relationships* (pp. 79–94). Mountain View, CA: Mayfield.

Keeley, M. P., & Hart, A. J. (1994). Nonverbal behavior in dyadic interaction. In S. Duck (Ed.), *Understanding relationship processes, 4: Dynamics of relationships* (pp. 135–162). Thousand Oaks, CA: Sage.

Mehrabian, A. (1981). *Silent messages: Implicit communication of emotion and attitude* (2nd ed.). Belmont, CA: Wadsworth.

Montgomery, B. (1988). Quality communication in personal relationships. In S. Duck (Ed.), *Handbook of personal relationships* (pp. 343–366). New York: Wiley.

Riessman, C. (1990). *Divorce talk: Women and men make sense of personal relationships*. New Brunswick, NJ: Rutgers University Press.

Rubin, L. (1985). *Just friends: The role of friendship in our lives*. New York: Harper and Row.

Swain, S. (1989). Covert intimacy: Closeness in men's friendships. In B. Risman & P. Schwartz (Eds.), *Gender and intimate relationships* (pp. 71–86). Belmont, CA: Wadsworth.

Tannen, D. (1990). *You just don't understand: Women and men in conversation*. New York: William Morrow.

Watzlawick, P., Beavin, J., & Jackson, D. (1967). *Pragmatics of human communication: A study of interaction patterns, problems and paradoxes*. New York: W. W. Norton.

Wood, J. (1996). She says/he says: Communication, caring, and conflict in heterosexual relationships. In J. T. Wood (Ed.), *Gendered relationships* (pp. 149–162). Mountain View, CA: Mayfield.

PART 2

. . .

Misunderstandings in

Perceiving Others

. . .

| 7 |

IT'S ONLY SKIN DEEP

. . .

Stereotyping and Totalizing Others

> *I want to be known as a talented young filmmaker. That*
> *should be first. But the reality today is that no matter how*
> *successful you are, you're black first. (p. 92)*

Those are Spike Lee's words. In an interview with Diane McDowell, reporter for *Time* magazine, the gifted filmmaker lamented the reality that most people see and respond to his blackness more than his other qualities and achievements. Sometimes, awareness of Lee's blackness overrides all other perceptions of him.

Distinguished historian John Hope Franklin made the same point in an interview with Mark McGurl, reporter for the *New York Times*. According to Franklin, many people assume that because he is an African American historian, he must study African Americans. He is often introduced as the author of 12 books on black history. In reality, Franklin points out, he is *not* a historian only of African Americans. His specialty is the history of the South and, as he notes, that history includes both whites and blacks. In fact, several of his books have focused primarily on whites in the South. Franklin has been elected president of the American Historical Association, the Organization of American Historians, and the Southern Historical Association — none of which is specifically an African American organization. Still, many people perceive his skin color above all else and they assume his ethnicity defines his work.

The misunderstanding of identity and achievement that Spike Lee and John Hope Franklin confront is not unique to people of minority races. Women report that they are often asked to serve on committees. Many times the person asking says, "We need a woman on the committee" or "We think you can provide the woman's perspective on the issues." Like Lee and Franklin, professional women may feel that all their accomplishments and abilities are erased by those who ask them to be "the woman on the committee." The language in the request communicates that all that is noticed is biological sex: She can fill the "woman slot" on the committee.

In this chapter, we focus on communication that highlights one aspect of a person — usually race, sex, sexual orientation, disability, or economic status. We discuss common instances of such communication and explore how it fosters misunderstandings and often offense.

Understanding the Misunderstanding

Scholars use the term *totalize* to describe communication that emphasizes one aspect of a person above all others. When someone totalizes, he or she acts as if a single facet of an individual is the totality of that person or as if that single aspect is all that's important about the person. For example, describing Spike Lee as a *black* filmmaker spotlights his race as what is worthy of attention. Calling John Hope Franklin a *black* historian emphasizes his race and obscures his professional expertise and accomplishments. Asking a professional to provide the *woman's* perspective highlights sex as the criterion for serving on committees. Referring to a person as *gay* stresses sexual orientation and obscures all the person's other qualities. Describing people as *blue collar* or *white collar* makes their class visible and everything else about them invisible.

Totalizing affects both those who do it and those who are its targets. When we feel that someone totalizes us, we are likely to be offended and resentful. We may also be hurt that we have been reduced to a single part of our identity — perhaps not the part most important to us in a particular context. These feelings create barriers to open, healthy communication and comfortable relationships.

Less obvious but no less important is the impact of totalizing on people who engage in it. Language shapes our perceptions by calling certain things to our attention. When we use language that focuses our attention on race, class, sex, or any single aspect of another person, we limit our perception of that person. In other words, we tend to perceive others through the labels we use to describe them.

Kenneth Burke, a distinguished critic of language and literature, observes that language simultaneously reflects, selects, and deflects. In his book, *Language as Symbolic Action*, Burke writes: "Any given terminology is a *reflection* of reality, by its very nature as a terminology it must be a *selection* of reality; and to this extent it must function also as a *deflection* of reality" (p. 45). Burke means that the words we use to reflect our perceptions select certain aspects of what we are describing while simultaneously deflecting, or neglecting, other aspects of what we are describing. When we select *woman, black, gay,* and so forth to describe people, other aspects of those people are deflected (neglected or added as an afterthought). Consequently, we may not see in others whatever our labels deflect. Thus, we are unlikely to interact with those others in their wholeness.

Most of us wouldn't intentionally reduce another person to one aspect of who he or she is, but it happens. One motive for totalizing is the desire for reducing uncertainty. We tend to be uncomfortable when we are unsure about others and situations. To ease discomfort, we often attempt to reduce our uncertainty about others and circumstances. One way to do this is to define others as belonging to a group about which we have definite ideas (although the ideas may not be accurate). It is easier to think of Spike Lee as black than to try to perceive him as a unique individual who is—among other things—male, young, a filmmaker, educated, and African American.

In the classic book, *The Nature of Prejudice*, psychologist Gordon Allport observed that stereotyping and prejudice grow out of normal—not deviant or unusual—cognitive activities. Specifically, Allport identified classification and generalization as commonplace mental activities that can foster stereotypes and prejudice. One reason we use stereotypes, then, is that they reduce our uncertainty by grouping people into broad classes that obscure individual characteristics.

A second reason we stereotype is that we rely on what psychologists call implicit personality theory. Most of us have certain unspoken and perhaps unrecognized assumptions about qualities that go together in personalities. Many people assume that attractive individuals are more extroverted, intelligent, and socially skilled than less attractive individuals. Another common implicit personality theory (one that research does not support) is that people who are overweight are also lazy, undisciplined, and happy. In both examples, we attribute to others a constellation of qualities that we associate with a particular quality we have noticed.

If we meet an individual who is overweight (in our judgment), we may assume that the person meets our implicit personality theory of overweight people and is happy, lazy, and undisciplined. Our implicit personality theories may also lead us to think that a nice-looking person must be intelligent, outgoing, and socially skilled. When we rely on our implicit personality theories, we latch onto one quality of another person—often a characteristic we can see, such as race, sex, or weight—and attribute to the person other qualities that we perceive as consistent with the quality we have identified.

In many, perhaps most, cases, stereotyping occurs because we don't understand how our language reduces another person and narrows our own perceptions of him or her. A few examples should help us understand the anatomy of totalizing so that we can recognize some of the forms it takes and try to avoid them when we communicate with and about others.

Isiah Thomas is a professional basketball player. He is also an African American. In an interview with *New York Times* reporter Ira Berko, Thomas expressed resentment of the unequal ways that reporters describe black and white players. Thomas said, "When Bird [Larry Bird] makes a great play, it's due to his thinking, and his work habits." Yet, continued Thomas, that isn't the case for blacks: "All we do is run and jump. We never practice or give a thought to how we play. It's like I came dribbling out of my mother's womb." Thomas claims that reporters describe him and other great black players such as Magic Johnson and Michael Jordan as "wild in the jungle" and "playing on God-given talent" (p. D27), whereas white players are portrayed as having intelligence, strategy, and ambition.

Thomas recognizes the racial stereotypes that underlie the description of blacks as jungle animals who react from instinct, not intelligence. Another stereotype of African Americans is that they are naturally talented at dancing: "They are just born with rhythm." I've asked several African American students and friends about this. They tell me that music— dancing, singing, rapping—is emphasized more in their communities than in white communities. However, they add, we practice, we work to develop skill in dancing. The same is true of my white friends who are skillful dancers. The only difference is that they are *perceived* as devoting thought, time, and discipline to achieve their skill.

Another example comes from spectacular golfer Tiger Woods. In conversations with biographer John Strege, Tiger Woods said he was tired of being called "the best black golfer." He wants to be known as the best golfer. In Tiger Woods's case, there are other reasons not to refer to him as black; he is part American Indian, Thai, Chinese, white, and black.

The examples we've discussed illustrate one form of totalizing, which involves defining individuals by their membership in a specific group. Years ago sociologist Louis Wirth conducted classic studies of racial prejudice. One of his more important conclusions was that when we perceive people primarily in terms of their membership in a particular racial or ethnic group, we tend to think about them and interact with them in terms of our stereotypes of race, regardless of their unique qualities, talents, and so forth. In other words, their individuality is lost, submerged in our preconceptions of the group to which we assign them.

A second form of totalizing reduces individuals to one quality or aspect of their identities. This type of totalizing is evident in some of the language used to describe persons who have disabilities. How we perceive and label people with disabilities is the research focus of Dawn Braithwaite, a communication scholar at Arizona State University West. From interviews with persons who have disabilities, Braithwaite learned that the term *disabled person* is likely to offend. The reason is that the term suggests that their personhood is disabled—that they are somehow inadequate or diminished as persons simply because they have disabilities. One of the people Braithwaite interviewed asserted, "I am a person like anyone else" (1994, p. 151). Another interviewee said, "If anyone refers to me as an amputee, that is guaranteed to get me madder than hell! I don't deny the leg amputation, but I am me. I am a whole person" (1994, p. 151).

Individuals who have disabilities have been vocal in resisting efforts to label them *disabled*. They point out that calling them disabled emphasizes their disabilities above all else. "We're people who have disabilities. People first," a deaf student explained to me. When someone with a disability is described as disabled, we highlight what they cannot do rather than all they can do. (Chapter 10 offers a fuller discussion of communication with persons who have disabilities.)

Totalizing isn't limited to one-to-one communication. The mass media sometime define people by their membership in particular groups and ignore other aspects of them. Think about news programming on television. How often do you see someone from a minority race featured as an expert in a news story? How often is the news story *not* about minorities or minority issues?

Communication Professor Robert Entman studied national nightly news programming. He reports that in stories about black issues, 33 black experts and 27 white experts appeared. In news stories about issues not specifically relevant to African Americans, 94 white experts and only 15 black experts appeared. This pattern encourages viewers to assume that African Americans can speak knowledgeably only about African American issues, whereas whites can speak with authority about African American and other issues alike.

When we think stereotypically, we expect people to conform to our perceptions of the group to which we assign them. Sometimes, however, we meet someone who doesn't fit our stereotypes of the group to which we think he or she belongs. Have you ever said or heard the phrases "woman doctor," "male nurse," or "woman lawyer"? Notice how they call attention to the sex of the doctor, nurse, or lawyer. Have you ever heard or used the phrases "man doctor," "woman nurse," or "man lawyer"? Probably not—because it is considered normal for men to be doctors and lawyers and women to be nurses. Many people perceive it as unusual for women to practice law or medicine or men to be nurses. "Woman doctor," "male nurse," and "woman lawyer" spotlight the sex of individuals as the element worthy of notice. The phrases also reflect stereotyped views of the professional groups.

When we mark an individual as an exception to his or her group, we unknowingly reveal our own stereotypes. In fact, we may reinforce them because marking an individual who doesn't conform to the stereotype as unusual leaves our perceptions of the group unchanged. All we do is remove the "exceptional individual" from the group. Consider these statements:

White manager to black manager:	"You really are exceptional at your job." [*Translation:* Black women aren't usually successful.]
Male professional to female professional:	"You don't think like a woman." [*Translation:* Most women don't think like professionals.]
Able-bodied individual to person in wheelchair:	"I'm amazed at how well you get around." [*Translation:* I assume that people who use wheelchairs don't get out much.]

Upper-class person to working-class person:	"It's remarkable that you take college classes." [*Translation:* Most working-class people aren't interested in higher education.]
White person to African American:	"I can't believe you don't like to dance." [*Translation:* I think that all blacks dance, have rhythm.]
Heterosexual to lesbian:	"I think it's great that you have some male friends." [*Translation:* Most lesbians hate men.]
Homeowner to maid:	" You speak so articulately. " [*Translation:* I assume most domestic workers don't speak well and/or aren't educated.]
White man to black man:	"I never think of you as black." [*Translation:* You don't fit my views of blacks; you're an exception to my (negative) stereotype of blacks.]
Christian to Jew:	"I'm surprised at how generous you are." [*Translation:* Most Jews are tight with money.]
African American to white person:	"You're not as stuffy as most of your people." [*Translation:* Most whites are stuffy, or up-tight, but you're not.]

Would any of the above statements be made to a member of the speaker's group? Would a heterosexual say to a heterosexual woman, "It's great that you have some male friends"? Would a white man say to another white man, "I never think of you as white"? Would a maid say to his or her employer, "You speak so articulately"? Would a white person say to another white person, "I can't believe you don't like to dance"? In each case, it's unlikely. By changing the speakers in the statements, we see how clearly the statements reflect stereotypes of groups.

Communicating that you perceive an individual as an exception to his or her group invites two dilemmas. First, it expresses your perception that the person belongs to a group about which you have preconceptions. Understandably, this may alienate the other person or make her or him defensive. The person may feel compelled to defend or redefine the group from which you have removed that individual. An African American might, for instance, say "Lots of blacks don't enjoy dancing." A working-class person might inform an upper-class person that "education has always been a priority in my family."

A second possible response to communication that marks an individual as an exception to her or his group is the effort to deny identification with the group. A professional woman may strive not to appear feminine to avoid being judged by her colleagues' negative perceptions of women. A white person may try to "talk black" or play music by black artists to prove he or she isn't like most whites. The group stereotypes — no matter how inaccurate — are left unchallenged.

Whether individuals defend or redefine their groups or separate themselves from the groups, one result is the same: The possibilities for open communication and honest relationships are compromised.

Improving Communication

Several years ago, Marsha Houston and I collaborated in a dialogue about communication between people of different races and classes. Marsha is African American and I am European American. Over the years that we have known each other, we have developed enough trust to talk openly about misunderstandings between people with different backgrounds.

Perhaps the single most important conclusion to come out of our conversations and our writing is that it's important to acknowledge, but not totalize, any aspect about others. It is neither honest nor confirming of others to pretend not to notice ways in which they and we differ. Repeat-

"I FORESEE THE DAY WHEN RACIAL AND RELIGIOUS DIFFERENCES WILL BE OF NO IMPORTANCE WHATEVER, AND PEOPLE WILL HATE ONE ANOTHER FOR COMPLETELY PERSONAL REASONS."

© *1994 by Sidney Harris*—The Wall Street Journal.

edly, African American, Hispanic, Asian American, and Native American students tell me how frustrating it is to have white people say, "I never think of you as black" or Asian or Hispanic or Native American. "Of course they do," insist my students. As one of my students remarked, "They're so busy working not to notice that I am Asian that it's all they do notice about me." Another student who is an African American pointed out that she's insulted when people say that they don't think of her as black. She is proud of her heritage and being told "I never think of you as black" erases a cornerstone of her identity. Through our dialogues, Marsha and I realized that acknowledging real differences is a foundation for healthy communication.

In addition, we should try to keep those differences in perspective. Generally, it's not honest or constructive to focus on differences to the exclusion of similarities. It is especially ill advised to focus on any one particular characteristic of a person when we think about and communicate with that individual. Marsha and I acknowledge that we are of different races. We also recognize that one of us is married and the other is not, and one of us has a child and the other does not. Our differences are part of who we are and the relationship between us.

At the same time, Marsha and I have much in common. We're both middle class, we're both faculty members at universities, we're both middle aged, we're both women, we're both writers, and we're both heterosexual. These similarities between us are also part of who we are and of the relationship we have. Both our commonalities and our differences affect our dialogues. Neglecting either would impoverish our relationship and what we learn from communicating with each other.

In an essay that we wrote, Marsha and I identified a number of phrases that can be "red flags" when spoken by members of one group to members of another. To close this chapter, I restate some of the phrases we identified, along with other phrases I've learned since Marsha and I published our essay in 1996.

What's the black (or woman or Asian) perspective on this?

I think of you as just like me.

You're really exceptional.

I didn't know lesbians (or women or blacks) did that (thought that, felt that, believed that, cared about that).

You people.

Disabled, or disabled person.

Your people.

People like you.

You don't act like (think like, look like, talk like) most gays (or African Americans or people with disabilities).

I never think of you as a Native American (or an African American, or a gay, or a person with a disability).

I know a black (or woman, or Asian, or Native American, or gay) doctor (or lawyer, or accountant, or executive, or college president).

I'm not racist. I have lots of black and Asian friends.

I know men can't understand feelings, so I don't expect that from you.

I try to overlook your sexual orientation (or race or disability).

This isn't something white (or men, or able-bodied) people can understand.

Love the sinner; hate the sin.

Key Words

- implicit personality theory
- people with disabilities
- reducing uncertainty
- stereotyping
- totalizing

Reflecting on This Chapter

1. Have you ever felt that someone totalized you by the way she or he spoke to or about you? Describe what the other person said and how you perceived the communication.

2. Is totalizing something another person says or does to an individual, or is it the individual's interpretation of what another person says or does? What does each view of totalizing imply about the nature of communication and the ethical responsibilities inherent in totalizing?

3. Are there phrases about you or groups to which you belong that are "red flags" for you? Does what you've learned in this chapter enhance your understanding of why those phrases anger or upset you?

4. How can a person respond effectively to someone who totalizes her or him? Does an effective response require diplomacy? Is an aggressive or self-righteous response likely to invite the other person to reflect on his or her communication and the assumptions underlying it?

5. Think about your relationships with people you perceive as different from you in some important way. Identify differences between you and those people. Identify similarities between you. Which list is longer? How do both differences and similarities shape your relationships?

6. How do you label yourself? What do your self-labels include and exclude (select and deflect)? What do they erase and make visible?

7. How do you perceive and respond to phrases such as "women of color" [are there no men of color?], visible minority [what's an invisible minority?], and women and minorities [are no women minorities?]? What alternatives to these problematical phrases might we develop?

8. Read crime reports in several newspapers. Notice when the category of race is specified. How often is race identified as white? How often as a minority race? What does identification of race, or failure to identify it, convey about the media's perceptions of the "normal" race?

9. Think about phrases such as "the woman's perspective" or the "African American point of view." Do they imply that all women and all blacks think alike, have a single perspective? Is this accurate?

10. Communication over the Internet and via e-mail offers us useful insights into our own prejudices and how much they may shape (and misshape) our perceptions of others. Have you ever "met" someone on the Internet and developed a friendship and/or respect for the person and later discovered that the person belonged to a group you would not normally interact with? Many people interact with others on the Internet over substantive matters but would never have entered into the conversation if they had known at the outset that the other person was of a particular race, gay or lesbian, homeless, or of a certain religion.

References

Allport, G. (1979). *The nature of prejudice*. Reading, MA: Addison-Wesley.

Andersen, M., & Collins, P. H. (1995). Preface: Toward inclusive thinking through the study of race, class, and gender. In M. Andersen & P. Collins (Eds.), *Race, class and gender: An anthology* (2nd ed., pp. xi–xx). Belmont, CA: Wadsworth.

Berko, I. (1987, June 2). The coloring of bird. *The New York Times*, p. D27.

Braithwaite, D. (1992). "Isn't it great that people like you get out?": Communication between disabled and ablebodied persons. In E. B. Ray (Ed.), *Case studies in health communication* (pp. 149–159). Hillsdale, NJ: Lawrence Erlbaum.

Braithwaite, D. (1994). Viewing persons with disabilities as a culture. In L. Samovar & R. Porter (Eds.), *Intercultural communication: A reader* (7th ed., pp. 148–154). Belmont, CA: Wadsworth.

Braithwaite, D. (1996). "Persons first": Exploring different perspectives on the communication of persons with disabilities. In E. B. Ray (Ed.), *Communication and disenfranchisement: Social health issues and implications* (pp. 449–464). Hillsdale, NJ: Lawrence Erlbaum.

Burke, K. (1966). *Language as symbolic action*. Berkeley, CA: University of California Press.

Childers, M., & hooks, b. (1990). A conversation about race and class. In M. Hirsch & E. F. Keller (Eds.), *Conflicts in feminism* (pp. 60–81). New York: Routledge.

Entman, R. N. (1994). Representation and reality in the portrayal of blacks on network television news. *Journalism Quarterly, 71*, 509–520.

Folb, E. (1980). *Runnin' down some lines: The language and culture of black teenagers*. Cambridge, MA: Harvard University Press.

Houston, M. (1997). When black women talk with white women: Why dialogues are difficult. In A. González, M. Houston, & V. Chen (Eds.), *Our voices: Essays in culture, ethnicity, and communication* (2nd ed., pp. 187–194). Los Angeles: Roxbury.

Houston, M., & Wood, J. T. (1996). Difficult dialogues, expanded horizons: Communicating across race and class. In J. T. Wood (Ed.), *Gendered relationships* (pp. 39–56). Mountain View, CA: Mayfield.

Kramarae, C. (1996). Classified information: Race, class, and (always) gender. In J. T. Wood (Ed.), *Gendered relationships* (pp. 20–38). Mountain View, CA: Mayfield.

McDowell, D. (1989, July 17). He's got to have his way. *Time*, pp. 92–94.

McGurl, M. (1990, June 3). That's history, not black history. *The New York Times Book Review*, 13.

McIntosh, P. (1995). White privilege and male privilege: A personal account of coming to see correspondences through work in Women's Studies. In M. Andersen & P. Collins (Eds.), *Race, class and gender: An anthology* (2nd ed., pp. 76–87). Belmont, CA: Wadsworth.

Penelope, J. (1990). *Speaking freely: Unlearning the lies of the father's tongues*. New York: Pergamon Press.

Schneider, D. J. (1973). Implicit personality theory: A review. *Psychological Bulletin, 27*, 294–309.

Strege, J. (1997). *Tiger: A biography of Tiger Woods*. New York: Bantam Doubleday.

Wirth, L. (1945). The problem of minority groups. In R. Linton (Ed.), *The science of man* (pp. 347–372). New York: Columbia.

Wood, J. T. (1997). Diversity in dialogue: Commonalities and differences between friends. In J. Makau & R. Arnett (Eds.), *Communication ethics in an age of diversity* (pp. 5–26). Urbana: University of Illinois Press.

8

THE RAP ON RAP

. . .

What Is Gangsta Rap Communicating?

In the song "Iceberg," popular rap performer Ice-T sings about Evil E who

> Fucked the bitch with a flashlight
> Pulled it out, left the batteries in
> So he could get a charge when he begins.

Great White, another rapper, describes having sex with a woman and says to her he's "Gonna nail you to the floor," while one of the songs by Guns 'N' Roses describes a sexual encounter in which the woman is "Tied up, tied down, up against the wall."

According to Richard Johannesen, professor of communication ethics at Northern Illinois University, sexism and extreme violence are trademarks of much rap music, especially gangsta rap. If you don't listen to this kind of music, you may not know how explicitly some of it describes sex and violence. The Public Agenda Foundation studied lyrics in rap songs and report that in the song "S and M," 2 Live Crew explicitly refers to male genitals 117 times, refers to women as bitches over 100 times, and uses the word fuck 226 times.

It is not new for popular music to be accused of being dirty or even immoral, yet many people think that rap music has ushered in a qualitatively different and worse level of violence and sexism. And the opposition to much rap music isn't confined to white people. Leonard Pitts, Jr., an African American music critic, says, "There's something vile and evil moving beneath the surface of this music. Something that hates you. And shames me" (p. 7E). What is the "something evil" that concerns Pitts? Consider a song from 2 Live Crew's album, *As Nasty as They Want to Be*. The song, titled "The Fuck Shop," includes these lyrics:

> Whole lotta suckin' and fuckin' at the Fuck Shop
> Please come inside and make yourself at home
> I want to fuck 'cause my dick's gone to bone
> You little whore behind closed doors.

This song, as well as the entire album on which it is featured, were declared obscene in a Florida District Court ruling of June 1990. Yet only four months later, in October 1990, a local court, again in the state of Florida, decided that 2 Live Crew was not committing obscenity by performing songs from the *Nasty* album.

Like the local and district courts in Florida, people disagree about rap music in general and gangsta rap in particular. Is it obscene? Does it debase women and encourage violence and meaningless sex? Even if it does debase women and celebrate violence, isn't it protected by the guarantee of free speech in the First Amendment? Does the music have redeeming artistic or social values? Different people answer these questions in different ways.

Music is a form of communication. Like talk, music relies on verbal and nonverbal symbols. Also like talk, music describes relationships and expresses ideas, feelings, identities, and experiences. Just as some kinds of talk offend some people (hate speech, for example), some kinds of music offend some people. As we've learned in previous chapters, communication is powerful and can arouse powerful responses in us. This is especially the case with much gangsta rap. Some individuals passionately condemn it; others just as passionately defend it.

In this chapter, we explore different views of rap music in general and gangsta rap in particular. The goal of the chapter is not necessarily to change your opinions about the music—you may have the same personal judgment at the end of this chapter that you have now. If you like it, you may like it just as much after reading this chapter. If you find gangsta rap vulgar and offensive, you may still hold that opinion when you've finished the chapter.

Even so, considering different views and the reasons for them may allow you to understand why people differ in how they perceive and value rap and gangsta rap. In turn, this understanding may give you insight into others and an increased appreciation of the values and experiences that have shaped their views. Even if you don't agree with their views, understanding why reasonable people can perceive music in dissimilar ways is worthwhile.

Understanding the Misunderstanding

How we evaluate music is not a strictly personal matter. Our perspectives on music, like many things, are influenced by the views and opinions of others in our social groups. When people disagree about the value of music, chances are good that they identify with and participate in different groups.

Often different perceptions of music reflect generational divides. My parents thought Elvis was vulgar and the Beatles were weird; I disagreed as did most of my peers. Now I often find myself telling teenagers and college students that I disapprove of some of the music they like. And they tell me, as I told my parents, that "your generation can't understand."

Different responses to music may also reflect membership in different social groups. Do you like opera? If so, you probably grew up in a family and social group that appreciated opera and taught you to enjoy it. Hymns and spiritual music are appreciated by people who were raised in religious communities. Communication scholars Travis Dixon and Daniel Linz found that appreciation of black communication styles is related to viewing rap music as having artistic merit.

To understand different opinions about the value of rap and gangsta rap, let's consider a specific case in which those differences erupted. In 1996, Professor Michael Eric Dyson delivered the commencement address at my school, the University of North Carolina at Chapel Hill. Dyson is one of the most vocal defenders of hip-hop culture and rap and gangsta rap, and that became obvious in his speech. But first, let me give you some background information on Dyson.

After a rough childhood and adolescence in the ghettos of Detroit, Dyson went on to become an ordained Baptist minister and to earn a doctorate from Princeton University. Since receiving his Ph.D., Dyson has been a professor who refuses to confine himself or his ideas to the "ivory tower" of campuses. Considered one of the most visible public intellectuals of our time, Dyson appears regularly on television shows, such as "Oprah" and "Good Morning America" and he speaks in other public venues such as at the Million Man March in 1994.

Professor Dyson is a man who fuels controversy, and he does so deliberately. He believes that controversy, even conflict, provokes thinking and enlarges perspectives. Whether talking with a small group of students or presenting a public speech to thousands, he is outspoken and electrifying. And he delivers his ideas with dazzling style, combining the oratorical skills of preachers, teachers, and popular celebrities.

Rapping Rap

Never did Dyson stir more controversy than when he delivered the mid-year commencement address at the University of North Carolina at Chapel Hill. Dyson opened his address by recalling the Reverend Martin Luther King, Jr.'s "I Have a Dream" speech. He then told the graduating seniors and their families that the American dream is not available to many black youths. For them, the American dream is more like a nightmare, Dyson declared.

The message itself was not especially controversial, but Dyson's choices of how to present the message were. He quoted verbatim lyrics from gangsta rappers such as Snoop Doggy Dogg to dramatize the anger felt by black youths who don't have access to the American dream. The lyrics Dyson quoted were sexually explicit and violent and included the "f-word." He made no effort to sanitize the lyrics for the comfort of parents, grandparents, and young brothers and sisters of members of the graduating class.

Some members of the graduating class threw down their caps and stalked out of the ceremony, flanked by their angry families. And the negative reaction wasn't confined to the commencement service. For days after Dyson delivered his address, citizens responded with letters to the editor of the area paper. Most responses were negative and the writers said they were offended by the vulgarity and profanity that Dyson included in his address. Some lamented that Dyson's "locker room profanity" had plunged what should have been an auspicious, uplifting, and celebratory occasion into the sewer.

In the People's Forum, the letters to the editor section of the area newspaper, Rowland and Lourdes Shelley lambasted Dyson's speech as "a screaming racial tirade laden with epithets, locker room profanity and degrading analogies to sexual intercourse, including the 'F' word. . . . He owes a personal apology to every graduate and the North Carolina taxpayers, who pay his salary." Roland Hales, who had attended commencement to see his granddaughter graduate, wrote that the speech was "vulgar remarks, rap lyrics quoted verbatim and white trash slurs." Chancellor Michael Hooker, after receiving numerous and vociferous complaints, admitted he was working on damage control.

Singing the Praises of Rap

Dyson didn't agree with his critics. He said the commencement ceremony was a "teachable moment" and he chose to use it as an occasion to talk about issues important to the youth of America. He argued that it's impossible to talk about the dire circumstances of many black youths without using language that captures the anger, violence, and hopelessness that too often pervade their lives. He claimed that rap and gangsta rap express that hopelessness.

Some of those present at commencement appreciated Dyson's intent and the speech. Mary Beth Lackey, who attended the ceremony, wrote, "I must say it was one of the best speeches I've ever heard. . . . Dyson's speech did contain some bad words. But if that is all you got out of his speech, you weren't listening very hard. Look past the few bad words, and you'll see a very eloquent speech that orders our generation not to forget where we came from and to make a difference."

How can the same speech be described as "very eloquent" and "a screaming tirade . . . with locker room profanity"? How can one court rule that "The Fuck Shop" is obscene while another court judges it not obscene? Why do some people say gangsta rap offers important messages that we all need to hear while others say it isn't fit to be heard?

Perhaps we can learn something about these different views if we explore the opinions of some people who defend and some who disparage rap and gangsta rap. Both the defenders and detractors merit a hearing and thoughtful consideration.

Dyson argues that many black youths live lives of not-so-quiet desperation. He claims they are disaffected from a society that has not made good on its promises for equality of opportunity. In violent and sexually explicit lyrics, Dyson hears the angry, bitter rage of young black men who have grown up in a racist world that regards them as unworthy and inferior to whites.

Dyson acknowledges that much rap and gangsta rap denigrates women and he does not support or condone this. However, warns Dyson, we would be unwise to let the misogyny in the music keep us from hearing other important messages it communicates. Dyson asks us to pay attention to the environment in which many rappers grow up, an environment that cultivates the very rage and violence that surfaces in their music. Listen, says Dyson, and you can learn something about the oppressive, joyless world of many black youths. It is a world in which violence may seem the only way to respond to injustices, and rage may be rampant because more calm, considered emotions are inadequate and seldom have any impact on unsympathetic, privileged people. It is a world in which there is no hope for the future and no security that there even will be a future.

On the other side of the controversy are those who denounce rap music. bell hooks, a black social critic and professor, says that sexism among black males is a serious problem in black communities, and she urges black women to resist violence and sexism from their black male friends and romantic partners. Dolores Tucker, who chaired the National Political Congress of Black Women in 1993, denounces music that celebrates impersonal sex, rape, and murder and encourages black men to mistreat black women. Notice that some of the strongest detractors (as well as defenders) of rap are themselves African Americans.

Public Opinion

A 1990 survey conducted by the American Society of Newspaper Editors found that a majority of U.S. citizens believed music that explicitly describes sexual acts should not be protected by the First Amendment, which guarantees freedom of speech.

When and how much First Amendment protection should be given to music that deals with sexual acts?

No protection whatsoever	61%
Protection sometimes	24%
Full protection all the time	13%

The controversy about violent and sexually explicit rap music is not just about the music or the lyrics. It's also a debate about freedom of speech, and it's a disagreement about whose voices and experiences deserve to be heard. The controversy is also dramatic testimony to the power of words. Some people feel very strongly that the words in rap are harmful to society in general and women in particular; other people feel that the words are important expressions of the experience of one group of Americans.

Improving Communication

How can we respond to those whose opinions of rap and gangsta rap differ from our own? How can we increase our understanding of perspectives that may seem repugnant (if we disapprove) or narrow minded (if we approve)? Many courses of action are open to us.

Censorship

One option is to ban sexually explicit and violent lyrics. Should we support prohibiting it, because a majority of citizens in the United States do not favor freedom of speech protection for sexually explicit music? To do so would be to engage in censorship, which may create more problems than it solves. Censorship of any speech, including music, jeopardizes what many consider the most important of our constitutional freedoms.

First Amendment scholars argue that even (and perhaps especially) ideas that are unpopular deserve a hearing. Only by allowing unpopular communication, or outright objectionable speech, can we have public debate on controversial ideas and issues. According to the Public Agenda Foundation, the impulse to silence anything that offends or alienates some people represses the vibrant diversity that is part of our culture.

Increasing Information for Choices

Censorship isn't the only way to address violent and degrading speech. Tipper Gore was one of the founders of the Parents' Music Resource Center. This center strongly opposes censorship or government regulation of music that some people find objectionable. Members of the center say censorship is not the answer. Instead, they asked the music industry to package music with information that explains how sexually explicit and

Dana Summers, The Orlando Sentinel.

violent particular albums are. This center persuaded the Recording Industry of America to provide warning labels on potentially offensive record-
ings: Explicit Lyrics—Parental Advisory.

Conversations

Conversation is a particularly constructive path to increased understanding of those who regard rap and gangsta rap differently from the way we
do. We can't understand perspectives other than our own if we don't talk
with and listen to people who hold them. Willingness to listen thought-
fully reflects both respect for others and commitment to our own growth.

   In the early 1990s, I firmly disapproved of music that included sexually explicit language and positive portrayals of violence. Although I
would never argue for censorship, I did think such music was violent and
degrading of women, and I did think society would be better off without it.

   When I listened to gangsta rap, all I heard was denigration of women
and glorification of violence. Then Michael Eric Dyson joined the faculty
in my department. I quickly learned that he was a strong defender of equal
rights for women and that he treated women students, colleagues, and

friends respectfully. I also learned that he was a deeply religious man who counseled against violence.

Given my opinions of Dyson, I was stunned when I first heard him defend gangsta rap as offering a vital message. He presented a public talk in which he argued that all members of our society should pay attention to gangsta rap. I couldn't reconcile the decency of the man and his respect for women with his support of music that I found indecent and radically degrading of women.

So I talked with him. I asked him why he thought gangsta rap was important. I asked him what message he was urging people to hear in the music. Michael explained that he shares my disdain for the sexism and violence in the music. But, he pointed out, if that's all you hear, you're missing what's most important. He said, "Hear the sexism and condemn it. Hear the violence and condemn it. But also hear the pain and the anger and pay attention to it. That's the message none of us can afford to ignore." Michael talked passionately about the lives of many young black men. He informed me about their struggles and the scorn that routinely is inflicted on them.

Through conversations with Michael, I also came to understand that violent and sexually explicit lyrics are more than words. They are also symptoms of a specific way of life — a way of life that I never had to endure but that I want to recognize. Not to acknowledge this sphere of life and the hopelessness and anger it fosters is failure to be aware of the world beyond my own horizons.

After Michael and I talked, I listened again to music by Snoop Doggy Dogg and Tupak Shakur. I still heard language that I deplore and I still heard incitations to violence that I abhor; but I also heard something I hadn't heard before. I began to hear the anger, the rage, the despair of people who feel they've been left out of the American dream and I heard how different lives can be in one country.

How do I now feel about rap that extols violence and is sexually explicit and degrading? Personally, I still don't like it and it still doesn't represent society as I have experienced it; *but* now I do listen to the music because it has the power to teach me things I can't learn from my personal experiences. I have learned that some of this music represents a sphere of society that I don't know — a sphere less generous, less just, less promising, and far less kind than the sphere of society that I have been fortunate to inhabit. I've learned to hear the brutal lyrics as embodying with accuracy the brutal reality of too many people's lives. And I've learned that people who are decent, smart, spiritually committed, and fair-minded can defend gangsta rap with as much integrity and insight as those who denounce it.

Like any kind of communication, music has the power to move us — to lift our spirits, fuel our anger, and expand our understanding of our own lives and those of others. People may differ in their attitudes toward rap and gangsta rap. What people have in common, however, is the capacity to listen critically and to be open to learning from all communication, including music.

Key Words

- censorship
- First Amendment
- gangsta rap
- obscenity
- rap music

Reflecting on This Chapter

1. Imagine that Michael Eric Dyson had given his speech at your commencement. How would you feel? Would you follow the example of those who walked out on his 1996 speech, or would you listen to the message Dyson claims he was trying to express?

2. Dyson claims that rap lyrics accurately represent the rage and violence that is endemic in the environment of many black youths. Assuming that is true, are the profane and explicit lyrics justified? Could less inflammatory lyrics convey the reality of the world in which many black youths live?

3. Should we ban lyrics that are judged obscene by prevailing standards of communities? As communities differ in values, this would lead to banning certain lyrics in some communities and not in others. Are there any universal standards that we can use to guide our judgments about the obscenity and social value of music lyrics?

4. There is a tension between a commitment to free speech and commitments to other values such as nonviolence, respectful treatment of all people, and civility. How can we balance these commitments in specific cases such as judgments of gangsta rap?

5. We can learn by taking the perspective of others who differ from us. If you are white, try to imagine how you might feel and how you might view others and society if you had grown up feeling you were despised and devalued because of the color of your skin. If you are a person of color who grew up in poverty, try to imagine how gangsta rap lyrics

might sound to you if you had grown up in a suburban middle-class white family.

6. Do you perceive any inconsistency between responses to Douglas Hann's hate speech (discussed in Chapter 2) and court rulings that violent and sexually degrading lyrics are protected by the constitution? Are only some forms of communication free speech that is entitled to protection?

7. Assume Michael Eric Dyson is correct that gangsta rap is a powerful scream of rage and hopelessness. Does that justify celebrating degrading women and endorsing violence against them? In other words, at whose expense is the rage expressed?

References

Dixon, T., & Linz, D. (1997). Obscenity law and sexually explicit rap music: Understanding the effects of sex, attitudes, and beliefs. *Journal of Applied Communication Research, 25,* 217–241.

Dyson, M. E. (1995). Personal communication.

Dyson, M. E. (1995). *Between God and gangsta rap.* New York: Oxford University Press.

Dyson, M. E. (1996). *Race rules: Navigating the color line.* New York: Addison-Wesley.

Dyson, M. E. (1996, December 15). Commencement address delivered at the University of North Carolina at Chapel Hill.

Dyson speech still drawing complaints. (1996, December 18). *Raleigh News and Observer,* p. 2A.

Gore, T. (1995, September 25). Raising PG kids in an X-rated society. Speech delivered to the Junior League in Greenville, SC.

hooks, b. (1994). *Outlaw culture.* New York: Routledge.

Johannesen, R. (1997). Diversity, freedom, and responsibility in tension. In J. Makau & R. Arnett (Eds.), *Communication ethics in an age of diversity* (pp. 157–186). Urbana: University of Illinois Press.

Lackey, M. B. (1996, 21 December). The people's forum: A timeless message. *Raleigh News and Observer,* p. 21A.

Pitts, L., Jr. (1993, June 30). Music's new wave of sexism is especially discordant. *Miami Herald,* pp. 1E, 7E.

Public Agenda Foundation. (1992). *The boundaries of free speech: How free is too free?* New York: McGraw-Hill.

The rap on the speech (Editorial). (1996, December 19). *Raleigh News and Observer,* p. 30A.

Shelley, R. M., & Shelley, L. O. (1996, 21 December). The people's forum: Dismissing Dyson. *Raleigh News and Observer*, p. 21A.

Stanley, L. (Ed.). (1992). *Rap: The lyrics*. New York: Penguin Books.

Tucker, D. (1993, December 23). Quoted in Ransom, F. Black women man the ramparts for war on "gangsta rap" sexism. *Raleigh News and Observer*, p. A6.

UNC-CH commencement speech draws ire of parents. (1996, December 22). *Raleigh News and Observer*, p. 2B.

Will, G. (1990, July 30). America's slide into the sewer. *Newsweek*, p. 64.

Wyatt, R. O. (1991). *Free expression and the American public: A survey commemorating the 200th anniversary of the First Amendment*. Washington, DC: American Society of Newspaper Editors.

9

I DON'T APPROVE OF
THEIR LIFESTYLE

. . .

Perceiving Gays, Lesbians,

and Heterosexuals

Tyler Bourne is an associate in a successful law firm. He attended Harvard Law school, and then served a five-year stint in the Marines, earning the rank of lieutenant, before returning to civilian life and joining an Atlanta law firm. Tyler drives a three-year-old Honda Accord and lives in a nice but modest home in downtown Atlanta.

Like many of his colleagues, Tyler enjoys watching action films, reading good books, and sipping an occasional scotch on the rocks. Also like many of the associates in his firm, Tyler likes to attend sporting events and is an ardent fan of the Atlanta Braves. Like the other unmarried members of the firm, Tyler dates and hopes one day to settle into a permanent relationship. Unlike his colleagues, however, if Tyler does settle down, his health insurance policy won't cover his partner. Tyler is gay.

Tyler is accustomed to disapproval from people who learn he is gay, yet he's never gotten used to the phrase "your lifestyle." Whether people say "I don't approve of your lifestyle," or "Your lifestyle doesn't bother me," Tyler finds the phrase irritating and inaccurate.

"What is a lifestyle, anyway?" he asks. "Is a lifestyle how you live? If so, I live like most of the other people in my profession—no more or less extravagantly. Is it what foods and recreational activities you prefer? Mine are pretty much like those of everyone else I know. Is it how much money you make and spend? I make about the mean average for attorneys of my age and I live fairly modestly. Is it the social and political opinions you have? Mine are pretty middle-of-the-road. No, when people use that phrase about me, they are referring to the fact that I date and sleep with men, not women. Now why is that a lifestyle? And why isn't it also a lifestyle if men date and sleep with women?"

In this chapter, we focus on how we perceive and communicate about sexual orientation. We begin by surveying information about gays and lesbians and the basis of sexual orientation. Following that, we discuss perceptions of gays and lesbians. We see that people are more likely to perceive differences than commonalities among people with different sexual orientations. We also learn that gays and lesbians are more likely than heterosexuals to be perceived and defined by their sexual orientation. Finally, we reflect on language that has been and is used to refer to gays and lesbians, and we ask how different language reflects and affects perceptions. The purpose of this chapter is to provide information that could affect how you perceive and communicate about gays and lesbians.

Gays and Lesbians: Perceptions and Knowledge

Do you have personal relationships with any gays or lesbians? Are you gay or lesbian? If you answer no to these questions, the chances are good that your perceptions of gays and lesbians don't reflect personal knowledge and observation. Without direct knowledge of people and events, our perceptions tend to be shaped by what we hear from others and what the media present to us. To test the accuracy of your perceptions about gays and lesbians, answer the following six questions:

1. In which, if any, branches of the U.S. armed forces have gays served?

2. Do gays and lesbians equal, exceed, or fall below national levels of voting?

3. Are gays and lesbians more likely to work in the computer field or the fashion industry?

4. How many gays and lesbians are in steady relationships?

5. How important are religious and spiritual beliefs to lesbians and gays?

6. Is sexual orientation fixed and stable?

Getting the Facts

General opinion and media are not always reliable sources of knowledge. Often, popular beliefs are based more on stereotypes and misinformation than on evidence. To provide a factual basis for our thinking about gay men and lesbians, let's consider what research tells us. Some of the information that follows contradicts many stereotypes that circulate in society. Read it and see how your answers to the foregoing questions square with the facts.

1. Randy Shilts reports that during the past decade gay people have served as generals in every branch of the U.S. armed forces.

2. According to a broad survey titled *Overlooked Opinions*, 82% of lesbians and 87.9% of gays voted in recent presidential elections. Nationwide, only 61.3% of citizens voted.

3. Mark Fefer's 1991 survey of professional life found that 10 times as many gays and lesbians work in the computer field as work in the fashion industry. In 1993, *Overlooked Opinions* reported that the three most common job categories for gay men are management, health care, and education.

4. John Gonsiorek and James Weinrich report that 75% of lesbians and 40% to 60% of gays were in steady relationships in 1991.

5. In a 1991 survey of readers of *Out/Look*, a gay and lesbian magazine, 58% of respondents said spirituality was a very important part of their lives and 28% said religion was very important to them.

6. Sexual orientation often is not fixed for life. John Gonsiorek and James Weinrich's survey of research on sexuality reported that between 74% and 81% of self-defined lesbians had engaged in heterosexual intercourse. *Time* reporter Anastasia Toufexis reviewed Alfred Kinsey's pioneering studies of human sexuality and reported that 50% of men could be classified as bisexual. Kinsey himself

*"We don't believe in pressuring the children. When the time is right,
they'll choose the appropriate gender."*

Drawing by Mankoff; © 1995 The New Yorker *Magazine, Inc.*

reported that 18% of men he studied between the ages of 11 and 55 showed as much homosexual as heterosexual inclination. Adding to these findings, sociologists Michelle Huston and Pepper Schwartz report that many people do not identify themselves as being strictly homosexual or heterosexual throughout their entire lives. Their studies reveal that many people who currently define themselves as gay or lesbian were once married and heterosexually active. These studies demonstrate that for many people sexual orientation is not necessarily a stable part of identity.

In addition to information about the six questions you answered, there is other knowledge that challenges common (mis)perceptions about gays and lesbians, such as the examples here:

Charlotte Patterson estimates that in the United States, between 1 million and 5 million lesbians are mothers and between 1 million and 3 million gays are fathers.

In 1992, *Overlooked Opinions* reported that 43% of lesbians and 48% of gays own their homes.

Of 35,000 gay respondents to a *Publishers Weekly* survey, 82% said reading was a favorite hobby.

According to Michelle Huston and Pepper Schwartz, only a small minority of lesbians conform to the butch-femme stereotype. The majority of lesbians—as many as 90% in some studies—prefer egalitarian relationships.

Were your perceptions of gays and lesbians consistent with findings from research? If not, you're not alone. Many people have inaccurate perceptions about gays and lesbians as well as other groups they don't know personally. In addition, many heterosexuals don't know anything about gays and lesbians except their sexual orientation.

In Chapter 7, we discussed totalizing, which is the tendency to think about people as if one aspect of them — in this case, sexual orientation — is the totality, the only relevant facet, of who they are. When we totalize people or when we hold inaccurate perceptions of people, we often misunderstand them. Reducing the likelihood of misunderstandings begins with a willingness to consider perspectives and information beyond what we currently have. Next, we explore some facts and viewpoints that may enlarge our understanding of gays and lesbians.

Genes or Choice?

One of the most heated debates surrounding sexual orientation is whether it is determined genetically or whether it is a personal choice. In 1993, *U.S. News and World Report* informed us that 46% of Americans believe homosexuality is a chosen lifestyle, whereas 32% of Americans think sexual orientation is innate. Bennett Singer and David Deschamps, who compile information on gays and lesbians, ask the disarming question, "How many [Americans] believe that being *heterosexual* is a choice?" (p. 55, emphasis in original). Their question is insightful because it calls to our attention the inconsistency between viewing one sexual orientation as a choice and considering a different sexual orientation as natural, or innate.

Research on the causes of sexual orientation is relatively recent, so findings are not conclusive. Increasingly, however, studies suggest there is at least some biological basis for sexual orientation. In 1992, *Newsweek's* David Gelman published a brief report on Dr. Simon LeVay's study of the brains of 41 male cadavers, 19 of whom had been gay men. Dr. LeVay found notable differences in the size of the hypothalamus, the part of the brain thought to control sexual activity, when he compared the brains of the gay and the heterosexual men.

But Is It "Normal"?

Even if sexual orientation is partially or entirely biological in origin, many people still wonder if it is "normal." The answer to that question depends on how we define normal. If normal is what biology and genetics dictate, then preliminary evidence suggests more than one sexual orientation is normal.

Normal, however, usually refers not only to biological directives but also to social attitudes. The word *normal* is based on the root word *norm*, which refers to what is average or conventional. When we speak of norms, we refer to what is customary or standard. It turns out that what we perceive as standard depends as much on social codes as on biology.

Biological and genetic factors never exist in isolation. Instead, biology is interpreted and shaped by cultures to suit the values and goals of those cultures at particular moments in time. Social context is a major influence on the extent to which we realize various biological inclinations. For example, social conventions dictate that we wear clothes, even though nudity is our "natural" state. Similarly, most of us control our aggressive tendencies because laws and mores require such restraint.

Consider more dramatic examples of social values that shaped perceptions of what is normal. For the first 200 years of U.S. history, women were the property of men (fathers and then husbands) and couldn't vote —and this was normal. Only a few decades prior to women's enfranchisement, white people could own black people and force the latter to work without pay—and this, too, was thought to be normal. Today, most of us would consider it highly abnormal (not to mention immoral) to allow slavery or to prohibit women from voting.

Sexual orientation—at least the extent to which we act on it and how we view it—is influenced by social attitudes. What we consider normal at any moment in history is a matter of social judgment, not absolute truth. In ancient Greece, sexual relationships between men were regarded as the ideal; they were seen as superior to heterosexual unions. Homosexual acts were decriminalized in France in 1810, Poland in

1932, Switzerland in 1942, New Zealand in 1946, and Spain in 1980. Denmark and Norway legally recognize gay and lesbian marriages, and 90% of the population in the Netherlands favors equal rights for gays and lesbians.

What about the United States? The Lambda Legal Defense and Education Fund reported that in 1993, same-sex sexual activities were prohibited in 20 states. Hawaii is the only state that wants to recognize gay and lesbian marriages, and the other states refuse to recognize gay and lesbian marriage ceremonies performed in Hawaii. Some states prohibit gays and lesbians from adopting children or becoming foster parents, and a number of states refuse to allow gay or lesbian parents to have legal custody of their biological children.

Although gays and lesbians continue to experience limited civil rights in the United States, they have greater legal protection and social acceptance than in earlier eras. For example, since Wisconsin led the way in 1982, a number of states have passed civil rights laws that protect gays and lesbians against discrimination. As of 1994, laws had been passed in 11 states declaring sexual orientation to be irrelevant in child custody cases. A number of municipal governments provide health benefits to partners of gay and lesbian employees, and a growing number of private-sector companies cover same-sex domestic partnerships in employee benefits.

Another interesting shift in perceptions of gays and lesbians is evident in the way sexual orientation has been and is now classified by the American Psychiatric Association (APA). Until 1942, the APA took no official stand on sexual orientation, perhaps because alternatives to heterosexuality were not widely acknowledged in this country. In 1942, the organization designated homosexuality as a disease. Thirty-one years later, however, in 1973, the APA declared that homosexuality was not a disease and removed it from the list of psychiatric disorders. There is no evidence that the nature of homosexuality changed in the 31 years between the two APA rulings. What did change were social attitudes about sexual orientation.

Shifts in legal protections, social attitudes, and psychiatric judgments testify to the changeable definitions of what is normal, acceptable, and standard. As social and legal acceptance increase, so does the number of people who publicly define themselves as gay, lesbian, or bisexual. Social acceptance does not occur evenly throughout the society, however. Sociologists Michelle Huston and Pepper Schwartz note that gays and lesbians are more likely to be closeted in isolated rural areas than in urban areas where acceptance is greater.

Perceiving Gays and Lesbians

What do you recall about Tyler Bourne whom you met in the opening paragraphs of this chapter? If you're like most people, what first comes to your mind is that he is gay. But if you reread his description, you'll discover that his sexual orientation is no more prominent than many of his other personal aspects, including his profession, the kind of car he has, the home he owns, and the ways he spends his spare time.

The Tendency to Totalize

We are more likely to perceive qualities we've learned to consider unusual than those we've been socialized to perceive as usual. Thus, if we think it is uncommon to be gay, we're likely to notice a gay person's sexual orientation. If we perceive heterosexuality as usual, a straight man's sexual orientation is unlikely to stand out in our perceptions. In many cultures, heterosexuality is currently normalized, as is whiteness, being able-bodied, and belonging to the middle class. What a culture defines as normal, standard, or regular is very difficult to notice. It may be invisible to us, so that we don't see our race, sex, sexual orientation, and so forth if they are the ones our culture defines as typical. What a culture defines as atypical, or abnormal, on the other hand, is very visible and noticeable to us. We perceive it.

Not only are we more likely to perceive what our culture has taught us to regard as unusual and not to perceive what is culturally defined as normal; we are also likely to exaggerate the importance of what we perceive as unusual. We are likely to give disproportionate weight to sexual orientation in our overall impressions of people who are gay or lesbian. In fact, that may be the singular aspect that we notice most and think most about in relation to these individuals.

If we know that someone is gay or lesbian, we may define that person largely or entirely by his or her sexual orientation. This perceptual error may lead us not to recognize many other aspects of the individual—profession, hobbies, family life, spiritual commitments, intelligence, ambition, athletic abilities, and so forth. One way to recognize the degree of distortion that totalizing by sexual orientation causes is to ask whether we focus on the sexual orientation of heterosexuals. For most of us, the answer is no. Because our awareness of heterosexuals' sexual orientation doesn't dominate our perceptions of them, we are likely to perceive a range of qualities in these individuals.

Language About Gays and Lesbians

As we have seen throughout this book, language reflects and shapes individual and collective perceptions. Consider the changing language used to refer to people that today we think of as African Americans. Originally, people of African descent who lived in America were called *Negroes, darkies,* or *niggers.* The civil rights activism and black pride emphases of the 1960s led to linguistic reforms, and *black* became the agreed-upon term. Today, the most widely accepted terms are *African American* and *African.* The shifts in language reflect changes in social perceptions. At the same time, linguistic changes prompt revisions in individual and collective perceptions.

Language about gays and lesbians has also changed markedly over the years. For many years, the most widely used term was *homosexual.* Other pejorative terms that were less often used in public contexts were *pansy, fairy, dyke, faggot,* and *queer.* In the late 1960s and 1970s, the negative connotations of the word *homosexual* led to a new term: *gay.* In 1987, the prestigious *New York Times* first allowed gay to be used as a synonym for homosexual. Soon after, the appropriateness of gay came under challenge, primarily from lesbians who perceive gay men and lesbian women as distinct groups. And in the 1990s, some gay men and lesbian women reappropriated the term *queer* as a self-description. This is an effort to take a term that has been used against them and claim it as a positive self-reference.

Currently, there is some confusion and perhaps controversy over other language used to refer to gays and lesbians. The term *sexual orientation* is not universally accepted or preferred. Some heterosexuals, as well as some gays and lesbians, favor the term *sexual preference,* which implies that being gay or lesbian is a choice, not a genetic determination. And some people, primarily gays and lesbians, use the term *affectional preference* to signal that their preference is not merely a matter of sex but, more important, a preference for partners for affection and love. The verdict is not yet in on terminology.

Another interesting insight about linguistic change comes from the work of Warren Blumenfeld and Diane Raymond. According to their research on versions of the Bible that have been published over the years, the word *homosexual* did not appear until its use in a 1946 edition. Further, Blumenfeld and Raymond note that although there are Greek words for sex between members of the same sex, those words never appeared in the original, untranslated version of the New Testament.

What difference do the different terms make? A great deal of difference to those who are being described. If you are Jewish, you probably don't want to be called a kike or hymie; if you are African American, you probably don't want to be called a nigger; if you are of Asian descent, you'd probably resent being called slant-eyed or chink; and if you are a devout Christian, you probably wouldn't welcome being called a god squader or Jesus freak. All of us feel strongly about our identities and we don't like to have them degraded by labels that we find inappropriate or offensive. In other words, language matters a great deal.

Before leaving this chapter, ask yourself four questions whose answers may be influenced by issues that have been woven throughout our discussion.

1. Did you learn anything in this chapter that affects how you perceive and describe gays and lesbians?

2. Is it appropriate, accurate, or useful to define some people (gays and lesbians) and not others (heterosexuals) by their sexual orientation or sexual preference?

3. If researchers could prove that sexual orientation is either biologically determined or freely chosen, what difference would this discovery make in social attitudes and public policy?

4. How important is sexual orientation within the range of qualities, inclinations, and behaviors that make up any human being?

Key Words

- affectional preference
- gay
- heterosexual
- homosexual
- lesbian
- lifestyle
- normal
- queer
- sexual orientation
- sexual preference
- totalizing

Reflecting on This Chapter

1. Does it matter why people are gay, heterosexual, lesbian, or bisexual? What difference does the cause make in our perceptions of sexual orientation? Would you feel differently about gays and lesbians if you knew for certain that sexual orientation is biologically determined? How and why might such knowledge affect your opinion?

2. If you are heterosexual, imagine that your sexual orientation is declared abnormal. Imagine that you face discrimination on your job and that you cannot cover your life partner on your insurance policy. Imagine that the laws in your state don't allow you to be a legal parent. Imagine that you cannot gain legal or religious recognition of your commitment to another person. Would you hide or try to change your heterosexuality?

3. Reflect on the ways your parents influenced you. Think about their social and political values, religious and spiritual beliefs, professional ethics, involvement with community, and other aspects of their lives. How much did your parents' sexual orientation affect your identity, self-concept, and sexual orientation? How important and influential was that single facet of their identity on who you are, what you do and believe, and how you live your life?

4. Speculate on the implications of declaring that the state and nation will not assist people in dealing with the consequences of personal choices. What would happen to people who were injured while driving under the influence of drugs or alcohol; people who develop cirrhosis of the liver from heavy drinking of alcohol; people who need heart surgery because they chose to eat a high-fat, high-cholesterol diet; people who were paralyzed as a result of skydiving or racing cars; people who choose to have children although prenatal testing reveals that these children will have serious mental retardation?

5. Reverse the scenario in question 4 so that you consider the implications of withdrawing government support of genetically determined conditions. What would happen to individuals who have diseases such as Lou Gehrig's or Parkinson's disease? What would become of people with genetic predispositions toward alcoholism, breast cancer, schizophrenia, or depression?

6. How much do media influence social attitudes about gays and lesbians? In 1993, *Married . . . With Children* was the first prime-time series to have a character (Amanda Bearse) come out of the closet.

Regular gay or lesbian characters have appeared on a number of prime-time television series including *Soap, Roseanne, Melrose Place,* and *Dynasty.* And in 1997, Ellen became the first lead character on a prime-time program to announce that she was lesbian. Do you think the presence of gay and lesbian characters on prime-time television affects general perceptions of gays and lesbians?

7. What terminology do you use to refer to people who have romantic and sexual relationships with members of the same sex? Do you prefer *homosexual* or *gay* or *gay and lesbian*? Do you use the term *sexual orientation* or *sexual preference*? What do your choices reflect about your perceptions of men and women who have same-sex partners?

8. Is sexual orientation a matter of inclination or behavior? If a person has sexual desires and fantasies about members of her or his own sex but lives a celibate life, is the person homosexual?

9. Is sexual orientation fixed or somewhat fluid? Can a person "be" heterosexual at one point in life and "be" homosexual at other points in life?

10. How different would you be if you woke up tomorrow and had a sexual orientation different from the one you identify with today? Would you have different tastes in music, recreation, food, or films? Would you have different social or political values? Would you change your career goals? Would you care more or less about children? Would your spiritual beliefs and practices shift? What do your answers to these questions suggest about the significance of sexual orientation in overall identity?

References

Blumenfeld, W., & Raymond, D. (1988). *Looking at gay and lesbian life*. Boston: Beacon.

Dynes, W. (Ed.). (1990). *Encyclopedia of homosexuality*. New York: Garland.

Fefer, M. (1991, December 16). Gay in corporate America. *Fortune*, pp. 48, 102.

Fletcher, L. (1992). *The first gay pope and other records*. Boston: Alyson.

Gonsiorek, J., & Weinrich, J. (Eds.). (1991). *Homosexuality: Research implications for public policy*. Newbury Park, CA: Sage.

Gross, J. (1991, February 11). New challenge of youth: Growing up in a gay home. *New York Times*, pp. B1, B6.

Huston, M., & Schwartz, P. (1996). Gendered dynamics in the romantic relationships of lesbians and gays. In J. T. Wood (Ed.), *Gendered relationships* (pp. 163–176). Mountain View, CA: Mayfield.

Lambda Legal Defense and Education Fund, Inc. (1993). New York.

Overlooked opinions. (1992). The gay market. Chicago: Overlooked Opinions, Inc.

Overlooked opinions. (1993). Chicago: Overlooked Opinions, Inc.

Patterson, C. (1992). Children of lesbian and gay parents. *Child Development, 63,* 85–96.

Readers' survey. (1991, Fall). *Out/Look,* 4–6.

Rutledge, L. (1987). *The gay book of lists.* New York: Alyson.

Shilts, R. (1993). *Conduct unbecoming.* New York: St. Martin's Press.

Singer, B., & Deschamps, D. (1994). (Eds.) *Gay and lesbian stats.* New York: The New Press.

Summer, B. (1993, June 7). Gay and lesbian publishing: The paradox of success. *Publishers Weekly,* p. 15.

U. S. News and World Report. (1993, July 5). p. 7.

Toufexis, A. (1992, August 17). Bisexuality: What is it? *Time,* p. 58.

| 10 |

I'M ALREADY SPOKEN FOR

. . .

Speaking For and About Others

Years ago, if a woman who was dating someone steadily was asked out by another person, she might say, "I'm already spoken for." Translated, she was telling her would-be suitor that another person had already asked for her commitment and she had agreed.

Today, the idea of being spoken for has taken on new and more complex meanings. When one person speaks for another person or a group, the individual or group that is spoken for may feel erased, ignored, or misrepresented. The person or group may feel disempowered and may be inhibited from speaking for themselves in the future. Dawn and Charles Braithwaite provide this example, which was recounted by a man who uses a wheelchair:

> People do not consider you, they consider the chair first. I was in
> a store with my purchases on my lap. The clerk looked at my
> companion and not at me and said, "cash or charge?" (p. 161)

Dawn Braithwaite is on the faculty of Arizona State University West, where she studies communication with and about people with disabilities.

In a 1990 study, she interviewed many people with disabilities and every one of them told some version of the story you just read. Because a person uses a wheelchair doesn't mean she or he cannot select merchandise and decide how to pay for purchases. The sales clerk ignored the customer and acted as if he wasn't capable of engaging in a simple commercial transaction. It's understandable that the customer resented the clerk's assumption that he couldn't speak for himself simply because he used a wheelchair.

Another interviewee in Braithwaite's 1990 study told of a time, like many others, when she felt she was erased as a person because of her disability. The woman, whose multiple sclerosis required her to use a wheelchair, was shopping for lingerie. Her husband accompanied her on the shopping trip. In the lingerie section of the department store, the woman explained to a clerk what she wanted and asked the clerk to help her find the items. The clerk turned to the husband and asked him, "What size does she want?" The woman identified her size, then the clerk turned to the husband and asked, "And what color?" As the exchange continued, the clerk repeatedly asked the husband questions that could and should have been addressed to the woman, who was the customer and who was able to speak for herself.

Consider an example of a different context in which speaking for others became controversial. Anne Campbell wrote several semifictional accounts of the lives of Native Canadian women. In her writing she adopted a first-person voice and assumed a Native identity, which was not her birthright. In 1988, Campbell was invited to speak about Native Canadian Women at the International Feminist Book Fair in Montreal. A delegation of Native Canadian writers asked Campbell to *move over* (their term) to allow them to speak for themselves. They explained that when she writes in the persona of a Native Canadian, she disempowers authors who are natives. To her credit, Campbell indeed agreed to move over and let Native Canadians speak for themselves.

In this chapter we explore some of the more common forms of speaking for others, and we consider how it can have consequences other than those we intend. By the time you finish the chapter, you should have a better understanding of the perspective of some people who are spoken for and you should have insights into when and how it may be appropriate to speak for others.

Understanding the Misunderstanding

We want to explore the reasons that people sometimes speak for others and some of the problems associated with doing so. We begin by identifying some of the most common motivations behind speaking for others. Next we consider the range of contexts in which this occurs. We then discuss some of the dangers of or objections to speaking for others. Finally, we consider guidelines that may help us decide when it is appropriate or useful to speak for others.

Reasons to Speak for Others

Speaking for and about others occurs for many reasons. Sometimes we speak for others because we like to hear ourselves talk. Sometimes we assume we understand others well enough to speak for them as they would speak for themselves. The most common motive for speaking for others, however, is probably the belief, which may not be conscious, that they cannot speak effectively for themselves. Sometimes this is correct, but in many cases, this is an erroneous assumption. Speaking for others can cause offense and can lower the self-esteem of those for whom we speak, however good our intentions may be.

Contexts in Which People Speak for Others

Let's begin unraveling this misunderstanding by considering the range of contexts in which it occurs. We discover that speaking for others happens in personal interaction, family communication, intercultural encounters, and mass communication. Across varying contexts, the basic issues involved in speaking for others are similar.

Last year I went to a party that was also attended by Celia and Vince, a couple I'd not seen in several months. I approached them and we engaged in the usual "Gee, it's been a long time" chatter. Then I asked Celia how she liked working outside the home after 10 years of being a full-time homemaker and mother.

"She really enjoys getting out, but it is a stress to meet her job responsibilities and still take care of the children," Vince replied.

I established eye contact with Celia and asked, "Do you have any help? Maybe a housekeeping service?"

"No," Vince said. "We can manage it all. It just keeps us pretty busy."

Once again, I tried to make it clear that I was directing my conversation to Celia, not Vince: "So, Celia, is work outside the home more or less stressful than working in your home?"

"It's not either-or," Vince said. "She's doing both."

As soon as I could politely leave ("Oh, gee, there's Ann. I've got to talk with her"), I moved away from Celia and Vince. Why, I wondered, did he presume he had the right to speak for her? Why did he presume he could give more informed answers about her feelings than she could?

Another common example of speaking for others is parents who speak for their children. Georgia, a colleague of mine, has a 5-year-old daughter named Lisa who has a superior vocabulary for so young a child. Once the three of us were having lunch. When the server came to our table, Georgia and I placed our orders. The server then asked Lisa, "And what would you like, young lady?" Lisa began to reply, but Georgia spoke over her, saying "She'll have the grilled cheese sandwich with a salad, no fries."

After the server left, Lisa said, "Mommy, I wanted a hamburger and french fries." Georgia smiled and said, "No, honey, you don't want all that fat, and you know red meat isn't good for you, right?" Lisa didn't reply. When our lunches arrived, Lisa nibbled at her cheese sandwich and ignored the salad altogether.

After lunch, the three of us stopped in a clothing store to select a new dress for Lisa. Georgia picked out a plain loden green dress and showed it to Lisa, who shook her head and wrinkled her mouth. "It's ugly," she said. Then Lisa pointed to a dress on a mannequin. The dress was royal blue and had rose piping and buttons. "No, honey," said Georgia, "Blue isn't a good color for you and that dress is too frilly. This green one is more your style." Lisa pouted as Georgia purchased the green dress.

Georgia is not a domineering person. She is a loving and thoughtful mother who wants what is best for her daughter, but in speaking for Lisa, Georgia may diminish Lisa's confidence in her own judgment and her ability to speak for herself. Unintentionally, Georgia may be teaching Lisa not to trust her perceptions or use her own voice.

Now an example from mass media. The nightly television news comes on. One of the seven stories reported is about low-income African Americans who live in inner cities. Each of the three experts interviewed in the story is a middle-class white person. The white experts confidently describe the circumstances, beliefs, and behaviors of people who differ

Reprinted with special permission of King Features Syndicate.

radically from them in race, economic status, education, and other conditions of life. They speak for others.

Robert Entman is a professor of communication studies at Northwestern University who conducts research on how television news shows portray African Americans. According to his studies, most nightly news programs feature black experts almost exclusively for stories that pertain directly to African Americans. White experts, however, are featured on stories about almost anything, including African Americans. The problem here is twofold. First, African Americans are often presumed to have no expertise unrelated to their race, an issue we discussed in Chapter 7.

The second problem is that white experts are presumed (both by programmers and many listeners and viewers) to have the knowledge and the right to speak for African Americans and other groups of which they are not part. The converse is not true as African Americans are generally not assumed to be competent to speak authoritatively about issues other than those clearly pertinent to minorities. This situation suggests that authority is associated generally with people who belong to privileged groups — those who have greater status, wealth, power, and opportunities than many groups in society.

Dangers in Speaking for Others

Linda Alcoff, a social critic, wrote an important article titled "The Problem of Speaking for Others." In that article, Alcoff focused on how common it is for people who are privileged to speak for and about oppressed groups. So whites speak for Latinos and Latinas, U.S. citizens represent women in Third World countries, economically comfortable people define the causes and effects of poverty, and European Americans speak for Native Americans. When this happens, there is danger that the spokespersons will misrepresent the experiences and interests of those for whom they speak. Such misrepresentation can occur even when the people speaking intend to help or act as advocates for those about whom they speak.

Each of us has a social location, which is our place in particular social communities. Each social location allows some experiences and knowledge and limits access to other experiences and other kinds of knowledge. Can a middle-class, heterosexual, white professional man speak in an informed way about people who are homeless, poor, minorities, or homosexual? Can a well-educated U.S. feminist, who enjoys a comfortable lifestyle in a relatively liberal society, speak with authority about the meaning of genital mutilation of women in certain countries in Africa? Can a person who has never experienced physical limitations understand what having a disability means?

In her essay, Alcoff states that privileged locations are especially dangerous. She means that when privileged people speak for those who are less privileged, they may reinforce the oppression of those for whom they speak. Alcoff is concerned that speaking for others can have the unintended effect of disempowering those whose interests we are trying to advance. When we speak for others, they may not gain the confidence and ability to speak for themselves. Also, when we speak for others, they lose the opportunity to demonstrate that they are authorities who merit a hearing.

And Dangers in Not Speaking for Others

Despite the problems of speaking for and about others, Alcoff does not advocate never doing it. Instead, she urges us to consider when speaking for others is appropriate and constructive. She specifically cautions against what she calls "the retreat response" (p. 17). This involves thinking or saying, "I only know about my personal experience, so I can't speak for anyone else." Although we may be unable to appreciate fully the experiences of people who differ significantly from us, we are not confined to knowledge based on strictly personal experience. Because one person is

Jamaican and heterosexual does not mean that she or he has nothing in common with Asians and/or lesbians.

Social critic and author Christopher Hitchens cautions us not to fall prey to the retreat response. In an interview with *Progressive* columnist Sasha Abramsky, Hitchens described the "narcissism of the small difference," which he defines as people's tendency to concentrate on their individual circumstances, identity, and problems (p. 35). Consequently, says Hitchens, we recognize only how we differ from others and not how we are like them. When we think only about our own circumstances, we lose awareness of something larger than just ourselves: the human community.

Retreating from whoever and whatever differs from us deprives us of the opportunity to learn about others. It also allows us to abdicate responsibility for speaking against conditions, laws, and people that oppress them. Further, retreat is not the neutral response some people assume it is. Not to speak is to allow continuation of oppressive conditions, attitudes, and behaviors. Sometimes those who benefit from inequities are the most persuasive agents for challenging the inequities.

To illustrate when speaking for others can be desirable, Alcoff cites the example of Rigoberta Menchu, a Quiche Indian who was born and raised in Guatemala. Like many poor people in Guatemala, Rigoberta Menchu and her family suffered extreme exploitation by propertied Guatemalans and the Guatemalan government. Menchu felt she had a responsibility to help all poor Guatemalans. To do so, she learned Spanish and traveled to many other countries where she told the story of her people.

In 1984, she published her autobiography, *I . . . Rigoberta Menchu.* She opens her book by asserting that it is about "not only *my* life, it's also the testimony of . . . all poor Guatemalans" (p. 1). Although Menchu had escaped the personal tyranny of poverty, she had the authority to speak for others who could not speak effectively for themselves. This example shows that sometimes it is appropriate and fruitful to speak for others. It is appropriate because Rigoberta Menchu knew about those for whom she spoke and because she spoke respectfully of them.

Improving Communication

There is no simple, one-size-fits-all answer to the question of whether to speak for others. As we've seen, not speaking for them may foster or reinforce oppression. Yet speaking for others is not appropriate if we do it without adequate knowledge of those others or if we do it to satisfy egotistical beliefs that our voices should be heard.

Recognizing Our Own Social Locations

Perhaps the first step in avoiding inappropriate speaking for others is to understand that we may not understand them on their own terms. If you are white, you can't understand fully the lives, ideas, and feelings of blacks, Latinos and Latinas, and other ethnic groups. If you are able-bodied, you can't comprehend the world and the feelings of people with disabilities. If you are a man used to asserting yourself in conversation, you may not understand that many women are less quick to jump into conversations and you may not grasp what they would say if given a chance to speak for themselves.

Speaking to Others

If you start with the presumption that you may not understand others well enough to speak for them, you create an opportunity to learn about them. Gayatri Spivak encourages us to speak *to* others so that we can offer them our perspectives and can learn from theirs. It may be that privileged individuals can command audiences that oppressed people cannot. If so, there is a powerful opportunity to be an agent of positive change. We can do this, however, only if we engage in dialogue with others in an effort to learn about people whose lives differ profoundly from our own.

Ask questions. Invite others to explain how they see their experiences and others' actions toward them. Ask what they want and don't want. Invite them to tell you what they resent and appreciate from others who care about them and issues that affect their lives. Questions show that you are interested in learning more about others.

From her interviews with persons who have disabilities, Professor Braithwaite discovered that many people with disabilities view themselves as educators who want to change broad social views of them and their disabilities. All her interviewees said they welcome questions about their disabilities as long as the questions reflect a genuine desire to understand them *as persons*, not a debasing interest in their "deformities."

AXIS is an organization committed to educating the general public about how to interact with individuals who have disabilities. AXIS issued a list of guidelines that offer insight into what to do and not to do if we want to communicate effectively with people who have disabilities. These "Ten Commandments" are presented below.

Ten Commandments for Communicating with Persons with Disabilities

1. When talking with a person with a disability, speak directly to that person rather than through a companion or sign language interpreter who may be present.

2. When introduced to a person with a disability, it is appropriate to offer to shake hands. People with limited hand use or who wear an artificial limb can usually shake hands. (Shaking hands with the left hand is an acceptable greeting.)

3. When meeting a person with a visual impairment, always identify yourself and others who may be with you. When conversing in a group, remember to identify the person to whom you are speaking.

4. If you offer assistance, wait until the offer is accepted. Then listen to or ask for instructions.

5. Treat adults as adults. Address people who have disabilities by their first names only when extending that same familiarity to all others present. (Never patronize people who use wheelchairs by patting them on the head or shoulder.)

6. Leaning or hanging on a person's wheelchair is similar to leaning or hanging on a person and is generally considered annoying. The chair is part of the personal body space of the person who uses it.

7. Listen attentively when you're talking with a person who has difficulty speaking. Be patient and wait for the person to finish, rather than correcting or speaking for the person. If necessary, ask short questions that require short answers, a nod, or a shake of the head. Never pretend to understand if you are having difficulty doing so. Instead, repeat what you have understood and allow the person to respond. The reponse will clue you in and guide your understanding.

8. When speaking with a person in a wheelchair or a person who uses crutches, place yourself at eye level in front of the person to facilitate the conversation.

9. To get the attention of a person who is hearing-impaired, tap the person on the shoulder or wave your hand. Look directly at the person and speak clearly, slowly and expressively to establish if

the person can read your lips. Not all people with a hearing impairment can lip-read. For those who do lip-read, be sensitive to their needs by placing yourself facing the light source and keeping hands, cigarettes and food away from your mouth when speaking.

10. Relax. Don't be embarrassed if you happen to use accepted, common expressions that seem to relate to the person's disability, such as "see you later" or "did you hear about this?"

To the guidelines offered by AXIS, Dawn Braithwaite adds several others. First, she says, if you push a person's wheelchair, don't make car sounds (vrooom). One of Braithwaite's interviewees, a business executive, complained that many people feel compelled to make car sounds as they push the chair. The chair is not a toy, the executive pointed out. Another interviewee resented people who leaned on a wheelchair. Many people who use wheelchairs regard the chairs as part of who they are. Touching the chair is touching the person, invading his or her personal space.

Braithwaite also cautions able-bodied people not to avoid communicating with persons who have disabilities. Her research shows that many able-bodied people evade interacting with individuals who have disabilities because the able-bodied people feel uncomfortable. Avoiding interaction, however, doesn't help us become more comfortable and doesn't increase our ability to interact effectively with people who have disabilities or who differ from us in other ways.

A final suggestion from Braithwaite is that we should not assume that we need to speak for or do things for those with disabilities. Instead, we should realize that most people who have particular disabilities can do most of what people without disabilities can do. Failing to recognize this is to perceive only their disabilities rather than to respect them as persons who — like all of us — have specific limitations. Ideally, we should focus on what individuals with disabilities can do, including speaking for themselves.

Another enriching perspective results from discovering how people with disabilities view those who don't have disabilities. Many with disabilities switch the convention of comparing minorities to majorities (that is, people with disabilities presuming that able-bodied individuals are the norm). Thus, people who have disabilities often refer to able-bodied people as *nondisabled* or *nonhandicapped*. Indicative of the wit and humor of those with disabilities is their use of the acronym TAB, a term they coined to refer to a person who is temporarily able-bodied. This term prompts people who currently have no disability to realize that nobody is immune to becoming disabled.

The distinguished writer Reynolds Price was a physically active man until he was paralyzed by cancer of the spine. He refuses to define himself as "differently abled" or "physically challenged." Instead, he refers to himself as a "cripple," perhaps in an effort to challenge the negative connotations conventionally associated with the word, *cripple*. Price also refers to people who don't have disabilities as temporarily able-bodied—a reminder that abilities may not last forever.

A final suggestion for approaching the question of whether to speak for others is to remember that for anyone, speaking for himself or herself is a process. Some individuals cannot represent themselves effectively because they lack communication skills or understanding of the norms of speaking in public. This doesn't mean, however, that they can't learn to speak effectively, even eloquently, for themselves.

Empowering Others to Speak

An example of empowering others to speak comes from my partner, Robbie Cox. During his two-year term as president of the National Sierra Club, one of Robbie's principal objectives was to tackle environmental injustice. This occurs when environmental hazards are located in poor communities where racial minorities are often the primary inhabitants. One group that Robbie learned about was a small community of African Americans who had an unusually high incidence of cancer. Members of the community discovered barrels of toxic waste that were shallowly buried near their neighborhood. When community leaders called newspaper reporters, they got no response. Members of the community had no social status and they didn't persuade reporters the issue merited coverage.

Robbie learned of the situation and he traveled to the community, which was in the rural South. After talking with community leaders and examining the barrels of toxic waste, Robbie called not only the local press but the national wire services. Because he was the president of an important organization, he got immediate response from major presses. It didn't take long for the president of the chemical company that had buried the toxic waste to read the stories that appeared in newspapers around the country. The president called Robbie and suggested the two of them meet. Robbie agreed, but only on the condition that the leaders of the community also participate in the meeting. The president reluctantly accepted Robbie's terms.

For over a year Robbie and several other Sierra Club members worked with the community leaders to teach them how to get their message across forcefully and effectively. As the community leaders gained competence and confidence in speaking for themselves, Robbie gradually reduced his visibility and his role as an adviser. He empowered this group to represent itself. In so doing, he reduced their dependence on others and increased their ability to speak effectively for themselves.

In his work, Robbie was informed by material from Tools for Change, a San Francisco–based organization that works to raise awareness of privileges that are often invisible to those who enjoy them. When we are unaware of our privileges, we may not realize how this unconsciousness can lead us to misunderstand others. Tools for Change publishes guidelines for communication that equalizes relations between more and less privileged groups.

Sharing some of the Tools for Change guidelines seems an appropriate way to conclude this chapter. The guidelines below are adapted from a pamphlet co-authored by Margo Adair and Sharon Howell. The pamphlet is titled "Breaking Old Patterns, Weaving New Ties: Alliance Building."

Don't

- patronize
- challenge others' tone, attitude, or manner
- interrupt others — let them speak for themselves
- take responsibility for, think for, or speak for others
- assume an individual is exceptional to the "average" members of their group; don't assume there is an "average" member of any group
- assume an individual can represent his or her group
- ask others to justify themselves, their ideas, or their feelings
- always speak first
- equate all oppressions as equal
- expect others to educate you about their group's history, customs, or conditions
- expect others to be grateful for your support and interest
- defend your mistakes by asserting that your intentions were/are good
- expect to be trusted

Do

- expect discomfort when communicating with people who differ from you
- remember that others can speak about (have knowledge of) matters beyond those directly relevant to their group (don't totalize them by their group identity)
- take responsibility for equalizing power
- point out dominating and patronizing behaviors when you observe them
- encourage pride in every person's ancestry and history
- try to understand others and what they think and feel in the context of their social history
- ask questions about matters you don't understand; hiding ignorance doesn't diminish it
- respect disagreements
- appreciate the risk that others take in sharing their experiences with you
- appreciate it when others point out mistakes in your assumptions or claims; if others are willing to challenge and criticize you, it means they think you really are interested in them and their issues

---

Key Words

- people with disabilities
- retreat response
- social location
- speaking about others
- speaking for others
- speaking to others

Reflecting on This Chapter

1. Have you ever thought that someone spoke for you? How did you feel about that experience? Did you feel the person represented you accurately or misrepresented you? Did you feel the person was supporting you or taking away your voice?

2. When, if ever, is it appropriate to speak for others? Are there ways to do so that are not patronizing? Are there situations in which doing so can be constructive for others and appreciated by them? Are there times when others cannot speak for themselves?

3. What standards can you develop to justify the occasions when it is acceptable or even desirable to speak for others? To answer this question, you might find it useful to read the article by Linda Alcoff that appears in the references for this chapter.

4. Who is most likely to speak for others? To what extent is speaking for others linked to status, access to media and public forums, and membership in privileged groups? What does your answer imply about the place of power relationships in the practice of speaking for others?

5. In many professions it may not be possible to avoid speaking for and about others. For example, can speaking for and about others be avoided by teachers, attorneys, politicians, and social service workers?

6. Reread the guidelines for communicating with persons with disabilities on pages 137–138. Have you ever inadvertently violated any of the guidelines? After reading this chapter, do you understand why these guidelines are useful?

7. When you read Adair and Howell's guidelines for equalizing relations on pages 140–141, did you recall times when you have followed the suggestions for what you should do to empower others? Did you recall any instances in which you had engaged in behaviors that Adair and Howell claim are misguided? Can you recall experiences in which you have seen others who are privileged engage in behaviors that undermine empowerment of less-privileged individuals and groups?

8. Is there any irony between the subject of this chapter—and the book as a whole—and the idea that sometimes we should not speak for others? What authorizes me as an author to speak about groups that I am not part of?

References

Abramsky, S. (1997, February). Christopher Hitchens. *The Progressive*, pp. 32–36.

Adair, M., & Howell, S. (1992). *Breaking old patterns, weaving new ties: Alliance building* (pamphlet). San Francisco: Tools for Change, P.O. Box 14141.

Alcoff, L. (1991, Winter). The problem of speaking for others. *Cultural Critique*, pp. 5–32.

Allen, B. (1995). "Diversity" and organizational communication. *Journal of Applied Communication Research, 23*, 143–155.

AXIS. Center for Public Awareness of People with Disabilities. 4550 Indianola Ave., Columbus, OH, 43214.

Braithwaite, D. (1987). *If you push my wheelchair, don't make car sounds: On the problem of "help" between disabled and ablebodied persons.* Paper presented at the annual meeting of the Speech Communication Association, Boston, MA.

Braithwaite, D. (1990). From majority to minority: An analysis of cultural change from ablebodied to disabled. *International Journal of Intercultural Relations, 14,* 465–583.

Braithwaite, D. (1992). Isn't it great that people like you get out: Communication between disabled and ablebodied persons. In E. B. Ray (Ed.), *Case studies in health communication* (pp. 149–159). Hillsdale, NJ: Lawrence Erlbaum.

Braithwaite, D., & Labrecque, D. (1994). Responding to the Americans with Disabilities Act: Contributions of interpersonal communication research and training. *Journal of Applied Communication Research, 22,* 287–294.

Braithwaite, D., & Braithwaite, C. (1997). Viewing persons with disabilities as a culture. In L. Samovar & R. Porter (Eds.), *Intercultural communication: A reader* (8th ed., pp. 154–164). Belmont, CA: Wadsworth.

Cushner, K., & Brislin, R. (1996). *Intercultural interactions* (2nd ed.). Thousand Oaks, CA: Sage.

Entman, R. (1994). Representation and reality in the portrayal of blacks on network television news. *Journalism Quarterly, 71,* 509–520.

Gates, H. L., Jr. (1987). Authority, (white) power and the (black) crisis: It's all Greek to me. *Cultural Critique, 7,* 19–46.

Houston, M. (1997). When black women talk with white women: Why dialogues are difficult. In A. González, M. Houston, & V. Chen (Eds.), *Our voices: Essays in culture, ethnicity, and communication* (2nd ed., pp. 187–194). Los Angeles, CA: Roxbury.

Houston, M., & Wood, J. T. (1996). Difficult dialogues, enlarged horizons: Communicating across race and class. In J. T. Wood (Ed.), *Gendered relationships* (pp. 39–56). Mountain View, CA: Mayfield.

Lyons, R. F. (1991). The effects of acquired illness and disability on friendships. In D. Perlman & W. Jones (Eds.), *Advances in personal relationships, 3* (pp. 223–277). London: J. Kingsley.

Lyons, R. F., & Meade, D. (1995). Painting a new face on relationships: Relationship remodeling in response to chronic illness. In S. Duck & J. T. Wood (Eds.), *Understanding relationship processes, 5: Confronting relationship challenges* (pp. 181–210). Thousand Oaks, CA: Sage.

Menchu, R. (1984). *I . . . Rigoberta Menchu* (A. Wright, Trans.; E. Burgos-Debray, Ed.). London: Verso.

Padden, C., & Humphries, T. (1988). *Deaf in America: Voices from a culture.* Cambridge, MA: Harvard University Press.

Rose, H. (1995). Apprehending deaf culture. *Journal of Applied Communication Research, 23,* 156–162.

Spivak, G. (1988). Can the subaltern speak? In C. Nelson & L. Grossberg (Eds.), *Marxism and interpretation of culture* (pp. 271–313). Urbana: University of Illinois Press.

• • •

Thompson, T. L. (1982). Gaze toward and avoidance of the handicapped: A field experiment. *Journal of Nonverbal Behavior, 6*, 188–196.

Tools for Change. Post Office Box 14141. San Francisco, CA 94114.

Wood, J. T., & Cox, J. R. (1993). Rethinking critical voice: Materiality and situated knowledges. *Western Journal of Communication, 57*, 278–287.

PART 3

Misunderstandings Between

Social Groups

| 11 |

WHAT CAN I DO TO HELP?

. . .

Different Ways of Communicating Caring

Your mother's about the same," Natasha tells Milton when she returns from visiting his mother in the hospital. "She's still not responding to the chemotherapy, and the doctors don't know of anything else to try."

Milton nods.

"You really need to visit her," Natasha says, giving Milton a critical eye. "You should be with your mother."

"There's nothing I can do," he replies as he has dozens of times before.

"You don't have to *do* anything. Just go there and be with her," Natasha says firmly. "She needs you."

"I can't do anything to help her."

"How can you be so unfeeling when your mother is dying? Visiting her isn't a lot to ask."

"You just don't understand," he protests.

"I understand that you don't care enough about your mother to visit her in the hospital when she is dying." Natasha's tone is caustic.

"Just get off my case, will you?"

Natasha shakes her head and walks out of the room, leaving Milton to his own thoughts. His wife and children have been criticizing him relentlessly ever since his mother was diagnosed with cancer and went into the hospital. They say he should visit her, but he doesn't see the point. He went a couple of times, but he felt totally useless. He couldn't do anything to stop the cancer, couldn't do anything to make her well. He couldn't even do anything to make her feel better. All he could do was watch the woman who gave him birth, whom he loved with all his heart, grimace in pain and shrink day by day.

After his first two visits, Milton hasn't been back to the hospital. He can't stand seeing his mother in pain and dying when there is nothing he can do to help her. Natasha and the kids think he doesn't care, but really, it's just the opposite. He cares too much to watch his mother hurting and be unable to do anything to lessen her pain. At the hospital, he felt utterly ineffective. If there were something he could do for her, he would do it in a minute. But there isn't.

Socialized to think he should solve problems and achieve things, Milton is at a loss when there is nothing he can do to help his mother. He doesn't feel it's doing anything to be with her. Natasha, on the other hand, grew up believing that being with others is a primary way to express love and support. She knows she cannot cure Milton's mother, but she can be with her and, to Natasha, that's an important way to express her love.

Fueling the misunderstanding between Natasha and Milton (and perhaps between Milton and his mother as well) are different views of what it means to care for another person. The misunderstanding will persist unless Natasha and Milton realize that they have different meanings for caring.

Understanding the Misunderstanding

In 1974, three researchers conducted a classic study that illuminates different ways people express caring. Wills, Weiss, and Patterson wanted to know how affection showed by husbands affected wives' feelings about their marriages. To find out, they asked each wife in the study to keep a diary in which she recorded her feelings about her marriage at several points each day. What the wives didn't know was that the researchers were instructing the husbands to vary the amount of affection they showed their wives. Some days the researchers would tell the husbands not to show affection. On other days they would tell the husbands to make small displays of affection. And on still other days, the researchers directed the husbands to engage in dramatic demonstrations of their affection.

At first, the study went as the researchers expected. When husbands displayed more affection, their wives recorded feeling more positive about their marriages. Then something happened that the researchers couldn't explain. They had instructed one husband to make very strong displays of affection, yet his wife's diary didn't reveal the expected increase in positive feelings about her marriage. The researchers contacted the husband to ask why he hadn't shown affection as instructed. Confused, the husband said, "But I did. I washed her car."

The husband in this study, like many men in real life, felt he was expressing care by doing something for his wife. His wife, like many wives, didn't interpret a car wash as a sign of affection. Thus, his efforts weren't understood or appreciated by her. He thought he was telling her he cared about her by washing her car. She didn't get the message.

What might have communicated caring to this wife? Probably, she would have felt cared for if her husband had spent time talking with her or if he chosen to be with her quietly. The difference between these ways of caring can be expressed as being and doing.

Being and Doing as Ways of Communicating Care

Some people express care by being with others. To show affection or commitment, they give others their presence, attention, and communication. People who express caring by being with others tend to feel that communication and presence are key signs of affection. Consequently, they show love or liking by talking with others, and they feel cared for when their intimates talk to them.

Other people more comfortably express care by doing things with others and for others. Going together to a game or concert is a way to show you care. Doing something for another is also a way to express caring: washing a car or repairing an appliance is a sign of caring. For these folk, doing things is a concrete way to convey affection.

Gender Patterns of Caring

The only problem is that sometimes people don't understand each other's ways of caring, and the caring that one person intends to express is not felt by the other person. If this misunderstanding persists, friends and romantic partners may not feel that their partners care about them when, in fact, their partners do. This misunderstanding can diminish or even end a relationship.

Catherine Riessman interviewed divorced men and women to learn why they had been dissatisfied in their marriages and discovered gender patterns of caring. She found that men and women, in general, tend to communicate caring and feel cared for in rather distinct ways. Riessman's findings tell us a lot about gender-related tendencies in how people express and experience care.

The men in Riessman's study complained that their wives had not done certain things that mattered to them. Some men mentioned that their wives didn't fix them special meals. Others focused on wives' failure to meet them at the door when they came home from work. Men also remarked that their wives didn't do things with them. Consistently, the men's dissatisfaction was tied to things their wives didn't do with them, or for them, or both.

The women in the study told a different story. For them, the marriage waned when their husbands no longer spent time with them or talked with them. Typical of women's complaints were "we never talk any more," "we just don't communicate," "we don't tell each other about what's going on in our lives." The divorced women felt their marriages frayed when communication ebbed.

Francesca Cancian claims that men, in general, have a distinct way of showing love, one that many women underrate and underappreciate. Cancian's research shows that men are inclined to express affection in two primary ways. One is to do things for another person—help a friend paint his house, rewire a broken lamp, teach someone how to use a new computer program, or wash a car. A second way many men typically express affection is to do things with another person—go to a game together, travel to a new place, make love, play tennis, or watch television together.

Realizing that there are different ways to express love has helped me understand my relationship with my father. He was not a man inclined to express his emotions verbally. During my doctoral studies, twice a year I would drive the 500 miles from my school to my home. When I arrived home, I would walk in the house and hug my father and tell him I loved him. He accepted my affection—even enjoyed it, I think—but he never reciprocated by saying "I love you."

I was always hurt that he wouldn't tell me he loved me; yet while I was visiting, he would check out my car. Once he had all four tires

SALLY FORTH reprinted with special permission of King Features Syndicate.

replaced. Another time he tucked money in my wallet. I found it when I got back to school. With the money was a note that said, "I know you need dental work. This should pay for it." I now understand that my father *was* telling me he loved me. He was telling me by doing things to take care of me.

I've talked with a number of men about how they express affection in their relationships. Some of them emphasize talking and sharing emotions; but the majority of men I know say doing things with and for others is the primary way they show they care for them. In fact, a number of men don't feel that talking about feelings enhances a relationship. For them, talking is important only if there is some problem to be resolved, some news to be shared, something that needs to be discussed. Otherwise, talking is not necessary.

Ethnic Patterns of Caring

Of course, gender is not the only influence on how we express care. There are ethnic patterns of caring at work as well. For example, Stanley Gaines reports that African Americans, both men and women, are more emotionally expressive than most European Americans. Members of many Hispanic cultures are also socialized to be more verbally and emotionally expressive than the majority of European Americans. So ethnic background, as well as gender, affect how we express and experience care.

Our focus on how social groups shape our ways of caring shouldn't lead you to think that individuals reflect only the groups in which they participate. Personal influences also sculpt our ways of expressing and experiencing care. How your parents and other family members communicated love to you probably shaped the ways you show love to others, as well as what feels loving to you today. The friends you have and how you interact with them also affect your ways of showing affection.

Constitutive Rules

Recall our discussion of constitutive rules in Chapter 3. These define what counts as what, or what particular communications mean to us. Constitutive rules apply to both personal and social patterns of expressing and experiencing care. If your best friend shows affection by doing things for you, you may have a constitutive rule that states doing things for others = showing care. On the other hand, if your best friend shows affection by talking with you, your constitutive rule may be talking = caring. The ways our family members expressed caring may also shape our constitutive rules.

Social groups often develop and operate according to constitutive rules that are shared by members of the groups. Thus, someone socialized in a particular social group would be likely to internalize the group's constitutive rules for caring. In this chapter, we've seen that race-ethnicity and gender are two social groups that influence members' views of how to show care as well as their preferences for how others care for them. Socioeconomic class is another group influence on our rules for caring. Francesca Cancian's research revealed that members of the working class were more likely to do things for family and friends than members of more affluent classes. When money is scarce, material assistance is highly valued and thus a significant way to communicate affection, friendship, and support.

The being and doing difference in ways of showing care appears in many spheres of relationships. One of the more common ways is when friends and romantic partners talk about problems or worries. Consider two different conversations.

Elise says, "I'm worried about getting everything done before the semester ends."

"Maybe you should work out a schedule of priorities," Roger suggests.

"That's not the problem. Everything I have to do is a priority—three papers for classes, and I haven't even started one of them. Then there's studying for final exams. And I can't quit my job or I won't have money for food and rent."

"Why did you wait so late to start the paper?"

"Because I was doing everything else I have to do, that's why," Elise snaps.

"Well, maybe you can plan better in the future."

"Quit telling me what to do. I'm organized. That's not the problem."

"Then what is the problem?" Roger asks.

"It's that I have too much to do. In addition to everything for school, I'm working 20 hours a week."

"Why don't you work less until the semester is over?"

"I already tried that. My boss can't let me work less, because he doesn't have anyone to cover for me."

"Then you'll just have to organize your time very carefully."

"Thanks a lot," Elise steams.

Elise doesn't appreciate Roger's efforts to support her. She wants sympathy or empathy for her problems. She doesn't want him to offer solutions. When he does, she feels that he doesn't care about her feelings and that he thinks she hasn't already considered everything he suggests to her. She wants him to hear her frustration and respond to that. His efforts to provide practical suggestions and advice don't feel caring to her.

Now consider a second conversation, one that starts the same way, but progresses very differently from the one between Elise and Roger.

Elise says, "I'm worried about getting everything done before the semester ends."

"Gee, I know what you mean," Jennifer agrees. "Sometimes everything we have to do is just overwhelming."

"Yeah, that's exactly what it feels like right now," Elise nods. "I've got three papers to write, and I haven't started even one of them."

"Gosh, that's a lot. I only have to write two papers, but I have a big oral presentation, too."

"Think we should give up sleeping and eating for the next three weeks?"

"Either that or flunk out," Jennifer says. "And you have to work, too, don't you?"

"Yeah. I asked about getting reduced hours until the semester ends, but my boss says he doesn't have anyone to fill in for me," Elise sighs.

"That's really rough," Jennifer empathizes. "You've got so much on you right now."

"I guess I'll just have to manage somehow."

"Right, and you will. It's just not easy sometimes."

"That's totally true! It helps just to know somebody understands how I feel."

In this conversation, Jennifer expresses care in a way that Elise understands. Unlike Roger, Jennifer doesn't try to solve Elise's problems. Instead, she listens and communicates that she understands and cares about her friend's frustration and worries.

Is One Style Better?

The *being* style of showing care isn't always better. Sometimes and with some people, caring by *doing* is much more appreciated. Remember the men in Riessman's study. What they wanted from their ex-wives was concrete signs of caring. If Roger had Elise's problem he might appreciate practical advice more than empathy. The goal for people who care about each other is to understand how the other communicates caring and what feels caring to each one.

When you are sick with the flu or recovering from an operation, what do you want from others? What makes you feel cared for and comforted? For some of us, we want companionship, sympathy, another person's company. For others of us, we prefer to be left alone unless there is something specific we need. We don't want people hanging over us and telling us how sorry they are that we don't feel well. These differences in ways of expressing care surface and sometimes conflict when a person is sick.

When my father was ill and dying, I was one of his caregivers. Whenever I was in his room, he'd ask me to get him this or that, adjust his pillow, tell him the weather, call a friend, and so forth. There were things he couldn't do for himself that he wanted me to do for him. When I'd done everything he wanted, he'd often say, "Thank you. I'm all right now." I knew he was dismissing me. I knew it would not be important to him for me to stay and sit quietly with him or talk with him.

Years later when my mother was terminally ill, I was also her primary caregiver. I'd go into her room and ask if there was anything I could do for her. "Just sit a while," she often replied. She wanted my presence, wanted not to be alone. There were times when we said little and a few times when we maintained silence. For her, that was a major source of comfort, one that my father did not need as much. She also appreciated talk about topics ranging from trivial to important. Any kind of communication made her feel we were connected.

Twice I have had surgery after disks in my back ruptured. The first time, my partner, Robbie, came to the hospital with gifts and news. Before each visit, he'd call to ask if there was anything I needed. When he'd given me anything I'd asked for and taken care of anything I needed, he became restless. Much like Milton, he didn't think he was caring for me if he wasn't doing something for me. Once when he was getting ready to leave, I said, "I really wish you could be comfortable just staying here a while. Read a book or go through your mail, but stay if you can." That led to a conversation in which he discovered that his presence made a big difference to me. Providing company was something he could do that mattered.

When I had my second back surgery, Robbie and I had our signals straight. He'd bring the mail to the hospital each day and we'd each read our mail and discuss it with the other. Then he'd read a book or watch TV with me for a couple of hours. Sometimes he didn't *do* anything practical for me, yet he was there, and that was what I most wanted. Knowing that, he felt that he was taking care of me in ways that I understood.

When Robbie is sick, however, he likes to be left alone unless he needs something. I've had to learn that he doesn't appreciate my sitting by his bed or making small talk. As he's told me, "When I feel bad, I like to be left alone. I'll tell you if I need anything." And I've learned that tending to his needs and otherwise leaving him alone is how I can communicate love to him in a way he will feel and appreciate.

Improving Communication

People have different ways to show love, caring, or friendship. There is no single right way of caring. What is important is that people who matter to each other explain what makes them feel cared for so that those who care about them can express their feelings in ways that will be understood and felt.

Because Robbie loves me, he wanted to care for me when I was recuperating from surgery. But at first he didn't know what would make me feel cared for, so he did what would make *him* feel cared for — brought me things, did things for me. Once he understood that his presence and communication were what I most wanted, he was happy to give me those. And I, too, want to care for him in ways that register with him. He had to explain to me that my way of loving was not his way of loving. When we talked, we each learned how to care for the other on our own distinct terms, and our relationship is enriched by this understanding.

Let Others Know What You Want

Some people think they shouldn't have to ask for signs of caring. You've heard (and perhaps you've even said), "If I have to tell her/him what I want, it doesn't count." That way of thinking is counterproductive. It assumes others can and should read our minds. But there's no way they can do that, so we have to explain what makes us feel cared for. Only then can those who love us express their love in our vocabularies.

We should also ask people we care about what makes them feel loved or cared for. Just as they can't read our hearts and minds, we can't read theirs. Similarly, it's a good idea to tell friends what kind of support you're looking for when you discuss worries. Elise might have said to Roger, "Thanks for offering advice, but what I really need is just some sympathy." Also, when his first efforts at giving advice weren't appreciated, Roger might have said, "I want to help you, but I don't know how. What can I do that would help?" Elise would probably have told him that she'd like him just to let her ventilate and tell her he understood how frustrated she felt.

It is a sign of commitment to care enough about others to tell them what we need and appreciate and to ask them what makes them feel loved. Only by doing this can we learn how to communicate care in ways that are understood and experienced fully by those for whom we care.

Key Words

- being
- caring
- constitutive rules
- doing
- ethnic patterns of caring
- gender patterns of caring

Reflecting on This Chapter

1. Are being and doing equally valid ways of expressing care? Are both modes of showing care appropriate to all situations, or is each mode most suitable in certain circumstances? Can you identify situations in which you've appreciated each style of caring?

2. How should we define caring? Is caring based on motives of the individual who cares? Is it based on the perception of the person receiving care? If someone cares but the way she or he expresses caring isn't felt by another person, has caring occurred?

3. What do you find comforting when you are sick or recovering from an operation? Do you like having your friends and intimates sit with you? Do you like having people do things for you? How important is each style of caring?

4. Have you ever said or thought, "If I have to ask for something, it doesn't count"? Does reading this chapter change your mind about that idea? What would you say to someone who said this to you?

5. What are your constitutive rules for caring? Identify what counts as caring for you. Can you also identify sources for your constitutive rules — friends, family members, social groups to which you have belonged and/or currently belong?

6. Think about times when you've talked with friends about your worries. What did you want? What made you feel better? Were there some occasions when you wanted advice and others when you wanted a sympathetic ear? Can you identify factors that influence what you appreciate when talking with others about your troubles?

References

Bellinger, D. C., & Gleason, J. B. (1982). Sex differences in parental directives to young children. *Sex Roles, 8,* 1123–1139.

Cancian, F. (1987). *Love in America.* Cambridge, MA: Cambridge University Press.

Cancian, F. (1989). Love and the rise of capitalism. In B. Risman & P. Schwartz (Eds.), *Gender in intimate relationships* (pp. 12–25). Belmont, CA: Wadsworth.

Gaines, S. O., Jr. (1995). Relationships between members of cultural minorities. In J. T. Wood & S. Duck (Eds.), *Understanding relationship processes, 6: Understudied relationships: Off the beaten track* (pp. 51–88). Thousand Oaks, CA: Sage.

Inman, C. D. (1996). Friendships between men: Closeness in the doing. In J. T. Wood (Ed.), *Gendered relationships* (pp. 95–110). Mountain View, CA: Mayfield.

Johnson, F. (1996). Friendships among women: Closeness in dialogue. In J. T. Wood (Ed.), *Gendered relationships* (pp. 79–94). Mountain View, CA: Mayfield.

Miller, J. B. (1986). *Toward a new psychology of women* (2nd ed.). Boston, MA: Beacon Press.

Riessman, C. K. (1990). *Divorce talk: Women and men make sense of personal relationships.* New Brunswick, NJ: Rutgers University Press.

Swain, S. (1989). Covert intimacy: Closeness in men's friendships. In B. J. Risman & P. Schwartz (Eds.), *Gender and intimate relationships* (pp. 71–86). Belmont, CA: Wadsworth.

Wills, T. A., Weiss, R. L., & Patterson, G. R. (1974). A behavioral analysis of the determinants of marital satisfaction. *Journal of Consulting and Clinical Psychology, 42,* 802–811.

Wood, J. T. (1994). *Who cares?: Women, care and culture.* Carbondale: Southern Illinois University Press.

Wood, J. T., & Inman, C. C. (1992). In a different mode: Masculine styles of communicating closeness. *Journal of Applied Communication Research, 21,* 279–295.

| 12 |

I'M THE GREATEST

. . .

Understanding Black English

DATE: 18 December 1996
PLACE: Oakland, California
EVENT: Ebonics is recognized as a primary language

Toni Cook, a member of the Oakland School Board that passed the resolution recognizing Ebonics, was interviewed for a *Newsweek* story on Ebonics. She stated, "African American students come to school with a home language other than English. We're going to bridge that gap and make sure our children learn" (Close, p. 78). Concurring opinion came from linguist Megan Crowhurst, who asked, "Why do we call a language pattern that many speak as naturally as breathing 'bad' English, rather than accepting it as a legitimate though non-standard variety of English?"

Bill Cosby offered an answer to Crowhurst's question. In a column in the *Wall Street Journal*, Cosby wrote that "legitimizing the street in the classroom is backwards." Agreeing with Cosby was Reuben Abati, a journalist who was born and raised in Nigeria, a West African country. Abati asserted that African Americans shouldn't "be encouraged to cling to a dialect that is bound to increase their alienation. . . . The success of African Americans and all black men who speak and write good, proper English proves the point that Ebonics is not in the genes."

Further opposition to the Oakland decision came from the Reverend Jesse Jackson, who appeared on NBC's *Meet the Press* to denounce the Oakland decision. In unequivocal terms Jackson asserted that teaching Ebonics was a disgrace and would deprive African American children of learning that they need if they are to succeed. Jackson later softened his criticism after the Oakland School Board insisted it didn't intend to teach students to speak Ebonics, only to teach teachers to accept it as a native language of some students. Secretary of Education Richard Riley didn't waver in his condemnation of calling Ebonics a language. In an interview with *Newsweek*, Riley stated that "elevating black English to the status of a language is not the way to raise standards of achievement in our schools" (p. 79).

The Oakland School Board countered not with more opinions, but with a clarification and some evidence. The clarification was assurance that the board had no intention of teaching students to speak Ebonics. Instead, the board encouraged teachers to recognize that Ebonics is the native language of many African American students. Board members also wanted teachers to help students translate Ebonics into standard English.

The school board justified its recognition of Ebonics by citing increased academic achievement of African American students in classes where Ebonics was recognized and treated respectfully. According to *Newsweek* reporters John Leland and Nadine Joseph, Oakland's experiment in using Ebonics in the classroom has shown positive effects. Since 1980, when some schools began using Ebonics to teach standard English, data show that students who enter school speaking Ebonics learn standard English better when teachers know and respect Ebonics and use it to teach standard English.

What is Ebonics, and how can people who are all committed to education disagree about its value? We explore those questions in this chapter. In addition, we consider misunderstandings of communication practices common among many African Americans. To begin our discussion, we define Ebonics and trace its linguistic history. Next we trace how the cultural heritage of Ebonics surfaces in current African American communication practices. By the time you finish this chapter, you may understand why educators disagree about the character and value of Ebonics, and you may understand and appreciate the richness of African American communication. Regardless of your conclusion on whether Ebonics should have a place in curricula, reading this chapter will give you insight into communication practiced by many members of our culture.

What Is Ebonics?

The word *Ebonics* was coined in 1973 to refer to a grammatically consistent and rule-governed form of language believed to have roots in West Africa. Ebonics is a combination of two root words: *ebony* and *phonics*. Basic features of Ebonics include dropping final consonants from words (runnin' instead of running), using unconjugated forms of the verb to be (I be leaving), using distinct sounds such as *x* for *s* (ax, not ask), and eliding words together (sapnin? for what is happening?).

Origins of Ebonics

There are different theories about the origins of Ebonics, which is also called Black English and African American Vernacular English. One of the more informed explanations comes from linguist Megan Crowhurst, who is a member of the Academic Advisory Board of the Common Sense Foundation. Crowhurst thinks that Ebonics evolved from a pidgin, or jargon, language used for communication between English-speaking slave traders and members of West African societies who spoke a variety of languages and dialects. Within the pidgin language, English words were modified to fit the sound and syntax patterns characteristic of West African languages. This pidgin language is also called a creole language, specifically what some linguists label Gullah or Geechee.

In the United States, children born to slaves grew up hearing their native West African language spoken by newly arrived slaves, the pidgin language spoken by their parents, and the English language of white landowners. Thus, the first generation of African Americans born in the United States heard three separate languages, which they blended into a single way of communicating.

The process of linguistic evolution continued. Once slavery was outlawed in the United States, African Americans were increasingly exposed to standard English. The result is what can be thought of as a decreolized form of the Gullah or Geechee language. It is more like standard English than the Western African or pidgin language, yet it retains some African linguistic qualities.

A Brief Linguistic History of Africa

Like all languages, African languages reflect the values and beliefs of their culture. According to Jonheinz Jahn, a scholar of African culture, traditional African philosophy places very high priority on words and artistry in using them. The term *nommo* refers to the magical power of words and historically it is a power that was widely respected among Africans. *Muntu*, the African word for mankind, emphasizes nommo as what distinguishes humans from things, places, and times. So important was the magical power of the word that only those who were skillful users of language were thought to be qualified as leaders in traditional African societies.

A second quality of African philosophy that is evident in language is the belief that all things are interrelated. People are deeply connected to animals and the natural world. Communities also take precedence over individuals, so each person is thought to be part of the whole and responsible to the whole. The interrelatedness central in the African world view extends to communication. Speakers and listeners are understood to be connected, interacting, responsible to one another. Ideally, says communication scholar Shirley Weber, speaker and audience become one in interaction. This happens as members of audiences speak back to speakers to add their ideas, express approval and disapproval, and guide the speaker. The ongoing interaction typical of African American communication is not routinely practiced by European Americans. In traditional African American churches, members of the congregation are vocal in responding to and directing preachers. They regard themselves as full and active participants in the collaborative communication encounter. Calling out responses would be decidedly unusual in most white churches.

Black English in Operation

Understanding the emphasis of traditional African culture on the magical qualities of language and the interrelatedness of all things helps us appreciate the communication patterns practiced by some African Americans and seldom by European Americans. African American communication is as intricate and rich as African Americans themselves. It reflects both African and U.S. heritages and cultures. In the next sections we consider five forms of communication common in many African American communities.

Braggadocio

The title of this chapter, "I'm the greatest," is taken from boxing champion Cassius Clay, who later renamed himself Mohammed Ali. When Clay/Ali first came into the national spotlight, he did so with style. Clay proclaimed on television and radio that "I'm the greatest." Repeatedly he sang his own praises loudly and clearly. Although some European American boxing fans found the young boxer's self-congratulatory style refreshing, many perceived him as brash and arrogant. After all, they thought, it's inappropriate for an individual to boast about himself.

What few European Americans understood was that Clay/Ali was not boasting — at least not in the way a white person would have been had she or he announced "I'm the greatest." Instead, Clay/Ali was engaging in braggadocio (also called woofin'). Geneva Smitherman, a scholar of African American language, explains that braggadocio is not intended to be taken seriously. It involves outrageous boasting — the more outrageous, the better. The purpose is to demonstrate humor and verbal artistry in bragging about oneself. Judged by European American standards, such behavior is tasteless, self-serving boasting. Judged by the standards of African American communication, however, braggadocio is a display of verbal skill that isn't meant to be taken at face value.

Signifyin'

Imagine this scene. Martin and Sheryl go to a party together. During the evening each of them talks and dances with others. On the way home, Sheryl says, "You sure were talking to Rochelle a long time." Martin replies, "Aw, don't be looking for trouble where there isn't any. You know there's nothing between me and that sister." Does Martin's reply make sense to you? Does it seem logical in response to Sheryl's comment? It does if you understand the practice of signifyin' (or signifying), which is speaking indirectly. Instead of making the direct comment, "I think you were coming on to Rochelle," Sheryl signifies on Martin by making an indirect comment.

Signifyin' allows a person to make a criticism in a roundabout fashion, which doesn't bluntly challenge another person's worth, motives, or behaviors. Rather than stating directly, "You didn't clean the house," an African American might signify by saying, "I'm going to buy you a vacuum cleaner." Instead of fussing at someone for being late, a person could signify on them by saying, "I'm going to buy you a watch." In preference to accusing a friend of being a hopeless spendthrift, a person could signify by saying, "I sure hope you win the lottery to cover these purchases."

Direct Expressiveness

But indirect communication, or signifyin', is only half the story. Scholars of African American communication also note that African Americans tend to speak more forcefully, dramatically, and confrontationally than is typical of European Americans — to use direct expressiveness. Emotionally charged exchanges are particularly common in interactions between African Americans. A clear illustration comes from writer and social critic bell hooks. She recalls that when she flew home and walked off the plane, her sisters and mother greeted her by saying, "I can't believe you got on the plane looking like that." There's no subtlety and no qualification in those words.

Sidney Ribeau and his colleagues think the dramatic, vigorous quality of African American talk reflects traditional African regard for personal involvement. In other words, talking isn't a passive process but a drama of active engagement. Communication occurs when not just words but also feelings are exchanged. To be reserved or emotionally restrained is to be uninvolved, and that is to be ineffective. For example, it shows more involvement to say, "What is wrong with you? Man, are you crazy?" than to say, "I don't understand what you're doing." Likewise, greater involvement is reflected in "You are one lazy bum. It's plain worthless to skip classes and sit in front of the TV all day" than to say, "Aren't you worried about missing classes?"

Marsha Houston observes that different degrees of emotional expressiveness often lead to misunderstandings when European Americans and African Americans interact. Houston's research on black and white women's perceptions of each other revealed that white women often perceive black women as confrontational, loud, or rude. Equally important is Houston's finding that black women perceive many white women as cold, unfeeling, and dishonest because they are so emotionally reserved. Some African Americans perceive the less dramatic language typical of European American speech as indicating a lack of interest or genuineness.

Call and Response

Traditional African belief in interconnectedness explains a third communication practice common among African Americans. The call-and-response pattern occurs in public contexts and involves a call (speech, proclamation, sermon) made by a speaker (teacher, preacher, politician) and responses made by listeners (students, congregation, audience). Both the call and the response are part of the communication event — they are joined, inseparable in the whole. Shirley Weber, a scholar of African American culture at San Diego State University, explains that African American congregations assume that a preacher's ability to deliver an effective sermon depends on their encouragement, their "amens" and "right ons." An African American congregation that doesn't interact with a preacher is insulting the preacher and disrespecting cultural values.

European Americans are sometimes unsettled by the vocal and vigorous participation of African American audiences and congregations. Because quiet listening and waiting your turn to speak are norms for most public communication of European Americans, "speaking out" may be perceived as disruptive and plain rude. That perception, however, is based on a particular cultural perspective, one that is different from the perspective that informs communicators who engage in and enjoy call and response. Conversely, African Americans may perceive the quiet, constrained listening of European Americans as displaying a lack of enthusiasm and a desire to keep distance between communicators.

Joanin' and Playing the Dozens

"Your face is so ugly nobody would go out with you. Even your mama couldn't love a face like yours."

"Yeah, but at least mama claims my face."

This exchange exemplifies an African American communication practice called playing the dozens, or joanin'. The practice consists of exchanging insults, with each communicator trying to outdo the other. Usually the dozens is played before others who judge which player displays the greater originality, creativity, and verbal skill. Despite the presence of insults, the dozens is not mean spirited. It is a stylized verbal sport designed to allow individuals to display wit and verbal skill and to engage in a friendly, genial competition. Shirley Weber reports that in many African American communities, playing the dozens is considered the highest form of verbal skill (remember the significance of nommo).

The dozens is often misunderstood by people outside of African American communities. "Your face is so ugly a mama couldn't love it" may be perceived as fighting words rather than an invitation to engage in sociable verbal dueling. Similarly, a European American who hears two African Americans playing the dozens may mistakenly assume they are on the brink of a serious fight.

We've discussed only five forms of communication common among many African Americans. There are others that are as interesting and reflective of African heritage as the ones we've examined. If you want to understand additional ones, consult the references for this chapter.

Improving Communication

Misunderstandings are not uncommon between people who belong to different racial and ethnic groups. Perhaps the greatest source of misunderstanding is interpreting the communication patterns of one group according to the standards of a different group. When we impose (however inadvertently) our own perspectives on others, we risk misunderstanding them and their communication. The issue is less the communication itself than the perspective from which it is interpreted.

A key to reducing misunderstandings between people of diverse ethnic and racial groups is recognizing that different groups often have different ways of communicating and different meanings for the "same" words and nonverbal behaviors. By extension, we should be cautious about using the standards of our social groups to interpret the communication of people who were socialized in and who identify with other social groups.

Communication Reflects Cultures

In Chapter 2 we discussed the Sapir-Whorf hypothesis, which asserts that language reflects and expresses cultural values and priorities. That idea pertains to our discussion of Black English. How people communicate echoes the history, values, and ways of life of their culture. For example, many traditional Asian cultures esteem emotional restraint and politeness, and this is reflected in communication practices such as veiling feelings, expressing ideas indirectly, and avoiding disagreements. Because Asian cultures emphasize harmony and respect, members of these cultures tend to negotiate with the goal of making sure nobody loses face. That's very different from Western negotiation in which the goal is usually to win and to beat the competition. Korean culture places high priority on family relations, so its language includes words that designate many specific relationships that are not named in the English language: my grandfather's sister, my mother's aunt, my youngest daughter, my oldest son.

In this chapter we've explored some of the roots of Ebonics in traditional African societies. The value that traditional African culture places on interrelationships and the power of communication is evident in particular features of Black English spoken today. Braggadocio, signifying, and other black communication practices reflect the traditions, beliefs, and values of the culture in which they arose.

Communication Rules

Communication rules are also pertinent to our discussion of diverse communication patterns. Constitutive rules, which we first discussed in Chapter 3, define what particular verbal and nonverbal behaviors mean. In other words, constitutive rules tell us what communication counts as, or expresses. Every social group develops distinct constitutive rules that allow members of the group to communicate smoothly. The rules of one social group may not be shared by people outside that group.

In this chapter, we've identified a number of communication practices whose meanings differ according to the particular constitutive rules used to interpret them. For example, according to constitutive rules endorsed by many European Americans, using the call-and-response pattern may seem disrespectful, playing the dozens may seem hostile, and dropping consonants on words may seem incorrect. Turning the tables, the constitutive rules learned by many African Americans may lead them to perceive quiet listening as aloof, restrained interaction as impersonal, and pronouncing all final consonants as sounding stuffy.

Also pertinent are regulative rules, which we discussed in Chapter 4. Regulative rules specify when and in which contexts certain kinds of communication are appropriate. In this chapter, we've seen that African Americans are more likely than European Americans to operate according to a regulative rule that defines as appropriate, even desirable, making comments while a speaker or preacher is speaking. A playful insult is an appropriate response to another's bantering if you are playing the dozens, but it may not be acceptable in other contexts.

Recognizing Pluralism as Usual in Cultural Life

Every social group has a unique history, and that history invariably surfaces in the group's communication patterns. Except for the rare closed society, social groups and their languages are not homogeneous or unchanging. Rather, most societies and most languages reflect pluralism —a mixture of influences from different peoples and the customs they fol-

low. Over time, most societies evolve and, as they do, their communication patterns also change.

What we call *Americans* are really people of many origins with distinct heritages; the United States was developed by Native Americans as well as people from England, Ireland, Scotland, Europe, Africa, and other countries and continents. By extension, what we call *English* is infused by language from many different cultures. Words that you may consider English were imported from other places: *Chocolate* was originally a word used by the Nahuatl, a Native American tribe; *cotton* came from the Arabic language; *khaki* was taken from Hindi; and *zombie* was taken from the Congo. What we think of as English, then, isn't the language of England in a strict sense. Instead, it is a richly multicultural language, which is appropriate for a country that is graced by people from many cultures.

At the same time the United States is multicultural, it is also a nation in which the distinctiveness of various groups survives. A resident of this country can claim heritage as both an African and an American, or as both a European and an American. Perhaps our best hope for a healthy pluralistic culture is for us to respect our commonness as a people while we also acknowledge the distinctive heritages that shape our individual and collective identity.

The debate over Ebonics is the topic that opened this chapter. To gain insight into it, however, we had to explore a larger context of cultural life and meanings. The controversy over Ebonics cannot be understood apart from African philosophy and heritage that have influenced and continue to influence the communication patterns of many African Americans. Regardless of how we feel about the place of Ebonics in academic curricula, perhaps what we've discussed in this chapter increases our understanding of the character of African American communication patterns and the cultural heritage they reflect and preserve.

Key Words

- braggadocio
- call and response
- constitutive rules
- direct expressiveness
- Ebonics

- nommo
- playing the dozens (joanin')
- pluralism
- regulative rules
- signifying

Reflecting on This Chapter

1. If you are an African American, do you speak so-called standard English in predominantly white contexts and black language in black communities? How do you feel about changing the way you talk, depending on interaction contexts?

2. If you are a European American, do you speak two different languages in your everyday conversations, or do you consistently communicate using so-called standard English? Compare your answer to the answer African American students gave to question #1 above. What do the differences in answers suggest about relationships between communication and majority and minority social groups?

3. Do you think "black English" or Ebonics is a distinct and legitimate language or a deficient form of so-called standard English?

4. What are your thoughts regarding the Oakland School Board's decision to declare Ebonics a separate and distinct language?

5. Who has the right to define what is and is not a language? If the legitimacy of languages is decided by only people who enjoy mainstream positions, can a culture and its communication represent all citizens? If any group can declare their way of communicating a language, would there be no standard language in a culture? How do you wrestle with the tension between these two questions?

6. Notice that opinions on the Oakland decision are not divided along strict racial lines. Some African Americans support recognizing Ebonics and others oppose recognizing it. European Americans also weigh in on each side of the decision. What do differences among members of each race reveal? How do differences within groups pertain to issues such as stereotyping (see Chapters 1 and 7)?

7. Should learning standard English be a requirement for gaining citizenship in the United States? Should languages other than standard English be included on instructions that accompany products sold in this country?

8. To learn about and appreciate other ethnicities and their ways of communicating, we need to step outside the contexts that are familiar to us. Attend a meeting of a racial-ethnic group other than your own. If you are white, you might attend services in an African American church. If you are African American, you could attend services at a church that has a predominantly or exclusively white congregation. How is the communication in the unfamiliar context like and unlike what you experience in your customary environments?

References

Abati, R. (1997, January 28). Ebonics: In Africa, forget it. *Raleigh News and Observer*, p. 13A.

Bates, E. (1994, Fall). Beyond black and white. *Southern Exposure*, pp. 11–15.

Close, E. (1997, January 13). Why Ebonics is irrelevant. *Newsweek*, p. 80.

Close, E. (1997). *Color blind*. New York: HarperCollins.

Cosby, B. (1997, January 10). Elements of igno-Ebonics style. *Wall Street Journal*, p. A10.

Crowhurst, M. (1997, 28 January). In linguistics, worth respect. *Raleigh News and Observer*, p. 13A.

Folb, E. (1980). *Runnin' down some lines: The language and culture of black teenagers*. Cambridge, MA: Harvard University Press.

Gaines, S., Jr. (1995). Relationships between members of cultural minorities. In J. T. Wood & S. Duck (Eds.), *Understanding relationship processes, 6: Understudied relationships: Off the beaten track* (pp. 51–88). Thousand Oaks, CA: Sage.

Garner, T. (1994). Oral rhetorical practice in African American culture. In A. González, M. Houston, & V. Chen (Eds.), *Our voices: Essays in culture, ethnicity, and communication* (pp. 81–91). Los Angeles: Roxbury.

hooks, b. (1981). *Ain't I a woman? Black women and feminism*. Boston: South End Press.

Houston, M. (1997). When black women talk with white women: Why dialogues are difficult. In A. González, M. Houston, & V. Chen (Eds.), *Our voices: Essays in culture, ethnicity, and communication* (2nd ed., pp. 187–194). Los Angeles: Roxbury.

Houston, M., & Wood, J. T. (1996). Difficult dialogues, expanded horizons: Communicating across race and class. In J. T. Wood (Ed.), *Gendered relationships* (pp. 39–56). Mountain View, CA: Mayfield.

Jahn, J. (1961). *Muntu.* New York: Grove Press.

Leland, J., & Joseph, N. (1997, January 13). Hooked on Ebonics. *Newsweek*, pp. 78–79.

Manly, H. (1997, January 12). Ebonics deemed "silly effort" to solve serious problems. *Raleigh News and Observer*, p. 24A.

McAdoo, H. P. (Ed.). (1993). *Family ethnicity: Strength in diversity.* Newbury Park, CA: Sage.

McDaniel, J. (1995). *The lesbian couples' guide.* New York: HarperCollins.

Mitchell-Kernan, C. (1972). Signifying, loud-talking, and marking. In T. Kochman (Ed.), *Rappin' and stylin' out* (pp. 315–335). Urbana: University of Illinois Press.

Ribeau, S. A., Baldwin, J. R., & Hecht, M. (1994). An African-American communication perspective. In L. Samovar & R. Porter (Eds.), *Intercultural communication: A reader* (7th ed., pp. 140–147). Belmont, CA: Wadsworth.

Smitherman, G. (1977). *Talkin' and testifyin': The language of black America.* Boston: Houghton Mifflin.

Smitherman, G. (1994). *Black talk: Words and phrases from the hood to the amen corner.* Boston: Houghton Mifflin.

Turner, L. D. (1949). *Africanisms in the Gullah dialect.* Chicago: University of Chicago Press.

Weber, S. (1994). The need to be: The socio-cultural significance of black language. In L. Samovar & R. Porter (Eds.), *Intercultural communication: A reader* (7th ed., pp. 221–226). Belmont, CA: Wadsworth.

| 13 |

I NEVER KNOW WHICH FORK TO USE

. . .

Understanding Differences in

Economic Class

It was the holiday season, and the most extravagant party of the season was, as usual, being hosted by a group of alumni and alumna who are major financial supporters of my university. I knew all the bigwigs would attend, partly to enjoy sumptuous foods and spirits and partly to admire the ornate decor. I asked my colleague Eileen if she would like to ride with me to the party.

"No. I never know which fork to use. Those fancy shindigs are beyond me. Besides," she added, "I hate that sissy wine they serve."

"Oh, come on, you should go," I encouraged her. "Don't worry about the fork. We'll have fun."

"You may. I wouldn't. I don't belong."

"How can you say that?" I asked. "The party is for faculty. You're faculty. Don't be stubborn."

"I'm not being stubborn," she insisted. "I really don't belong. I may be faculty, but I'm not from the right social group. You just don't understand how much difference that makes."

"But your social group is faculty and professionals — just like mine is. We both belong."

"No, I'd be out of place," she said firmly. "It's not my kind of thing. I wouldn't fit in. I'd just be uncomfortable."

Eileen seemed resolute, so I didn't try to persuade her further. I did, however, think about her comments — the reasons she gave for not going: I wouldn't fit in. It's not my kind of thing. I don't belong there.

Why, I wondered, did Eileen feel she didn't belong? The party was for faculty, and Eileen is as much a part of the university faculty as I am. Why does she, as a faculty member, feel she doesn't belong when I, also a faculty member, feel I do belong?

Reflecting on what I know about Eileen, I realized that she came from a working-class family whereas I grew up in an upper-middle-class family. She once told me that until she went away to college, she hadn't known there were any appetizers other than onion dip. In the community where Eileen grew up, money was always tight. People lived in small homes, children shared bedrooms, parents drove old cars if they could afford any cars at all, and they shopped at discount stores. Finances didn't permit expensive outings, so people in Eileen's community watched television in the living room for entertainment. They seldom went out for meals; if they did, McDonald's and Shoney's were the restaurants of choice. Only one fork was needed at Shoney's and none at McDonald's.

My family and our social circle, while not rich, were economically comfortable. We often had hors d'oeuvres before meals, and onion dip was rarely featured. Our home was an ample two-story home in which each of us had a separate bedroom. My father traded cars every few years. We shopped in nice stores and went to stylish restaurants. Our television was in the family room — my parents said a television should never be in a living room because living rooms are where people engage in conversations. Growing up, I learned not only which forks to use for which courses and foods, but also which type of wine glass is appropriate for bordeaux, chardonnay, chablis, and beaujolais. No wonder I was comfortable going to a posh party; no wonder Eileen was not.

How often do misunderstandings arise because of differences in social class background and current economic status? How much difference does it make whether we have discretionary money, whether we know which fork to use, whether we appreciate the qualities of different wines, or whether we drive late model cars? In this chapter, we consider some of the ways that class affects interaction and it may lead to misunderstandings.

SYLVIA   **by Nicole Hollander**

© *1996 by Nicole Hollander. Used by permission.*

Understanding the Misunderstanding

In our society, talking about class differences is difficult. In part, this is due to the myth that the United States is a classless society, one in which everyone is equal. The idea that everyone is equal and anyone can achieve success is what is often called the Horatio Alger myth, according to Edith Folb, communication professor at San Francisco State University. Many Americans want to believe that each individual rises on the basis of her or his personal abilities and merits, irrespective of age, sex, race, or background. We want to believe that anyone who is industrious can succeed.

Yet the reality of life in the United States is different. We may be equal under the law, but there are major inequalities and inequities among people of different economic groups. As sociologist Joan Ferrante notes, in the United States, economic and occupational status are quite often linked to factors over which individuals have little or no control. For example, social background; cultural views of and evaluations of race, age, sexual orientation, and sex; and economic transformations affect who we are, how we live our lives, and what we achieve.

What Is Social Class?

Economic standing and social class are not purely matters of current income. Instead, they involve the assumption of economic security or insecurity and all the material consequences of that assumption. Edith Folb describes social class as power and control over resources and wealth, along with the privileges and status that accompany power and control.

Our social class and, by extension, our experiences in class-based communities shape our views of who we are and what the world is like.

Class Shapes Individuals' Sense of Fit

Donna Langston explains that class and economic status are about much more than current income. She claims that social class has to do with our understanding of the world and where we do—and don't—fit in. This means that social class affects our ideas, attitudes, values, behaviors, and ways of communicating.

Let's think about the implications of belonging to different social classes. Answer the following questions.

1. Where do you shop? What kinds of stores do you regularly patronize?
2. Where do you go, if you go out for dinner?
3. What do you eat when you dine out?
4. What do you serve when you have guests for dinner in your home?
5. What do you drink at social occasions?
6. How do you serve food at your table? Do you use a table cloth, place mats that require laundering, cloth napkins, and good silver or do you use everyday dishes, stainless steel silverware, and paper napkins?
7. At what time do you typically eat your evening meal?
8. What do you do for recreation?
9. How traditional are your values, especially your values regarding sex roles?
10. What are your favorite leisure time activities?
11. How large was the home in which you grew up, if your family owned a home? Did you have your own room then? Do you now?
12. Did you and your family always assume you would attend college?
13. If your family owned cars, what kinds of cars were they? Do you own a car now? If so, what is its model and year?

How you answer the questions reflects your social class background as well as other influences in your life. The higher your economic status (both historically and currently), the more time you have for recreation and the more money you are able to spend on recreational activities. It costs less to go bowling or visit family over the holidays than to go to a Broadway play or take a cruise in the Mediterranean. Finding perfect coordinating accessories for dresses and suits is difficult and perhaps irrelevant if you buy your clothes at the Goodwill store.

Class Shapes Activities

Social class and economic status also influence leisure activities. Members of middle- and upper-income groups generally have more leisure time than working-class people. Langston reports that they also have the financial freedom to explore issues beyond basic survival. For example, members of middle- and upper-social classes may think and talk about improving self-esteem, take courses to enrich themselves, buy home exercise equipment and join spas for health and appearance reasons, and attend wine-tasting classes. These are not the leisure-time activities pursued by most members of the working class. Perhaps that's why Eileen turned down my suggestion a few years ago that we get season tickets to the theater.

Our social class also influences what, where, and when we eat. Members of the working class who work first shift generally eat soon after getting home—typically between 5 and 6—and eating is usually a quick affair. (Notice that the idea of a work shift and the possibility of being assigned to work night shifts rarely pertain to middle- and upper-income people.) Among members of the middle and upper classes, dining usually occurs later—7, 8, 9, or even 10 P.M., and lingering over meals is customary. For economically privileged people, the time between getting home and eating may be devoted to "quality time" with children and cocktails and hors d'oeuvres served in crystal and on china. More typical for working-class individuals is sipping a bottle of beer or a highball and having a handful of peanuts or chips while preparing a meal for the family. And savoring gourmet coffee, the current rage of people with discretionary income, is not likely to be part of the day for most members of the working class.

Once Eileen invited me to dinner at her house. I arrived at 5 P.M. as she had suggested and she served dinner promptly at 5:30. At the time, I felt she served dinner so early (from my perspective) that she was trying to rush me off. Later, I learned that she was simply serving dinner at what she regarded as the regular, normal time to eat the evening meal.

When Eileen came to my home for dinner a few weeks later, she too arrived at 5 P.M. And like Eileen, I served our meal at what I consider the regular, normal time to eat—8 P.M. When I later realized how mealtimes reflect social backgrounds, I asked Eileen if she thought I had served dinner late. "Are you kidding?" she laughed. "I thought you'd never feed me. I was starving."

Once while I was having my hair cut, I overheard the end of a conversation between two other women in the shop. One woman said, "I couldn't believe they served us meat loaf. Can you imagine inviting someone to dinner and serving meat loaf?" After years of struggling to find a lunch spot we could agree on, Eileen and I have found one that serves the foods we both consider our favorites. She always orders meat loaf with mashed potatoes and gravy, and I invariably order a Caesar salad. If Eileen served meat loaf to guests, she would be communicating that she thinks highly enough of them to prepare her favorite meal.

Class Shapes Social Roles

Social and economic backgrounds also influence our social roles, especially those concerning men's and women's places and responsibilities. Sociologist Arlie Hochschild studied families in which both husbands and wives worked outside the home. She found that traditional sex roles tend to be endorsed by members of the working and poor classes whereas middle- and upper-class families adhere to less rigid sex roles. In poor and working-class families, the man is defined as the breadwinner and the head of the house (even if the woman's salary equals or exceeds his). The woman is regarded as the homemaker who assumes primary responsibility for children (even if she works full time outside the home).

Spouses who have higher educations and greater financial resources are more likely to regard both adults as breadwinners and both as responsible for the home and children. Although women at all social and economic levels continue to do more of the housework and child care than men, the imbalance is less significant for people who are well educated and in the professional class. However, pursuing higher education, which is linked to more egalitarian values, is not equally available to everyone.

Class Shapes Attitudes and Options Regarding Education

Socioeconomic class turns out to be a major influence on the likelihood of attending college. In a recent article in the *Wall Street Journal*, David

Wessel reported that an 18- or 20-year-old from a family with income in the top 25% of U.S. incomes is three times as likely to attend college as the son or daughter in a family with income in the bottom 25%. Put another way, 75% of children from families with incomes in the top quarter attend college; 50% of children from families with incomes in the middle 50% attend college; and only 25% of children from families with incomes in the lowest 25% attend college. Higher education requires money, and not everyone has equal access to money. Thus, economic classes are reproduced by the constraints on people's options to move to higher economic status.

Social location and economic status are also linked to our early educational opportunities and how we view education. People tend to cluster in neighborhoods with families who have similar values, backgrounds, and incomes. Children attend the schools in their districts, and those districts are divided along economic lines. James Coleman was the principal investigator of a study reported under the title *Equality of Educational Opportunity*, government-sponsored research of inequalities in education in the United States. Coleman reports that he found few schools attended by students from diverse economic levels. Instead, he says, we have elite schools and low-income schools in the suburbs, inner cities, and rural areas. Coleman's conclusion is sobering: Family background, particularly economic standing, is the single most important influence on educational achievement.

Social class may also affect how we view education—our own and that of others. Todd Erkel, who straddles the line between working class and middle class, states that most working-class people are skeptical of higher education. Schooling is often regarded as less than useful. After all, what can you really do with knowledge of Kant's or Rousseau's philosophy? What's the use of knowing about ancient civilizations? Erkel says that most working-class people give lip service to the value of education. In reality, they measure people by what they do, not what they know. Erkel also points out that when children of working-class parents pursue higher education, a division between the children and parents often arises. The parents may feel their children have rejected them and their values. The children may feel shame for their parents' lifestyle.

Erkel describes leaving his working-class family to attend college:

> I arrived in State College Pennsylvania, with what I soon learned was more than a clothes problem. . . . There was no measure for the things I didn't know, nothing to suggest I might have to learn

everything about this new world of college from scratch. The system, like me, was blind to the ways in which my working-class background left me unprepared for this new world. It wasn't just poise or spending money I lacked. Everything from my colloquial speech to my primitive social skills to my wardrobe drew a discreet line between me and my new peer group. (p. 102)

Like my friend Eileen, Todd Erkel knew he didn't belong. Today, he is a writer who is professionally successful and economically comfortable. Yet, Erkel admits, he feels uncomfortable, adrift, and out of place in the middle-class world he now inhabits. He says he operates on borrowed knowledge and continuously represses his working-class values and instincts. He feels that he is an outsider in the social world he has joined.

Straddling Classes

Erkel's insight is important. He reminds us that our backgrounds echo into our current lives, no matter how different the two may be. A similar point was made by Carolyn Kay Steedman in her book, *Landscape for a Good Woman*, an autobiography about growing up in a working-class family and moving into the middle class. She comments that sometimes she goes to parties today and talks with other middle-class women. When she does, she thinks that because of her class background, a hundred years ago she would have been the cleaning woman for these people. Our history, then, is woven into our current lives and interactions. Eileen could easily learn which fork to use. It would be considerably more difficult for her to forget a background that taught her one fork is all anyone needs.

Improving Communication

Class differences exist and affect many aspects of our individual lives and our collective society. We cannot make them disappear. We can, however, lessen the misunderstandings that often arise because of differences in class and economic standing.

Recognizing Our Own Social Locations

A first step in reducing misunderstandings between members of different social classes is to become aware of our own historical and current social class and the ways in which it affects our ideas, lifestyle, identity, and sense of where we do and don't belong. This knowledge is especially important for members of middle- and upper-economic groups because they are less likely to be aware of their class and the privileges it bestows. As an example, in a published conversation with Mary Childers, bell hooks points out that upper-class women often don't see how they oppress working-class women by paying them minimum wages for domestic work. hooks asks those who are financially well-off to acknowledge the inequities in society and their personal role (and self-interest) in sustaining inequities that benefit them at cost to others. hooks thinks such acknowledgment is one key to reducing inequities. Presumably, genuine acknowledgment would lead employers to pay better wages.

The lack of awareness of privilege that many economically comfortable people have was humorously depicted in the film *Overboard*. In this film, Goldie Hawn portrays a rich woman who suffers temporary amnesia and winds up living with a working-class family. As a result of the experience, Hawn becomes aware of privileges she had always taken for granted and of the disparity between her lifestyle and that of people with less money and status. Her butler then tells her that she has gained a new perspective on life and that what she does with her newfound knowledge is up to her.

The media represent U.S. society as composed of two classes—the very well-off (programs such as *Dallas*, *The Cosby Show*, and *Thirtysomething*) and the poor and uneducated (the villains in many prime time shows and the focus of news stories on crime). Economic well-being is represented as good and normal, and this depiction makes seeing the character and effects of economic privilege more difficult than seeing the character and pragmatic consequences of groups that society portrays as substandard. Becoming aware of our own class location is a prerequisite for communicating effectively with people who have different economic and social backgrounds and current circumstances.

Resist Assuming That Your Values Are Superior

A second vehicle for communicating across social classes is to resist assuming that the patterns and values of your social groups are the only appropriate standard for everyone. When we eat, where we shop, what we do with leisure time, and how we view education reflect our socialization —what we have learned growing up in our particular social and economic situations. There is nothing that makes crab remoulade *intrinsically* superior to meat loaf, nothing that makes a well-aged burgundy superior to beer, nothing that makes expensive china better than paper plates. We serve what we like and serve it as we prefer. Yet what we've learned is that good food and appropriate ways of serving food vary among social groups.

Because membership in various economic classes affects how we spend time, we should be wary of judging the activities of others by the patterns of our own economic group. This means that people with working-class backgrounds don't need to disparage personal enrichment classes, and people with middle-class backgrounds don't need to look down on bowling. Our leisure time activities reflect what we've learned to enjoy, what we can afford, and the contexts in which we feel comfortable.

A lot can be learned by communicating openly with people whose backgrounds differ from our own. Once some trust is established in a relationship, people may feel safe exploring differences in their perspectives, lifestyles, and values. Doing so allows us to appreciate how various circumstances influence us and our lives.

Economic Class Is Not the Whole of Any Person

Finally, it's important to keep social and economic differences in perspective. We should be aware of them and acknowledge how they affect us and others. It's not constructive, however, to overemphasize differences or to focus on them to the exclusion of many similarities that transcend social and economic backgrounds and current status. In other words, we should avoid totalizing, which we discussed in previous chapters. Eileen and I enjoy different kinds of parties, yet we also read and discuss many of the same books, we both adore our cats, we share stories about our nieces and nephews, and we commiserate about academic responsibilities and pressures.

Social and economic differences are important parts of who we are, but they are only a part—not the whole. They do not define us totally. They do not mean that people of different social and economic circumstances do not have many commonalities. Both our differences and our similarities influence who we are and how we interact with others.

Key Words

- economic standing
- Horatio Alger myth
- leisure time
- social class
- social location
- social roles
- totalizing

Reflecting on This Chapter

1. Reflect on your social and economic standpoint. How did you answer the 13 questions posed in this chapter? What do those answers tell you about your social and economic background and current status?

2. Do you have friends and acquaintances whose social and economic backgrounds differ from your own? If so, how have these differences shown up in your interactions?

3. What messages that reflect social class did you hear when you were growing up? Did your parents ever talk about "right" and "wrong" ways to eat, where to place a television set in the house, and so forth?

4. How far can we and should we go in respecting differences of social class (and other matters)? Are some lifestyles and activities really "better" than others—more worthy, useful, or socially responsible? What criteria guide our evaluations of diverse lifestyles and activities?

5. Do you agree with this chapter's claim that the U.S. media tend to associate economic well-being with good people and a good lifestyle and to link poverty with a lack of education and antisocial inclinations? How do the media do this? What are the implications of defining middle- and upper-social classes as good and working or poverty classes as inferior?

6. What language do you use and do you hear from others to describe class? Have you heard terms such as *white trash, welfare class,* and *uneducated?* What assumptions are embedded in each of those terms?

7. Before reading this chapter, did you believe that in the United States individual merit and ability determine economic and occupational success? Did reading this chapter alter your views of the relative influence of social and economic background and individual merit on what people accomplish?

8. Do you agree that Americans are uncomfortable discussing class? What informs your opinion? Why is class so difficult for many people to discuss (or even acknowledge)?

References

Andersen, M., & Collins, P. H. (Eds.). (1992). *Race, class, and gender: An anthology.* Belmont, CA: Wadsworth.

Abel, E. (1990). Race, class, and psychoanalysis? Opening questions. In M. Hirsch & E. F. Keller (Eds.), *Conflicts in feminism* (pp. 184–204). New York: Routledge.

Cancian, F. (1987). *Love in America.* Cambridge: Cambridge University Press.

Childers, M., & hooks, b. (1990). A conversation about race and class. In M. Hirsch & E. F. Keller (Eds.), *Conflicts in feminism* (pp. 60–81). New York: Routledge.

Coleman, J. (1966). *Equality of educational opportunity.* Washington, DC: U.S. Government Printing Office.

Erkel, R. T. (1994, November/December). The mighty wedge of class. *Utne Reader,* pp. 100–103.

Ferrante, J. (1995). *Sociology: A global perspective* (2nd ed.). Belmont, CA: Wadsworth.

Folb, E. (1994). Who's got room at the top: Issues of dominance and nondominance in intracultural communication. In L. Samovar & R. Porter (Eds.), *Intercultural communication: A reader* (7th ed., pp. 131–139). Belmont, CA: Wadsworth.

Hochschild, A., with Machung, A. (1989). *The second shift: Working parents and the revolution at home.* New York: Viking Press.

Houston, M., & Wood, J. T. (1996). Difficult dialogues, expanded horizons: Communicating across race and class. In J. T. Wood (Ed.), *Gendered relationships* (pp. 39–56). Mountain View, CA: Mayfield.

Langston, D. (1992). Tired of playing monopoly? In M. Andersen & P. Collins (Eds.), *Race, class, and gender* (pp. 110–119). Belmont, CA: Wadsworth.

Ryan, J., & Sackrey, C. (1984). *Strangers in paradise: Academics from the working class.* Boston: South End Press.

Steedman, C. (1987). *Landscape for a good woman: A story of two lives.* New Brunswick, NJ: Rutgers University Press.

Wessel, D. (1996, December 30). Rising costs of college interest the politicians. *Wall Street Journal,* p. 1A.

Wood, J. T. (1997). Diversity in dialogue: Commonalities and differences between friends. In J. Makau & R. Arnett (Eds.), *Communication ethics in an age of diversity* (pp. 5–26). Urbana: University of Illinois Press.

| 14 |

SO, HOW WAS YOUR DAY?

· · ·

Different Styles of Relating

Ellen walks into the apartment, tired after a long day of dealing with problems at the hospital where she is a social worker. She finds her husband, Justin, in the family room working on a paper for one of his classes. After three years of working as a bank manager, Justin returned to school to earn an M.B.A.

"Hi," she greets him, "how was your day?"

He looks up at her and replies, "The accounting exam was rough, but I think I did all right. My other two classes were okay."

"Did you get a chance to talk with Mike about his father's surgery?" Ellen asks, remembering that Justin's friend's father was scheduled to have a double bypass operation today.

"Yeah, he's doing okay."

She sits in a chair near Justin. "What about lunch? Did you get together with anyone?"

"Yeah, Janice and I grabbed a pizza and worked on our team project." Justin fidgets with his pen. He hates it when Ellen pumps him for details on his day. He tells her about anything important. Why does she pressure him for details and small talk?

"Are you making good progress on that?"

"It's coming along."

Ellen waits, hoping Justin will ask about her day. When he doesn't, but returns to his paper, she says, "Aren't you going to ask about my day?"

"I figured you'd tell me if anything important happened."

"Well, I've had a horrible day," Ellen says, sinking into a chair near Justin. "Nothing but problems at work."

"Such as?" Justin looks up from his paper. He wants to know about anything important in her day.

"When I walked in this morning, Denise Granswold was arguing with a doctor who wants to discharge her husband too soon. It took me 20 minutes to straighten that out," Ellen begins. "I really understand how she feels, too. I mean, it's natural for her to be afraid of taking care of him at home when he still needs a lot of assistance. Denise isn't a nurse, after all."

"But you got it straightened out?"

"I finally got the doctor to agree to wait a couple more days to discharge him, and I'm going to work with Denise so that she feels able to take over at home. I think a nurse and I can teach her all she needs to know so she can take care of him at home."

"Sounds good."

"I guess, but it's so frustrating to deal with doctors who never think about the human factors in treatment."

"Anything else happen?" he asks, not wishing to encourage Ellen to ventilate about her frustrations with doctors. He's heard that too many times before.

"Then I had to talk with some new residents about how to interact with families of patients." Ellen lets out a sigh of exasperation. "Honestly, it is so hard to get them to understand that they need to deal with families, not just the patient."

"Families probably aren't emphasized in medical school."

"They're not, and that's the problem, so I have to convince these residents that dealing with families is part of their jobs." Ellen leans back in her chair. She waits for a response from Justin, but none is forthcoming.

After a couple of minutes, Ellen initiates a new topic. "At least Susan and I found time for lunch. We went to a new restaurant—I think you'd really like it. It's called Thai Times and the food is just wonderful—light, with lots of interesting spices, and the decor is very warm and friendly."

Justin nods and looks down at his paper. If Ellen doesn't have any more news, he'd like to get back to work.

"Susan and I talked about the home she's trying to buy. She's still negotiating with the realtor on some of the details, but I think she's going to get this deal through. She's asking for the current owners to fix the roof and regravel the driveway, and she wants them to pay for repainting the interior. If they'll agree to those terms, she thinks she can close in three or four weeks." Ellen smiles to herself, pleased that her friend will soon have a home of her own. She and Susan spent months house-hunting before finding a home Susan loved. For the past two weeks, they've talked daily about all the details of buying a home — the initial bid on the house, how to negotiate a final price and terms, and how to go through the process of applying for a mortgage. Ellen has been intensely involved in helping Susan buy the home, and she wonders why Justin doesn't seem more interested.

"I'm glad she's going to get the house," Justin says. He doesn't care about all the details and he finds it boring when Ellen recounts them, blow by blow. If she has any news, he's always willing to listen, but he gets frustrated when she buries him in minutiae. "Well, I'd better get back to my paper now."

Ellen frowns. She'd like to talk with Justin about some of Susan's ideas for decorating. She'd also like to tell him about the rest of her day, including a confrontation with one of the hospital administrators. And she'd like to know more about what his friend Mike is feeling about his father and how the project with Janice is progressing. But Justin clearly isn't in the mood for conversation tonight.

That seems to be the case most of the time. When she tries to tell him what's going on with her job or friends, he looks bored. He just doesn't seem to care what's happening in her world, and he doesn't seem to want to let her in on what's going on in his life.

What's going on between Justin and Ellen? Is he uninterested in her life? Does he not want to talk with her? What about Ellen? Is she "pumping" Justin for information? Is she drowning him in small talk and minutiae about her day? Is the interaction between Ellen and Justin normal? Is it healthy?

In this chapter, we examine different ways that people relate — how they share stories and information and how they stay in touch with others. We learn that there are distinct ways of relating. We also see why friends and romantic partners are sometimes confused and frustrated with each other's ways of relating news and stories.

Understanding the Misunderstanding

Let's return to Ellen and Justin. Perhaps we can get some clues about what's going on between them if we tune into what each of them is thinking during the conversation.

Communication as Instrumental

Like many men, Justin has been taught to view communication as instrumental — a tool that can be used to achieve things. He sees talk as a means to solve problems, state opinions, make plans, share news, give instructions. In other words, he regards communication as a means of conveying content that is significant. When there's nothing important to discuss, he doesn't feel a need to talk and sometimes finds talking annoying.

The guys he grew up with didn't spend time talking about every little thing that happened to them. The same is true of his friends today. They do talk, of course, but they talk when they have something to say. In just a few minutes, he and Mike touched base about Mike's father's surgery. He found out when the surgery was scheduled and asked whether Mike needed any help. What more did they need to discuss?

Justin's socialization also taught him that people speak up when they have something to say. If he wants to discuss something, he has no trouble initiating conversation. He doesn't wait for someone to ask him how his day was or whether he has something he wants to discuss. It seems silly to him that Ellen expects him to ask about her day. Why can't she just tell him whatever she wants to tell him?

Justin's perspective on conversation is like that of many men. Researchers report that masculine socialization teaches most men to see talk as a means of accomplishing instrumental goals. They talk when there is a problem or when there is a need to explain something, or inform or advise others. Research also indicates that masculine socialization encourages men to be assertive in taking the talk stage — they learn to initiate topics when they wish.

Although this is the general pattern of masculine socialization, it doesn't apply to all boys and men. Some boys grow up interacting primarily with women — mothers, sisters, and friends. Typically, this encourages a different view of communication — one more like Ellen's.

*"I'm your wife, Arthur. You talk to me.
You don't touch base with me."*

Drawing by Joe Mirachim; © 1988 The New Yorker Magazine, Inc.

Communication as Expressive

Like many women, Ellen regards communication as expressive — a means of communicating thoughts and a way to establish and sustain connections with others. She uses talk to build and nurture relationships. For her, the content of communication doesn't need to be significant for conversation to be valuable. Talking is relating. Communication is an end in itself, regardless of what is being communicated.

From Ellen's perspective, communication is also a way to include others and show she is interested in them. That's why she asks Justin how his day was. She wants to let him know that he matters to her and she wants to be involved with what's happening in his life. She doesn't care whether he has "big news" or not; the point for her is to be in touch with him and his life, whatever it involves. When he doesn't reciprocate by asking about her day or showing an interest in details of her skirmishes with doctors or conversation with Susan, she feels Justin doesn't care about being connected with her.

According to researchers, Ellen's view of communication is typical of many girls and women. Even at very early ages, young girls discuss the details of their experiences with each other as a way to share their lives. The details themselves aren't the point. Instead, the point is to be in touch, to share thoughts and feelings, even small ones. Today, for instance, Susan and Ellen spent 20 minutes talking about which shade of off-white paint would look best in the home Susan is trying to buy. Obviously, the exact shade of paint isn't an earth-shaking matter. Still, talking about the issue provided a connection between the two friends.

Feminine socialization also teaches people not to place themselves on center stage. Instead, they learn to include others in conversation, respond to what others say, and initiate topics that pave the way for others to speak. That's why Ellen expects Justin to ask how her day was instead of waiting for her to initiate the telling on her own. Generally, young girls learn not to dominate interaction and to invite others to enter conversation ("What do you think?" "Has that ever happened to you?" "How was your day?").

Not all girls and women learn feminine styles of communicating. Some girls learn to assert themselves, initiate topics, and dominate conversations. And some girls and women are as bored with details and small talk as Justin is. Despite exceptions, Ellen's way of communicating is more common in women than men, and Justin's style of communicating is more typical of men than women.

The problem between Ellen and Justin occurs because they don't share meanings about what communication is and what it is supposed to do. Another way of saying this is that they have different constitutive rules (see Chapter 3) or ways of defining what communication counts as.

Ellen's Meanings	*Justin's Meanings*
Talk = connecting with others.	Talk = accomplishing things.
Small talk = sharing lives.	Small talk = boring details.
Asking about another's day = showing interest.	Asking about another's day = intruding and probing.
Initiating talk about yourself = being self-centered.	Initiating talk about yourself = being assertive.

Asking another person about his or her life or day = showing interest and caring.	Asking another person about her or his life or day = insult because it assumes he or she can't speak for himself or herself.

The misunderstanding that Ellen and Justin experience is not unique to them. Many conversations are derailed by differences in how people view and use communication. As we saw in Chapter 11, students tell strikingly similar stories about what happens when they call home. Derek's description is typical. He says he calls home and his father answers. His father asks a series of questions, "Are you okay?" (yes). "Any problems with your grades?" (no) "Do you need money?" (no, but a little extra would be nice). Derek's father then says, "Okay, I'll put your mother on," after which Derek and his mother talk for 10 to 15 minutes.

(Not So) Small Talk

What do they talk about? Interesting things Derek's learning in classes, new people he's met, his mother's job, what's happening with his sister who lives 2,000 miles away. They talk about the rhythms in their lives and, after a phone call, they feel connected with each other. It's not that Derek's father doesn't care about his son. It's just that he doesn't see the point in talk that doesn't accomplish something he regards as specific and important.

Notice that in this example Derek enjoys small talk and sharing details about his and his mother's lives. This reminds us that not all men view communication only as a means to convey information and resolve problems. It's important that we recognize both generalizations (many men regard communication as an instrument to achieve goals) and exceptions to them (not all men use communication in only instrumental ways).

I recall my father's frustration when mother and I talked on the phone. After two minutes of talking, I would hear him in the background: "What are you talking about?" "Are you still on the phone?" "What's the point?" For mother and me, talking *was* the point. We didn't need major news or problems to enjoy communicating and to feel connected to each other.

. . .

Storytelling

Different views of what communication is about also surface in how people tell stories about events in their lives. For some people, storytelling is relatively linear. Their stories have a clear beginning, a sequential plot, and a climax. The stories are not embellished with details that don't add to the plot—for example:

> When I went to work today, my boss called me in. He said he was giving me a promotion and a raise. Starting next month, I'll be an assistant manager.

Other people relate stories in a weblike fashion that doesn't follow a linear sequence. Their stories include more details and more references to topics not directly related to the primary story line. It's not unusual for several story lines to be woven together in a single conversation, like this:

> When I went to work today, my boss called me in. I was afraid I'd done something wrong. You remember the last time a boss called me in was with Mr. Walters when I was working at the restaurant. Boy, had I blown it then! Then I thought maybe the bank was going to downsize. Remember when Pat was fired last year when her firm downsized? But this time there was good news, not bad. It turned out that he thinks I'm doing a great job and is going to promote me and give me a raise. That made me feel terrific because I've really put everything I could into this job. So I called mom and told her I was going to be an assistant manager starting next month. She was so excited and proud of me. She's coming up next week to take me out to lunch to celebrate and then we're going shopping together. It's been months since we made time for an afternoon with each other, so I'm really looking forward to that. I really miss talking and shopping with mom.

Both stories include the "news" of the promotion and raise. The first one is a bare-bones account of events. We don't hear how the speaker feels about the promotion and raise or how the events fit into the speaker's overall life. In the second story, the events are placed in the larger context of the speaker's work experiences and other relationships—with Pat, who was fired last year, and with the speaker's mother. In the second story, we also learn that the speaker was fearful of bad news, is excited about the good news, and misses time with her mother.

Is one style of telling stories better? Not necessarily. They are different, however. People who relate events in linear fashion may be irritated
by more weblike storytelling. They may be annoyed by what they perceive
as excessive details and comments unrelated to the point of the story. On
the other hand, individuals who nestle events in larger narratives that
include feelings and relationships may be frustrated by simple, facts-only
accounts. For them, the story is in the details and how a particular event
fits within the overall context of a life.

Improving Communication

Justin and Ellen have different preferences for communicating about hap-
penings in their lives. That may not change since their preferences grow
out of years of socialization. Even if they never develop a common preference for how to talk about events in their lives, there's a lot that they—and
the rest of us—can do to avoid feeling frustrated and hurt when they talk
with each other.

Focus on the Other's Meanings

First, each of them should try to understand what communication means
to the other. Justin might realize that small talk means different things to
Ellen than it does to him. He might respond differently if he figures out
that she shares details of her day as a way to connect with him more than
to share information. Understanding this could encourage Justin to
respond to Ellen and her meanings for communication instead of reacting
only to the informational content of what she says.

Ellen should also try to understand that Justin wasn't socialized to
view small talk as important and certainly wasn't taught to see it as a
means to building a relationship. If she can understand this, then she is
less likely to be hurt if he doesn't seem interested in the details of her days.
She may still wish he would be more involved in conversations, but she
won't misinterpret his lack of involvement as an indicator that he doesn't
care about her.

Recognize Differences and Their Sources

Second, Ellen and Justin should recognize that they have learned different meanings for asserting themselves in conversation. Their relationship

should improve if Ellen realizes that Justin doesn't need her to ask him about his day because he'll tell her about anything that matters to him. If she knew that Justin felt she was "pumping" him when she persists in asking about his day, she might be less persistent. She might also realize that he wants to hear about anything important in her day and she doesn't need to wait for him to ask.

Justin, too, could try to understand Ellen's perspective on communication. If he realizes that she interprets his asking about her day as a sign of caring, he might be more comfortable doing so. And he might respond differently to Ellen's questions if he learns that she asks about details in his life because she wants to feel connected, not because she wants to pump him.

For Ellen and Justin, and others of us who share the misunderstanding they experience, a key to better communication is to ask what the other person means. Imposing our meaning on another's style of communicating is bound to lead us to misinterpret what the person says and means. A much more satisfying course is trying to gain insight into what others mean by their ways of communicating.

Key Words

- constitutive rules
- expressive
- feminine socialization
- instrumental
- masculine socialization
- small talk
- storytelling

Reflecting on This Chapter

1. How can friends and romantic partners explain their ways of talking about events in their lives so they understand each other's style?

2. Think about people in your life who relate experiences in linear and in weblike styles. How does each style make you feel about the person? Do you feel more connected to people who use one style than the other? Do you feel you know a person better if she or he uses one style rather than the other?

3. Do we have any ethical responsibility to learn about and respect others' ways of telling stories and relating experiences? Do we have more

responsibility to do so in some relationships than in others? Why? What determines our level of responsibility?

4. What does it mean to "pump" someone for information or to "drown" someone in details? Are pumping and drowning actions done by a speaker, reactions to a speaker, or both?

5. Reread the conversation between Ellen and Justin. Based on what you've learned in this chapter, how might you rewrite the conversation so that Ellen and Justin understand each other and communicate more effectively.

6. Not all women and men communicate using patterns that research reports are typical for their sex. Think about women and men who are your friends. How many of them fit the patterns typical of sex socialization?

7. Try an experiment. Select two events or experiences you want to share. Relate the first story using a linear style of communication. Then, relate the second story to the same person using a weblike style of communicating. Do you feel different about the stories and the conversations when you use different styles of communicating? Does the other person respond differently to the two ways of relating stories?

8. Extend the ideas in this chapter to the context of the workplace. How might different styles of relating events and experiences surface in interaction on the job? How might they complicate communication between workers?

References

Baldwin, K. (1985). "Woof!" A word on women's roles in family storytelling. In R. A. Jordan & S. J. Kalcik (Eds.), *Women's folklore, women's culture* (pp. 149–162). Philadelphia: University of Pennsylvania Press.

Canary, D., & Dindia, K. (Eds.). (1997). *Sex differences and similarities in communication*. Mahwah, NJ: Erlbaum.

Coats, J. (1986). *Women, men, and language: Studies in language and linguistics*. London: Longman.

Coates, J., & Cameron, D. (1989). *Women and men in their speech communities: New perspectives on language and sex*. London: Longman.

Hall, D., & Langellier, K. (1988). Storytelling strategies in mother-daughter communication. In B. Bate & A. Taylor (Eds.), *Women communicating: Studies of women's talk* (pp. 107–126). Norwood, NJ: Ablex.

Johnson, F. (1996). Friendships among women: Closeness in dialogue. In J. T. Wood (Ed.), *Gendered relationships* (pp. 79–94). Mountain View, CA: Mayfield.

Maltz, D., & Borker, R. (1982). A cultural approach to male-female miscommunication. In J. J. Gumpertz (Ed.), *Language and social identity* (pp. 196–216). Cambridge, UK: Cambridge University Press.

Polanyi, L. (1979). So what's the point? *Semiotica*, 25, 207–241.

Swain, S. (1989). Covert intimacy: Closeness in men's friendships. In B. J. Risman & P. Schwartz (Eds.), *Gender and intimate relationships* (pp. 71–86). Belmont, CA: Wadsworth.

Tannen, D. (1991). *You just don't understand: Men and women in conversation*. New York: William Morrow.

Wood, J. T. (1995). *Relational communication: Continuity and change in personal relationships*. Belmont, CA: Wadsworth.

Wood, J. T. (Ed.). (1996). *Gendered relationships*. Mountain View, CA: Mayfield.

| 15 |

A SIGN OF THE TIMES

. . .

Misunderstandings Between Deaf

and Hearing Persons

Walter John Carl

How would you feel if you were an African American student at a historically black university and your president is, and has always been, European American? Or what if your college president spoke only German and could communicate with you only through an interpreter? What if you were a deaf student and the highest ranking official at your university couldn't communicate directly with you because she didn't know sign language? Would you feel that you could identify with this person? What would you do?

The deaf students at Gallaudet University, located in Washington, D.C., encountered this very issue in 1988 when the board of directors, composed of all hearing persons, selected a hearing woman as Gallaudet's new president. The students at Gallaudet University, the only liberal arts college in the world established exclusively for the purposes of educating deaf students and funded in large part by Congress, had never had a deaf

Author's Note: I would like to thank Lorelei Reed and Julia Wood for the valuable feedback on this chapter.

president. After another hearing president was selected in 1988, the students protested and shut down the campus by boycotting classes and blocking all entrances into the university. Students demanded that a new president be elected, one who was deaf. After a march to the Capitol building and nearly a week of protest, the board selected I. King Jordan as Gallaudet's first deaf president. The protest at Gallaudet thrust deaf people into the public limelight. For many people in the United States, this was the first time they'd been aware of issues in Deaf culture.

What exposure have you had to Deaf culture? Maybe you have seen a sign language interpreter in a bubble in the corner of your TV screen or a road sign that cautioned "Deaf Child Area." Maybe you've seen the movie *Children of a Lesser God* or films and television episodes starring Marlee Matlin, an Academy Award–winning actress who is Deaf. My experience with Deaf culture began in Rochester, New York, at the Rochester Institute of Technology (RIT). One of RIT's colleges is the National Technical Institute for the Deaf, the world's largest technical college for Deaf students. I lived in a mainstreamed residence hall (which means deaf and hearing students live together in the same building) for two years, learned sign language, and later became a student sign language interpreter on campus. During my time at RIT, I formed friendships with deaf people and I developed a strong interest in Deaf culture.

Understanding the Misunderstanding(s)

You may be curious about why I capitalized the D in "Deaf culture." You may also wonder why there's a chapter on deafness and not other topics that are commonly referred to as disabilities, such as mobility impairment or blindness. Deafness is unique for two reasons. First, many people who are deaf do not consider it a disability at all. In fact, many deaf individuals do not consider deafness a disadvantage, but a rich, textured cultural tradition with its own language. Second, many deaf individuals use a distinctive language — one that is not (as commonly misperceived) visual English. Instead, the language used in Deaf culture is as unique to its users as French, Hebrew, and Spanish. In this chapter, you will learn about misunderstandings between hearing and Deaf persons that can result from a failure to distinguish between the views of (small "d") deafness as a medical condition of hearing loss, and (big "D") Deafness as it defines a cultural and linguistic minority. Reading this chapter should increase your knowledge of deafness and Deaf culture. In turn, this insight will enable you to understand and communicate with deaf people more effectively. Toward this end, we'll discuss Deafness as a culture, historical views of deafness, issues of mainstreaming and technology with the Deaf community, forms of discrimination, and other common misunderstandings about deafness and Deaf culture.

The view that deafness is a medical condition, a physical impairment representing a lack of hearing, has been circulating for centuries. Thus, deafness is often regarded as a deficiency in what would otherwise be considered a "normal" person. This view is designated by "deafness" with a small "d." If we look at something as missing or broken, to want to replace it or fix it makes sense, and that's how some people in the (hearing) medical community, government, and larger public view deafness. This is the view against which the students at Gallaudet University protested.

Deafness with a big "D," however, is used to define the unique culture and language deaf people share. In their book *For Hearing People Only*, Matthew Moore and Linda Levitan write that the term *Deaf community* can be applied broadly to include those people who are deaf from birth (congenitally deaf), those who become deaf very early in life (prelingually deaf), those deafened later in life (adventitiously deaf), and hard-of-hearing persons of all ages. They go on to state that Deafness is a part of the rich and complex total identity of some individuals. Being deaf, then, is another way of being human. To Deaf people, deafness is a part of their wholeness. Many Deaf people, when asked if they would choose to become hearing, say no because they see deafness as basic to who they are and not as a disability. Throughout this chapter, I use "deaf" (small "d") to refer to the medical condition of hearing loss, and "Deaf" (big "D") to refer to the "Deaf community" or to Deaf people as a linguistic and cultural minority. A person can be medically deaf, but not culturally Deaf, which will become clearer as we understand Deafness as a culture.

Deafness as a Culture

If you've ever taken an anthropology class, you know that a culture encompasses an entire way of life — an interconnected system of institutions, beliefs, understandings, language, and practices that are shared by a group of people. Each culture has its own traditions, rituals, stories, and a common language. The Deaf community (and therefore Deaf culture) expresses all these features. For example, in the United States, members of Deaf communities use American Sign Language (ASL) to communicate with one another.

Many persons of the (hearing) scientific and linguistic community think that ASL is not a "real" language but merely a system of physical gestures, a manual code for spoken English. In the 1960s, Dr. William Stokoe, a hearing linguist working at Gallaudet University, demonstrated otherwise. He showed that ASL is a visual, spatial, and gestural language with its own distinct grammatical rules and syntax (sentence structure) that developed independently of English. American Sign Language does not have a written form, although people have attempted to create one. This language can be traced back to Martha's Vineyard in New England and old French Sign Language. In Martha's Vineyard there was an unusually high rate of hereditary deafness through many generations. In this community, both hearing and deaf residents communicated in Sign, and the hearing residents even used it to communicate among themselves when there were no deaf people around.

Each country has its own sign language and alphabet (Korean Sign Language and British Sign Language are two of many examples), which includes a manual alphabet (signing the letters of the alphabet with the hand is called "fingerspelling"). In the 1970s, an attempt was made to create a universal sign language, with the development of Gestuno, but this system was artificial and was never widely adopted. Two signers from two different countries, however, have the potential to break the language barrier more easily than two users of spoken language because both deaf people are communicating within a visual, spatial, and iconic system where words are pictures and pictures are concepts. Therefore, signed language is more tangible and thus potentially easier to "decode" by two users of two different sign languages than two spoken languages would be for their speakers. People who require spoken language to communicate lack the common iconic, gestural base of signed languages, and therefore the task of decoding separate spoken languages is more difficult.

American Sign Language is distinct from spoken English and other spoken languages because it is a visual-spatial language, rather than an auditory-oral language. Visual-spatial languages rely on the use of vision and the physical space around a signer to create meaning. Signs are produced with the signer's body (hand shapes, eyebrows, shoulders, and other body movements) and the space it occupies according to spatial reasoning. For example, to sign *I show you*, a signer makes one sign that moves from the chest of the signer outward to the recipient; to sign *you show me* the hand moves from the recipient inward toward the signer. In

THE FAR SIDE   By GARY LARSON

"Those snakes? Oh, they're just signing, honey."

ASL, the concept of "showing" (to you or to me) is expressed in one fluid
sign. In spoken English the same concept is expressed with three separate
words. Depending upon the movement and position of the hands, the
same base sign, "show," (similar to a "root word" in English) is used to
express *you show me, I show you, she shows them, they show us,* and other
related concepts.

American Sign Language also has its own grammatical structure that
is different from spoken English and from sign systems based on English
grammar. For example, in Signed English (a byproduct of ASL that was
developed by individuals interested in using manually coded representa-
tions of English words to teach English structure to Deaf children), the
word "forest" is often fingerspelled because there is no commonly accepted Signed English representation for the concept of a collection of

trees. In ASL, however, the sign for "forest" is the sign for "tree" repeated several times. As the above examples illustrate, English users tend to string words one after another in a linear, sequential manner, whereas ASL users place signs in a unique order (based on ASL structure and grammar rules) —vertically, horizontally, and overlaid, close to the body or distant. They make a sign large or small; they show it quickly or slowly. Within this structured yet personally devised and executed orchestration, exact concepts are brought to life.

American Sign Language binds together users of this highly textured language of the Deaf and makes it possible for them to share a rich cultural heritage and to develop a discrete sense of Deaf identity. The Deaf culture, however, is distinct from other cultures in at least two important aspects. First, an ethnic culture is usually transmitted from generation to generation. However, many deaf children are born to hearing parents who can't communicate with their deaf child or who know nothing about Deaf culture. Second, when we think of most cultures we usually picture a group of people who live near one another and interact regularly. Individuals and families who make up Deaf culture, however, are often scattered throughout the United States and the world, coming together in large numbers only at residential schools and in cities with a high deaf population like Washington, D.C., Los Angeles, and Rochester, New York. Because of the difficulty of passing Deaf culture across generations and because deaf people are so geographically dispersed, there is often a strong sense of community when members of the local, national, and international Deaf community do come together.

Deafness, Medicine, and Paternalism

Many misunderstandings result when we fail to distinguish between deafness as exclusively a medical condition and Deafness as it defines a cultural and linguistic minority. One misunderstanding revolves around medical attempts to cure deafness. For example, you may have heard of cochlear implants. A cochlear implant contains an array of electrodes; implanted in the skull, it acts as a "bionic ear." Some deaf individuals, for example late-deafened adults, have reported positive results with cochlear implants. However, some factions of the Deaf community view cochlear implants in less than a positive light. People who are deaf and don't view deafness as a deprivation may think it is inappropriate, even offensive, to attempt to "fix" for them something they don't consider broken. Matthew Moore and Linda Levitan, co-editors of the monthly magazine *Deaf Life*, argue that "an implant is the ultimate invasion of the ear, the ultimate denial of deafness, the ultimate refusal to let deaf children be Deaf" (p. 145).

Related to misunderstandings about "fixing" deaf individuals are paternalistic attempts to "help" them. For example, the students protesting at Gallaudet University were struggling against a tradition of hearing people making decisions for them, as if they were small children. According to Harold Orlans, a writer for the magazine *Change*, the chairperson of the board of directors at Gallaudet, Jane Basset Spillman, stated that "Deaf people are not ready to function in a hearing world." Although she insisted that her words were "*not* not ready," the view that deaf individuals can't function effectively in a hearing world has haunted deaf people for centuries.

Mainstreaming

There are many tensions between the views of deafness as a disability and Deafness as it defines a linguistic and cultural minority. One area where this tension surfaces is the issue of "mainstreaming." In general, mainstreaming efforts represent attempts to integrate minority groups into the larger majority population. For example, students who are mentally retarded or brain damaged often have classes in "regular" schools. Similarly, individuals who use wheelchairs often live and work in contexts dominated by persons who do not use wheelchairs. Mainstreaming deaf individuals into hearing culture has also been attempted. Two historical examples that continue to this day are initiatives to teach deaf people to speak English and attempts to integrate deaf children into public, hearing schools.

Attempts to teach deaf children English oral communication skills, referred to as the oralism movement, have been made for hundreds of years. Almost all deaf people have the physiological ability to speak, as the mechanics required for speech are present. However, because deaf people can't hear the vocalizations of others, they have no model to copy. Furthermore, people who are deaf can't hear their own voices and therefore lack the ability to make judgments about their own pitch, loudness, and inflection. You can't copy something you've never heard. In the United States, some hearing people (as well as some deaf people) insist that deaf children learn to speak English so they won't be cut off from the larger (hearing) society.

Immense pressure can be placed on deaf people to learn to speak English. This pressure can come from well-intentioned sources like parents, teachers, and speech pathologists. I remember a floormate of mine in college who was forced by her parents to learn to speak English as well as she could and was forbidden to use sign language. The implicit assumption was that if my friend learned how to sign, she would become a "deafie" (a pejorative label for deaf individuals) and not be a part of the (hearing) world. When her parents came to visit her, she asked me not to sign in front of them so her parents wouldn't know she was learning ASL, and thus, becoming "Deaf." Not all hearing parents have this negative reaction to signing and Deaf culture, but some do. This response perpetuates the view that deafness is a disease that should be cured.

Similar to the desire for deaf children to speak English is the effort to mainstream deaf children into the public, hearing schools. Residential schools are often state-run schools where students attend school and are raised together in a residence hall setting. Because most deaf children are dispersed around the United States, many deaf children congregate in residential schools and develop their own sense of a Deaf identity. Dr. Peter Seiler, superintendent of the Illinois School for the Deaf and deaf himself, argues that "there should be no stigma attached to attending a state school for the deaf which is no different from attending a private boarding school." Initiatives to mainstream deaf students into (hearing) public schools have led to a decline in the numbers and enrollments of residential schools for the deaf. Policies of mainstreaming, however, were not originally intended for deaf students. Rather, the "mainstreaming law," Public Law 94-142, was designed to ensure that the needs of handicapped/disabled children were considered and met by placing them into appropriate schools. Matthew Moore and Linda Levitan argue, however, that the mainstreaming law was used to justify shifting deaf children from residential schools to public schools.

Although some children who are mainstreamed into public, hearing schools experience positive results, others feel isolated because they have relatively few, if any, deaf classmates. Mainstreamed schools don't always have staff in sufficient numbers or with adequate training to work effectively with deaf students. Furthermore, many public school teachers have difficulty communicating with deaf children, and deaf students' participation in extracurricular and sports programs can be diminished. Leo Jacobs, a prominent deaf educator, argues that attempts to mainstream deaf children into regular public school programs will result in a "new generation of educational failures" and "frustrated and unfulfilled adults."

Matthew Moore and Linda Levitan also support residential schools and argue that they facilitate the transmission of Deaf culture and offer a place to cultivate Deaf identity.

Residential schools, however, also have disadvantages. One drawback concerns their academic standards. Although some residential schools have strong reputations for academic excellence, others struggle to attract the best teachers and to establish high-caliber curricula. Furthermore, deaf students who graduate from some residential schools historically have scored lower than their hearing counterparts in academic achievement skills, especially English skills. Parents of deaf children often struggle with the pros and cons of residential versus mainstreamed schooling. In making the difficult choice of where to educate their children, (hearing) parents often turn to medical doctors and other professionals rather than to experts on deafness—Deaf adults who are successful participants in the world at large and prominent members within the Deaf community.

Not all hearing people exhibit a paternalistic perspective on deafness and Deaf culture. For example, many hearing people are Children of Deaf Adults (CODAs) and may find themselves as adults working within Deaf culture as teachers, social workers, and sign language interpreters. Hearing people who have collaborated with the Deaf community include Thomas Gallaudet (who helped establish what was later named Gallaudet University) and the Abbé de l'Epée (a "neighborhood priest" who worked with deaf people in France in the mid-1700s). There are also many contemporary hearing scholars and activists such as Harlan Lane, Ursula Bellugi, sociologist Harry Best, linguist William Stokoe, and Iowa Senator Tom Harkin, who have supported the Deaf community and promoted international respect for ASL and Deaf culture.

Other Forms of Discrimination

In addition to discrimination rooted in paternalism, Deaf people face other forms of discrimination when sign language interpreters are not provided at public events, TV programs are not captioned, or pay telephones are not equipped with a TDD/TTY for deaf users. (TDD, a telecommunication device for the deaf, is also called TTY, or teletypewriter. This is an electronic device that allows deaf people to communicate over phone lines by typing on a keyboard and reading the other person's words on a display screen.) One attempt to redress these forms of discrimination is the Americans with Disabilities Act (ADA), which went into effect in

1992 and prohibits discrimination on the basis of disability in public accommodations, transportation, and access. The act is an attempt to mainstream people with disabilities into the larger culture. Some Deaf people, however, have mixed feelings about ADA and other mainstreaming attempts (for example, residential versus mainstreamed schooling) because they fear that such efforts could cause them to lose their unique sense of Deaf identity and the close relative of identity—language (in this case, ASL). At the same time, many Deaf people realize the political danger of cutting themselves off from the larger, wealthier, and more powerful groups that lobby for rights for disabled people. The ADA makes it illegal for organizations not to provide sign language interpreters for public events, job interviews, and doctor's appointments. Also, the powerful disability lobby helps to ensure TDD/TTY access, telephone relay services, and the provision and development of other essential products and services in the larger, hearing society.

In addition to discrimination based on views of deafness as a disability, paternalism, and issues of access, another common form of misunderstanding and discrimination concerns the practice of totalizing. We discussed totalizing in Chapters 1 and 7. It occurs when one aspect of a person's identity is taken to represent the total, or whole, person. If I look at a person who is deaf and I think that deafness is all she or he is, then I totalize her or him. This creates a barrier to our communication. Each deaf person is just as complex and multifaceted as each hearing person. Both deaf and hearing individuals are characterized by a race or ethnic background, sex, socioeconomic class, and sexual orientation; all have different hobbies, interests, and perspectives. When we totalize, we strip away all the other facets of a person's identity and focus on only one aspect. An example of totalizing occurs when hearing persons outside Deaf culture do not realize the tremendous richness and complexity of a deaf person's life and the diversity found within Deaf communities.

Some deaf people may be discriminated against from within Deaf culture. A phenomenon common to many cultures is the notion of an authentic member—one who is "really" or "truly" a member of the group. According to some people who live in the southern United States, a "real" Southerner is someone who is born in the South, not someone who was born elsewhere and then moved to the South. In Deaf culture, a "really" deaf person is a deaf child who has deaf parents, because this is as deaf as one can be, "untainted" by anything "hearing." Instead of bringing people closer together, rigid rules for authenticity can result in exclusion and division.

Some Deaf people argue that an "authentic" Deaf person communicates only in ASL while other deaf people may read lips (a difficult skill to develop) or communicate with Signed English (sign language based on English grammar and syntax), cued speech (spoken English accompanied by hand signals to assist lip-reading), or other variations of sign language. One reason that communicating with ASL becomes a defining characteristic of an authentic Deaf person is that ASL is one thing that is truly Deaf people's own; it owes little to hearing culture. Again, we see that language and identity are closely intertwined and, at times, inseparable.

Labeling someone as deaf is based simply on a medical condition of hearing loss. To label oneself, or to be labeled, as Deaf in a cultural sense, however, requires a definition of the characteristics of what makes one Deaf. What if a deaf person does not communicate with ASL but with Signed English? Can this person be a member of Deaf culture? Some people define the Deaf culture more broadly or more narrowly than others and this is a site of controversy within Deaf communities. Some people will exclude deaf people who don't sign in ASL or aren't "authentically" Deaf, however this is defined. Note that having criteria for authenticity is not unique to Deaf culture but is common to many social groups, based on notions of identity. Although not every member of the Deaf culture harbors negative feelings about those deaf people who do not use ASL or who have hearing parents (especially because most deaf individuals come from hearing families), it is important to realize that discrimination within one's own community can be just as damaging as discrimination from outside the community.

Improving Communication

The Story So Far

Understandings of Deaf and deaf individuals have progressed since 1773 when Dr. Samuel Johnson described deafness as "one of the most desperate of human calamities." Deaf communities have taught many hearing people that deafness is not a handicap or a disability, and that deaf people don't need to be taken care of or "helped." Rather, deaf people share membership in a unique linguistic and cultural minority. Members of Deaf culture in the United States unite around a common language, American Sign Language, which is held as an integral aspect of their identity. Deaf culture, however, is not homogenous or always harmonious. Rather, it is characterized by a great deal of diversity of interests and social standpoints, by disparate views of technology and mainstreaming, and by an uneasy political connection with disabled rights initiatives.

What You Can Do

Rather than thinking of deaf people as disabled, think of them more appropriately as belonging to a culture that differs from hearing culture. This approach paves the way for a better understanding of the individual and collective experiences of deaf people.

If you want to learn more about ASL and Deaf culture, there are many fascinating books you can read. The references at the end of this chapter will get you started. I suggest that you begin with *For Hearing People Only* as it contains a great deal of basic information about deafness and is written by individuals who are Deaf.

Probably the best approach to learning more about deafness and Deaf culture is to communicate with Deaf people. You can take classes to learn American Sign Language at your university or in your local community. Even if you don't know ASL, you can always communicate with a deaf person by fingerspelling (the sign language alphabet that you can learn by looking in a sign language dictionary) or writing back and forth on a piece of paper. A simple smile can go a long way in breaking the ice the first time you interact with people who are deaf.

When approaching a deaf person, however, be respectful of his or her privacy and use common sense. You probably wouldn't want a complete stranger coming up to you in a grocery store telling you that she is learning to speak English and is curious about your culture. For the same reasons, a deaf person might not appreciate a hearing person invading her or his privacy.

Matthew Moore and Linda Levitan suggest that if you want to learn more about the Deaf community you should learn Sign. They also advise hearing individuals to have an open mind about deafness and Deaf culture. Learning about Deaf culture teaches us both about people who are different from us and about ourselves.

Key Words

- American Sign Language (ASL)
- authenticity
- culture

- deafness
- Deafness
- mainstreaming

- oralism
- paternalism

- residential schools
- totalizing

Reflecting on This Chapter

1. Could a hearing president be effective at Gallaudet University? What if the hearing president could communicate in ASL? What are the advantages and disadvantages of a president who is hearing versus a president who is Deaf?

2. What meanings does the message on the road sign "Deaf Child Area" convey to you? Is this a sign that is beneficial to automobile drivers? Or does the message, although rooted in good intentions, reflect a paternalistic view that deaf children can't watch for cars themselves and need to be protected? Would it be sufficient to post signs saying "Children's Area" or "Children at Play"?

3. Should companies continue to invest in cochlear implant technology in attempts to correct deafness? What about developing better telecommunications devices like TDDs/TTYs, or closed-captioning television technology? How do you think hearing people's relationship with technology differs from that of individuals who are Deaf? What if we had a medical way to "correct" homosexuals so they were heterosexual? Should it be offered? Required? What if a decision was made in the United States that one and only one race was "normal" and scientists devised a way to "correct" "abnormal" races? Who defines what is normal?

4. How might the perception of deaf people as disabled be disabling to deaf people? How does the view of Deafness as it defines a cultural and linguistic minority provide a different perspective on deafness? If you are a hearing person, try thinking of yourself that way—always using the adjective "hearing" to describe your identity. How does doing so affect your self-concept?

5. Where do you stand on issues of mainstreaming? Is it better for Deaf children to learn in (their own) residential schools? Or is it better for Deaf children to be mainstreamed into public, hearing schools at an early age? Is separate equal? How might this be the same as or different from mainstreaming and integration efforts based on race?

6. How might the idea of authenticity work to bring people together? How might it be a divisive and fragmenting force? Are there other approaches to collective group efforts and identity that aren't based on authenticity?

7. How does my own standpoint as a hearing person affect my ability and right to write this chapter? Is this an example of speaking for or about others (refer to Chapter 10)? What considerations should be made when learning about and speaking for or about others?

8. How has this chapter affected your views of hearing people's relationship to deafness? How do you see your own relationship to Deaf culture?

References

Dolnick, E. (1993, September). Deafness as culture. *The Atlantic Monthly*, pp. 37–53.

Harris, J. (1995). *The cultural meaning of deafness: Language, identity, and power relations*. Aldershot, UK: Avebury.

Higgins, P. C. (1980). *Outsiders in a hearing world: A sociology of deafness*. Beverly Hills, CA: Sage Publications.

Lane, H. (1992). *The mask of benevolence: Disabling the deaf community*. New York: Alfred A. Knopf.

Moore, M. S., & Levitan, L. (1992). *For hearing people only: Answers to some of the most commonly asked questions about the Deaf community*. Rochester, NY: Deaf Life Press.

Orlans, H. (1989, January/February). The revolution at Gallaudet. *Change*, pp. 9–18.

Sacks, O. W. (1991). *Seeing voices: A journey into the world of the deaf*. London: Picador.

Spradley, T. (1985). *Deaf like me*. Washington, DC: Gallaudet College Press.

Taylor, G., & Bishop, J. (Eds.). (1991). *Being deaf: The experience of deafness*. London: Pinter Publishers.

Wrigley, O. (1996). *The politics of deafness*. Washington, DC: Gallaudet College Press.

PART 4

Misunderstandings in

Romantic and Family Relationships

| 16 |

WHAT'S A FAMILY, ANYWAY?

• • •

Different Views of What Family Means

In the autumn of 1992, the United States was engaged in its once-every-four-year ritual of presidential campaigning. One of the more memorable moments in the 1992 presidential race was when then–Vice President Dan Quayle castigated sitcom star Murphy Brown for choosing to be a single parent. Murphy Brown represents the decline of family values in America, proclaimed the vice president who, it turned out, was not to be reelected to a second term.

Who is Murphy Brown, and what did she do to earn such a chewing out from Dan Quayle? She was the female lead in a successful television situation comedy. Murphy was an accomplished professional, long parted from her former husband. She wanted a child and so she deliberately became pregnant (for the record, the father was her former husband) and gave birth to "baby Brown," who had to wait through several episodes to acquire a more personal name.

What's wrong with this picture? According to Dan Quayle, her choice to be a single mother was emblematic of the degeneration of morals and family values in America. Quayle spoke of the "right" kind of family as the traditional nuclear one—children who live with a married mother and father, who live together (that is, not separated or divorced and certainly not cohabiting without benefit of marriage). This is how the American family *should be*, insisted Dan Quayle. This kind of family is the only one that reflects "family values."

The problem with Quayle's definition of family is that it excludes the majority—yes, the *majority*—of people living in the United States as well as in the world. Instead of the singular model of family that Quayle championed, we have a cornucopia of different forms that are considered families by those who create and live in them. The family form Quayle endorsed, in fact, represents only a small portion of current U.S. families.

In the following pages, we consider the smorgasbord of families in the United States today. We also explore the ways in which failing to recognize multiple family forms can limit our personal growth and lead to misunderstandings and hurtful communication.

Understanding the Misunderstanding

There are several reasons that we may not wish to join Quayle in insisting there is one and only one "right" or "normal" family form. First, doing so limits our personal horizons and our opportunities to expand and enrich our own families. Second, recognizing only one form of family as legitimate disrespects the commitments of people whose families are unlike our own. Third, insisting that there is only one kind of "real," "moral," or "legitimate" family disregards the fact that society is always evolving, always in process. What family means, like the meanings of other things in the social world, changes over time. Finally, failure to recognize and respect different family forms can lead to misunderstandings in communication.

What Is Immediate Family?

One of the students I advise is an African American man who is preparing for a career in marketing. Franklin is an ideal student—smart, curious about ideas, responsible in getting his work done, and serious about his studies. Not long ago, Franklin came to me visibly upset, so I invited him to sit down and tell me what was bothering him.

"My grandmother had to go in the hospital for heart surgery, so I went home to be with her." I nodded. "I missed an exam in my history class. When I got back to school, I went to see Dr. Raymond to schedule a make up and he says he won't excuse my absence."

"Why not?" I asked. "Did he want some assurance that your grand-mother really was in the hospital?"

Franklin shook his head. "No, I brought a copy of her admission form as proof. That's not the problem. He says he only excuses absences for medical problems in the student's *immediate* family."

Dr. Don Raymond, like many middle-class white people, thought of family as a mother, father (or stepmother or stepfather), and children. After all, when he was growing up, Don lived with his parents and two sisters. His other relatives did not live nearby and he saw them only once or twice a year, if that often. Now 48 years old, Don lives with his second wife and their two children, ages 12 and 15. He seldom sees his sisters and visits with his parents and in-laws only over Christmas. Aunts, uncles, and grand-parents are not part of the immediate family that Don Raymond knows.

It wasn't difficult to resolve Franklin's situation. I simply called Don Raymond and talked with him about some of the typical differences between white and black family structures, and I emphasized that many African American families are more extended than those of most Euro-pean Americans. Large, extended families are also common among second-generation Americans of many ethnic origins. Once Don under-stood that grandparents were immediate family to Frankin, he was more than willing to schedule a make-up examination.

There was nothing mean spirited or intentionally discriminatory in Don's initial refusal to schedule a make-up exam for Franklin. The prob-lem was that he assumed—without even knowing he was making an assumption—that his definition of family was everyone's definition of family. He simply didn't understand that Franklin considered his grand-mother immediate family. After all, she had raised him for the first seven years of his life, a situation not uncommon in African American families. She was more like a mother (in white terms) than a grandmother to him.

Lesbian and Gay Families

Lesbian and gay families are also frequently misunderstood. Not long ago I was having lunch with Jean and Arlene, who have been in a committed relationship for 15 years. With us were their two children, Michael and

Arthur, age 6 and 8, respectively. A colleague of mine saw us in the restaurant and came over to our table to engage in small talk for a few minutes.

I offered the standard introduction: "Chuck Morris, I'd like you to meet Jean Thompson and Arlene Ross. And these are their sons, Michael and Arthur."

"Good to meet you," Chuck said. "Do you live here?"

"Yes, our home is just off Lystra Road," Arlene said. "And what about you?" Chuck asked Jean.

"Same place. The four of us are a family," she replied.

Chuck had made the mistake of assuming that the two women and the two sons constituted separate families. Once Jean clarified the relationship, Chuck understood and was not taken aback by the fact that Jean and Arlene were lesbians. Yet he was confused about the boys. "So how old were they when you got them?" he asked, assuming the boys were adopted.

"Depends on whether you count the gestation period," Jean said with a smile. She had run into this assumption before. "I carried Michael and Arlene carried Arthur."

"Oh, so they're your biological children?" he asked.

Arlene and Jean nodded.

Chuck made the mistake of assuming that lesbians (and gay men, too) can't be biological parents. Obviously they can, because sexual orientation has no bearing on a man's ability to produce viable sperm or a woman's ability to produce fertile eggs and carry a child in her womb. When we assume gay men and lesbians cannot have biological children, we conflate sexual orientation with reproductive ability.

Interracial Families

Misunderstandings also surround many interracial families. Matt and Vicky had been married for six years when they realized they weren't able to have biological children. They decided to adopt, first, James and, three years later, Sheryl. They love their son and daughter and consider themselves a close family. But, whenever they go out as a family, others subject them to stares and sometimes thoughtless comments.

"Are you baby-sitting?"

"Whose children are these?"

If you guessed that James and Sheryl are not the same race as Matt and Vicky, you're correct. The children are African American, and Matt and Vicky are European American. In recent years, two of my white friends have adopted children of other races—a young girl from China for one and a Native American girl for another. Like Matt and Vicky, they are hurt when people assume their children are not their children. Comments such as "Are you baby-sitting?" deny the families they have created.

Divorced and Blended Families

You have probably read the statistic that half of first marriages end in divorce. In addition, even more than half of second and subsequent marriages end in divorce. Divorce may end a marriage, but it doesn't end family. Instead, it changes the character and dynamics of family life.

If the former spouses had children, they are still parents, but how they parent changes. In some cases, one parent has sole custody of children and the other parent may have visiting rights. In other cases, parents agree to joint custody with each parent providing a home to children part of the time. Children experience two homes and two sets of rules, which may be inconsistent. One parent may have rigid requirements about dating, curfews, and household chores while the other parent is more relaxed.

If one or both parents remarry, families combine to create what are called blended families. Years ago *The Brady Bunch* was a popular television situation comedy. In it, two parents, each with several children, married and became a blended family. Among the Bradys, liking and comfort seemed effortless. Unlike the Bradys, many blended families find it difficult to reorganize into a functional, comfortable unit. Children may have to accommodate other children, from both former marriages and the current one, so jealousy and conflict often surface. New household rules may cause confusion, resentment, and resistance. Parents may have to accept the children's other parents and grandparents. And people outside the family may have to recognize multiple parents of children and both former and current spouses of parents.

Some children in blended families call their stepparent mother or father; other children reject that term. Similarly, some children in blended families consider their step-siblings and half-siblings brothers and sisters whereas other children don't accept those labels. When communicating with people who belong to divorced or blended families, we should be sensitive to how they perceive and name their family ties.

Families Without Children

My partner and I have been married for 23 years, and we have no children. We are a family without children. I am annoyed and hurt when people ask me, as they frequently do, "Why don't you have a family?" Sometimes I reply with a question: "What do *you* mean by family?" On other occasions, I respond by saying, "I *do* have a family—I have a husband, a sister, three nephews, and a niece." I consider all six of these people my immediate family. Like other people who don't have children, I resent it when others assume that I don't have a family just because Robbie and I don't have children.

What's a Family, Anyway?

Yet another kind of family was introduced by Kath Weston in her book, *Families We Choose*. Weston describes close friendship circles of gays and lesbians as the families they choose. For Weston, families are people who are bound together by commitment, regardless of whether there are biological or legal ties. Some biologically related people may have no commitment to each other and may refuse to interact. Siblings sometimes feel such animosity toward each other that they decide not to visit, write, call, or otherwise have contact. Some parents and children are estranged, and in extreme cases parents sometimes disown children. Biology, then, doesn't guarantee commitment.

Legal and religious procedures are also insufficient to ensure the level of commitment and caring most of us consider the crux of what a good family is. As noted earlier, current statistics indicate that approximately one-half of marriages in the United States will end in divorce. Laws that define marriage can be negated by laws that grant divorce. In a 1993 poll of the baby boom generation, only 58% of respondents said they considered it likely they would stay married to the same person for life. Pledging "until death do us part" before a magistrate or member of the clergy may create a legal marriage. It does not, however, guarantee that the people making the pledge will, in fact, be able or willing to stay together for life. These statistics show that the nature of family is neither as fixed nor as uniform as Dan Quayle suggested.

Thus, concludes Weston, it's reasonable to define family as people who elect to commit to each other in a sustained way—to have a family we choose. Their commitments may or may not be recognized by current laws or religious practices; but they are families, if by family we mean people who care about one another, organize their lives together, take care of one another, and intend to continue being together and caring for one another. This enlarged view of family pivots on the idea that people can commit to casting their fates together.

Improving Communication

When I teach about family diversity at my university, some of my students are uncomfortable. "I understand what you're saying," they often tell me, "but my church says that homosexuality is immoral. I can't approve of that." Others say, "It's wrong for members of one race to adopt children of a different race. The children will never understand their ethnic heritage. I just can't agree with interracial adoptions."

Distinguish Between Personal Choice and Respect for Others' Choices

What I try to show my students is that they don't have to embrace various family forms for themselves in order to respect them as legitimate choices for other people. In other words, there's a big difference between deciding what you personally want in a family (or career or spiritual practice or education or home life) and deciding to honor the choices that others make.

We already recognize and respect varied choices in many aspects of family life. For example, some parents believe that physically punishing children is wrong; other parents believe that if you spare the rod, you spoil the child. Some parents bring up children within strong religious traditions; other parents don't introduce children to any religious or spiritual path. In some families, children have to do chores and sometimes take on jobs outside the home to earn money; children in other families get automatic allowances. Few of us would label any of these choices wrong, deviant, or antifamily. Yet we sometimes find it difficult to accept other variations among families.

Recognize That Views of Family Change

Columnist Stephanie Salter interviewed Jane Collier, a professor of anthropology, who noted that people have continuously changed their views of what marriage is. Among the Nayars in India, a wife and husband often meet for the first time at their wedding and then part, never to see each other again. Meanwhile, she gives birth to children fathered by her lovers and the children are her husband's legal offspring and heirs. The purposes of Nayar marriages are to link families and establish lines of inheritance.

In some societies, it is acceptable for a husband to have more than one wife (called polygamy), and in fewer societies it's acceptable for a wife to have more than one husband (called polyandry). Arranged marriages are still practiced in some cultures, and communal marriages and families are accepted in still other cultures. Historically throughout the world, many people without property have lived together and raised children in common-law families. There was no practical need for them to marry because they had no property and the institution of marriage is designed to protect property rights of heirs.

We don't even have to look to other cultures to learn about diversity in family forms. The diversity is right here in our own society. Recently I collaborated with Steve Duck, who conducts research on communication and personal relationships, to co-edit a book. It includes chapters on different kinds of families, such as cohabiting couples, long-distance relationships, gay and lesbian commitments, and African American and Hispanic families. The chapters in this book document the diversity of family forms in the United States today.

Family historian Stephanie Coontz points out that during the 300 years since Columbus landed in this hemisphere, families in the United States have taken many forms. The Iroquois lived with extended and matriarchal families, whereas the more nomadic Indian groups had small families. African American slaves saw their nuclear families wrenched apart, so they developed extended communal networks, routinely engaged in co-parenting, and took orphaned children into their homes and raised them as their own, usually without formally adopting them.

The family form idealized by Dan Quayle came late in U.S. history and sustained its status as the dominant family form for only a short period. According to Coontz, only beginning in the 1920s did the majority of working-class white people in the United States live in families that had male breadwinners and female homemakers. Today, by contrast, the majority of women work outside the home, and approximately one-half of wives who work outside the home have salaries equal to or greater than those of their husbands. The male breadwinner/female homemaker model simply doesn't describe the majority of U.S. families today.

Intact families, also part of Quayle's model, are more the exception than the rule in this country as we approach the year 2000. Nearly half of first marriages (and an even greater percentage of second marriages) end in divorce. Only 50% of children live with both their biological parents, and nearly one-quarter live with single parents, usually their mothers.

The Census Bureau's 1996 survey of 60,000 U.S. households noted several trends in families. The greatest shift is in the number of single-parent households. Between 1990 and 1995, the number of single-parent families rose by a scant 3%. In the single year 1995–1996, families headed by single mothers rose 12% as did families headed by single fathers. Some single-parent households, such as Murphy Brown's, represent choices. In other cases, single parenting is not desired or anticipated, but it becomes the only or the most acceptable option.

Recognize Diversity in Family Forms

Demographic trends in the United States clearly challenge the accuracy of any singular view of what a family is. Effective participation in current society requires us to understand that people have diverse ideas about what counts as a family and they have equally diverse ways of structuring family life. As one gay man said to me, "I don't care if straights like me and my partner or not, but I do care that they recognize I have rights to love a person and have a family just like they do." Understanding this point can help us interact effectively in two ways.

First, when we recognize the normal diversity of family forms, we can communicate more respectfully with people who have varying family structures. No longer is there a universal definition of family. Dan Quayle says single mothers are an affront to family values, but single mothers are no more or less successful in parenting than married women. Just like mothers who are married, some single mothers are devoted and effective parents, and some are not. Just like married mothers, single mothers' effectiveness depends on a variety of factors including support networks, income, education, and employment.

Most states do not recognize gay and lesbian commitments, yet the evidence suggests they can be as healthy, stable, and enduring as heterosexual unions. Even if gay and lesbian families do break up, that doesn't mean they weren't families at one time. After all, if a heterosexual couple divorces, we don't assume they were never married. Like heterosexuals, gays and lesbians can pledge a lifetime of love and loyalty; like some heterosexuals, some gays and lesbians will not realize that promise.

And what about the children of lesbian and gay parents? Child development specialist Charlotte Patterson reports that there are currently between 1 million and 5 million lesbian mothers and 1 million and 3 million gay fathers in the United States and between 6 million and 14 million children who have a gay or lesbian parent. Many states don't allow gay or lesbian partners to be legal parents, even if one partner is the biological parent. These states argue that lesbians and gays cannot raise healthy children, but this argument isn't justified, according to *New York Times* columnist Jane Gross. Based on reviewing 35 studies of children who have gay or lesbian parents, Gross concluded that these children are as well adjusted as children of heterosexual parents and that they are no more or less likely to become gay or lesbian than the children of heterosexual parents. In a separate review of research, Charlotte Patterson found that children of gay and lesbian parents and children of heterosexual parents are no different in terms of intelligence, self-concept, and moral judgment. Existing evidence shows that both heterosexuals and gays and lesbians can raise children who are healthy and happy—and both can raise poorly adjusted children who have low self-concepts.

Learn from Differences

Diverse family forms also offer an opportunity for us to consider how we form our own families and live in them. Martha Barrett interviewed same-sex couples and concluded that they tend to relate to each other on equal terms more than do heterosexual couples. Barrett suggests that gays and lesbians have something to teach the heterosexual community about equality in rights and responsibilities in intimate relationships. Similarly, interracial families may discourage us from overemphasizing race in our thinking about personal identity and family. And families in which there are children may learn from child-free families about ways to keep couple communication alive and intimate.

We can learn about others and ourselves if we are open to differences in how people form and live in families. As long as we interact only with people whose families are like ours, it's hard for us to see some of the patterns and choices we've made in our own relationships. The particular ways that we charter our families remain invisible, unseen and unseeable because they seem "normal," "the only way to be a family." Yet when we consider some of the contrasts provided by interacting with people who have families different from ours, what was invisible and taken for granted in our own relationships becomes more visible. This realization allows us to reflect on the way we've created our families. In turn, this knowledge enables us to make more informed, more thoughtful choices about the kind of family we want to have.

In other words, heterosexuals don't have to change their sexual orientation to gain insight into their own relationships by observing gay and lesbian families. A heterosexual friend of mine once told me that only through her friendship with a lesbian couple had she realized how fully she centered her life around her male partner. She chose to stay married, but she and her husband communicated about ways they could be less centered on each other and enlarge their circle of friends.

A child-free family doesn't need to have children to learn something about their own relationship from interacting with families in which children are present. I've learned a lot about my relationship with Robbie by spending time with my sister Carolyn and her husband, Leigh, and their children, Michelle and Daniel. One of the insights I've gained from visiting them is that Robbie and I didn't include much play and frolic in our relationship.

Notice I used the past tense (didn't). Watching Carolyn and Leigh play with Michelle and Daniel and then blend into playfulness with each other allowed Robbie and me to notice that the playful dimension of relating was largely missing in our interaction. When Robbie and I played with Michelle and Daniel and then with them and their parents, we revived our dormant sense of how to be playful. Since learning this, Robbie and I have become more playful, even silly at times, with each other, and this enriches our marriage. Opening ourselves to various ways of being a family allows us to enlarge our personal identities and our relationships, including our own families.

Key Words

- blended families
- divorce
- family
- families we choose

- families without children
- immediate family
- interracial families
- lesbian and gay families

Reflecting on This Chapter

1. Social and legal definitions of family are arbitrary social conventions. What social institutions and policies benefit by defining family in traditional ways? Who benefits if family is defined more broadly?

2. Can you think of general characteristics of heterosexual marriage that are not present in gay and lesbian commitments? Some have argued that gay and lesbian unions don't produce children, but neither do many heterosexual unions. Also heterosexuals can adopt children, as can gays and lesbians in many states. If there are not qualities that firmly distinguish gay and lesbian commitments from heterosexual ones, what could be the basis for laws that refuse to recognize gay and lesbian commitments?

3. Is it "wrong" for a single woman to choose to have a child? Can you identify any criteria that affect your judgments of this choice—for example, financial resources, role models of both sexes? If you consider these criteria to justify disapproving of single women who have children, then what is your opinion of single mothers who are single because they are widowed or divorced? Can we condone some single mothers and not others?

4. Some members of racial minorities argue that minority children should not be adopted by people of different races—for example, European Americans should not be allowed to adopt Native American or African American children. Advocates of this position claim that children need their racial heritage and will lose it if they are raised by parents of a different race. Those who favor allowing interracial adoptions respond that what any child needs most is a loving, supportive family. They also argue that there are not enough minority adults who

want to adopt minority children, so many minority children will be left in orphanages if interracial adoptions are not allowed. How do you feel about the issue of interracial adoption?

References

Barrett, M. B. (1989). *Invisible lives: The truth about millions of women-loving women.* New York: Morrow.

Card, C. (1995). *Lesbian choices.* New York: Columbia University Press.

Changes in families reach plateau, study says. (1996, November 27). *Raleigh News and Observer*, pp. 1-A and 10-A.

Coontz, S. (1992). *The way we never were: American families and the nostalgia trap.* New York: Basic Books.

Coontz, S. (1996, May–June). Where are the good old days? *Modern Maturity*, pp. 36–43.

Ferrante, J. (1995). *Sociology: A global perspective* (2nd ed.). Belmont, CA: Wadsworth.

Goodman, E. (1997, January 17). Adopting across racial lines. *Raleigh News and Observer*, p. 13A.

Gross, J. (1991, February 11). New challenge of youth growing up in a gay home. *New York Times*, pp. 2B, 6B.

Guttmann, J. (1993). *Divorce in psychosocial perspective: Theory and research.* Hillsdale, NJ: Lawrence Erlbaum.

Indulgent "boomers" bring an unraveling of society. (1993, October 17). *Raleigh News and Observer*, p. 6E.

Marciano, T., & Sussman, M. B. (Eds.). (1991). *Wider families.* New York: Haworth Press.

Patterson, C. (1992). Children of lesbian and gay parents. *Child Development, 63,* 83–96.

Salter, S. (1996, April 7). With this ring I thee wed, or whatever. *San Francisco Examiner*, p. B-11.

Singer, B. L., & Deschamps, D. (Eds.). (1994). *Gay and lesbian stats: A pocket guide of facts and figures.* New York: The New Press.

Weston, K. (1991). *Families we choose.* New York: Columbia University Press.

Wood, J. T., & Duck, S. (Eds.). (1995). *Understanding relationship processes, 6: Understudied relationships: Off the beaten track.* Thousand Oaks, CA: Sage.

| 17 |

A FAIR SHARE

. . .

Perspectives On and Involvement

In Homemaking and Child Care

Last summer, I spent a week visiting my friends Andrea and Lewis. Andrea and I met in graduate school. We formed a close friendship then and it has lasted more than 20 years. A decade after we completed our graduate study, Andrea moved to Oklahoma where she met Lewis. After a whirlwind romance, they married and two years later had a son named James (Jamie) after Andrea's father.

During my visit, Andrea and I caught up on many things. We reminisced about our days in graduate school, and we talked about our current work — its pleasures and problems. We discussed our health, how we had changed over the years, and our dreams for the future. At one point we talked about our marriages. Often during graduate school, we had discussed our parents' traditional marriages and we had agreed that we didn't want the roles our mothers had held. We both pledged to have egalitarian marriages or none at all. I asked Andrea if her marriage with Lewis measured up to her egalitarian ideals.

"Well, we try," she equivocated.

"What does that mean?" I asked, wanting to know more.

"We both believe in equality between partners," she explained. "We both *want* to live out that belief, but, well, it just doesn't always work out."

"For instance?" I prompted.

"Housework."

"But I thought you told me you and Lewis had divided the household chores."

"We have divided them, but I still do more," she said, then added, "by a long shot."

We talked further and I learned that Andrea does jobs that aren't on the list if she notices they need doing. "Lewis vacuums once a week, just like it says on the list," she explained. "But sometimes the rugs get dirty during the week and I can't stand that, so I run the vacuum. And I always wind up spending more time taking care of Jamie. Lewis puts him to bed half the time, just like I do, but I fix his breakfast and lunch each day, and I'll make time to talk with him about what happens in his school. A lot of nights, Lewis says he's too busy or too tired. A six-year-old can't understand that! Lewis just doesn't pull a fair share."

Later during my visit, Lewis and I were hiking and talking about our lives. I asked him the same question I had earlier posed to Andrea: Do you and Andrea have an equal marriage? Lewis smiled and nodded, "Yes, we've really had to work at that, but we've created an equal partnership. We split the home chores and child care right down the middle."

"Does Andrea agree with you?"

"Sometimes she says I don't do enough," he admitted. "But I don't agree. I think about my father and how little he did. Once he came home each day, he didn't lift a hand to help mom. He never washed dishes or did the grocery shopping. It was always mom, never him, who took us to the doctor or dentist. Compared to my father, I'm doing great!"

"So you feel that you and Andrea share the work equally?"

"Sure. I'm always asking her if I can help her out."

Lewis believes he is doing a fair share of housework and child care. After all, compared to his father, he's "doing great." Yet Andrea tells me he "just doesn't pull his share." How can two people in the same marriage have such different perceptions of their contributions to homemaking and child care? Knowing both of them well, I am confident that Andrea isn't exaggerating her perceptions of the imbalance. I'm also sure that Lewis isn't inflating his perceptions of how much he contributes. Yet clearly, they have very different views of what's going on in their marriage. How can they hold such disparate understandings of how their relationship works?

In this chapter, we explore the ways couples distribute responsibility for homemaking and child care. Just as important as who actually does what is each person's *perceptions* of what she or he is doing. Thus, we also discuss how individuals talk to themselves and each other about responsibilities for domestic work and caregiving.

Understanding the Misunderstanding

Andrea and Lewis aren't alone. The majority of people in dual-worker relationships struggle to balance the demands of their paid jobs and their responsibilities for home and caregiving. And the majority of people don't manage to work out a truly 50–50 division of responsibilities for the "homework"—all of the work to be done in the home.

Perceived inequity in responsibilities for homes and children is a primary source of marital tension. Fewer than one in five marriages today is supported by a single wage earner. The vast majority of women now work outside the home, just as the majority of men do. And many of those women earn as much as or more than their husbands. Thus the traditional idea of the man as the family breadwinner is no longer a reality for many people.

The Second Shift

Despite changes in men's and women's financial contributions to their families, many people of both sexes continue to assume that women should and will be primary homemakers and caregivers. Sociologist Arlie Hochschild has dubbed this phenomenon "the second shift." According to Hochschild, many women work a full shift outside the home and then take on a second shift of work when they come home. In other words, most women today are working more outside the home and about as much inside the home as previous generations of women.

On the other hand, most husbands today continue to work about the same amount outside the home, but most haven't substantially increased the amount of work they do in their homes. Joseph Pleck reports that over three decades, from 1957 to 1987, the amount of housework and child care that husbands provide has risen a scant 10%—from 20% to 30%. So today, most women are doing 70% of the homework. Hochschild concurs, saying that in only 20% of dual-worker families do men's contributions to homemaking and child care match those of women.

Understand that Hochschild and others who have studied responsibility for housework and child care are not trying to "bash men." They are concerned about inequity, regardless of whom it burdens. At the present time, however, women are generally more likely than men to carry the bulk of domestic responsibilities.

Generally, husbands' contributions to homework don't increase significantly if their wives work outside the home. A recent *USA Today* survey reveals how much time young children in different countries spend with only their mothers, only their fathers, and both parents. The results show that, on average, mothers in the United States spend 10.7 hours each weekday caring for preschoolers—more than mothers in any of the other countries surveyed. On average, U.S. fathers spend 0.7 hour a day caring for their children—less than one hour a day. The table below summarizes the results of the survey.

Time Spent Daily Caring for Children

	MOTHER ONLY	FATHER ONLY	BOTH PARENTS
Belgium	5.2	0.5	3.2
Finland	7.7	0.8	2.1
Germany	10.0	0.6	1.9
Hong Kong	7.5	0.1	0.8
Nigeria	10.0	0.7	1.0
Portugal	8.2	0.4	1.6
Spain	7.6	0.3	2.3
Thailand	8.0	0.2	3.3
USA	10.7	0.7	0.9

As we will see, perceived inequities in homemaking and child care can't be blamed solely on one person. Both partners contribute to the perceived inequities and both can contribute to diminishing them. In other words, although research shows that most men don't do as much in homes as most women, we would be mistaken to conclude that men are the problem. Women, too, often behave in ways that maintain inequitable distributions of domestic responsibility.

Helping Out

Lewis says that he is always asking Andrea if he can "help her out." Many men do this. When their wives are preparing dinner, the husbands may offer to help by setting the table. When the wives are bathing children, the husbands may offer to help by getting fresh towels. But helping out is not the same as taking responsibility for doing something. Helping others implies that you are generously and voluntarily assisting them in doing *their* job. It reflects the assumption that the job is really theirs, not yours.

A few years ago, Pulitzer Prize–winning columnist Ellen Goodman wrote a column titled "When Grateful Begins to Grate." In this column she chronicled the feeling of many women whose husbands, like Lewis, offer to help their wives. Goodman noted that at first the women are grateful when men help out with housework or child care. Yet, continued Goodman, after a while, grateful becomes grating. It grates because women resent being grateful when men contribute in small ways to jobs that women think should be shared equally by spouses.

Goodman wrote, "The Grateful Wife began to wonder why she should say thank you when a father took care of his children and why she should say please when a husband took care of his house" (p. 93). When both adults in a family work outside the home, it's hard to justify inequity in their responsibilities for home and children. The Grateful Wife about whom Goodman wrote initially was grateful for a husband who would help, but that wife eventually wondered why her husband didn't share fully in the responsibilities of running their home and raising their children.

Taking care of the home and children is not the only kind of domestic responsibility that falls predominantly on women. As life spans increase, more and more people have parents and parents-in-law who are living to older ages and who require some assistance. A *Newsweek* article titled "The Daughter Track" reported that the average woman in the United States today will spend about 17 years raising children and 18 years caring for elderly parents and parents-in-law. In some cases the adult child will take over shopping, cleaning, and bill paying so that one or both parents can continue to live in their own homes. In other cases, adult children will invite parents and in-laws to move into their homes and will assist them there.

My own study of women's caregiving confirms the *Newsweek* report. The responsibility of caring for others usually falls on women, regardless of whether the others are blood relations or not. It tends to fall on women even when they don't live in the same town as the person who needs care and even if a son or brother does live in that town. Both others and women themselves seem to expect women to provide care, probably because women's role as caregiver is so firmly fixed in Western culture. From early childhood, many girls are socialized to view caring for others

BABY BLUES. *Reprinted by special permission of King Features Syndicate.*

as central to their identity. Typically girls are encouraged to be attentive, nurturing, and helpful to others.

As a result of their socialization, boys are less likely to see caring for others as central to who they are, and they are less likely to be taught that nurturing and helping others are priorities for them. Thus, the scripts that we learn as children may lead us as adult men and women to assume women should be more involved than men in caring for others. A key point to recognize is that both sexes are socialized to associate caregiving more with women than men. No wonder that Andrea and Lewis—and millions of other couples—play out this script in their families.

Psychological Responsibility

"And then there's all the other stuff," Andrea said.

"What other stuff?" I asked.

"All the stuff that isn't on the list. Who schedules appointments with the pediatrician? Who makes sure the dog gets his vaccines? Who remembers everyone's birthday? Who shops for holiday gifts? Who makes sure that we are stocked up on cleaning supplies? Who notices when there are sales? All that falls on me. Most of the time Lewis doesn't even notice all I do that isn't on the list."

The "stuff that's not on the list" is what Hochschild calls psychological responsibility. These are the obligations to remember, plan, coordinate, follow through, and so forth. For example, many spouses agree to share the responsibility of taking children to the doctor, but it is typically the mother who remembers when various inoculations are due and schedules appointments. It's usually the mother who notices when a child needs medical attention. More often than not, it's the mother who keeps track of whose turn it is to accompany the child to the doctor or dentist. Husbands often ask their wives "When is mom's birthday?" or, as December rolls around, "Have we gotten a present for my sister?"

All this remembering, planning, and coordinating is seldom counted in a couple's formal list of responsibilities for home and family. Typically, psychological responsibility is invisible work. Unnoticed and unappreciated are all the managerial tasks of taking care of a home and children. These tasks that women usually do amount to what Ellen Goodman calls the "moonlighting job of household manager," but because the job consists of invisible work, the manager is unlikely to receive thanks or even notice for the work. All of us, both women and men, are likely to be resentful when our work is taken for granted.

In her most recent book, *The Time Bind: When Work Becomes Home and Home Becomes Work*, Hochschild explains a primary reason that many people — both women and men — are working longer hours at their paid jobs and are increasingly resenting home responsibilities. Her research shows that many people feel their work in the paid labor force is more valued and recognized than their work in the home. All of us like to have our efforts acknowledged, so it's understandable that invisible labor may not feel rewarding. Historically, home was viewed as a retreat from the pressures of public and work life. According to Hochschild, that may no longer be true for the many people who work full days outside the home (often 10 to 12 hours) and then come home to different pressures awaiting them there.

Standards for Judging Men's Contributions

Like Lewis, many men believe they are doing their share of work in the home. And many women, like Andrea, feel that their partners aren't contributing equally. One of the reasons for the discrepancy in perceptions is that partners often use different standards for measuring men's contributions. When women and men think about how much each of them contributes to homework, they're likely to reach different judgments because they don't rely on the same criteria to measure men's contributions.

In her study of dual-worker couples, Hochschild found that many men, like Lewis, compare their contributions to those their fathers made. Their fathers belonged to a generation in which most men assumed little responsibility for household chores and child care. Today most men who contribute in any substantial way to housework and child care easily surpass their fathers. Not surprisingly, men who compare themselves to their fathers may conclude that they are carrying a fair share or, as Lewis says, "doing great."

Women in dual-worker families, however, tend to use a different standard of judgment. They compare what their husbands contribute to what they contribute. This does not cause them to conclude that their husbands are contributing generously. Instead, it leaves many women feeling, as Andrea does, that their husbands are not doing a fair share.

The Buffer Zone

"And when he's tired from a stressful day at the office, he expects to relax when he gets home," Andrea told me. "When I'm tired or stressed out, I'm still supposed to fix dinner and bathe Jamie and pay the bills. That's one of the biggest gripes I have. It's just so unfair for him to think he deserves down time but I never do."

Andrea's comments point to one of the more subtle inequities in many dual-worker marriages. Ann Coulter and Heather Helms-Erickson are human relation specialists on the faculty of the Pennsylvania State University who study this inequity. They label it the *buffer zone*, which is an allowance for a spouse not to do the usual household chores and child care. According to Coulter and Helms-Erickson and other researchers, the buffer zone is more often provided to husbands than wives. Many men seem to expect some reprieve from normal tasks in the home, and they often get it. When men come home stressed and tired from their paid jobs, many of them feel a need to relax, and they give themselves permission not to do their normal household chores and to reduce their time with their children. Customarily, wives accommodate husbands' need for down time by taking over the abandoned responsibilities. Yet when women come home stressed and tired from their paid jobs, typically there is no buffer zone that they or their husbands create for them.

Both women and men generally accept men's need to relax at times, and both think it is normal to provide men with a buffer zone from pressures and responsibilities in the home. Yet many men and some women don't assume women are entitled to the same buffering from life's stresses. The fact that men and not women are typically protected probably reflects traditional divisions of labor. The wife's conventional role as homemaker and mother seeps into current-day arrangements, even when it is no longer fair or reflective of the multiple responsibilities of both spouses.

Unequal access to a buffer zone after a taxing day in the paid work force may account for differences in how women and men feel when they are at home. Recent studies show that wives who work outside the home report feeling most positive about themselves and their lives when they are in their workplaces. For those who return home to the second shift, their sense of well-being and satisfaction decreases. Home offers them no haven, no reprieve from pressure and responsibility. Researchers believe the decline in wives' emotional mood is due substantially to the reality that they usually do the majority of housework and child care after putting in a full and stressful day's work in their paid jobs.

The same pattern doesn't hold for husbands. In general, they report feeling most negative in the workplace, where no buffer zone is provided for them. They are expected to perform their jobs, regardless of whether they are tired, sick, or stressed. For husbands more than wives, the home may still represent a haven in which they can escape responsibilities and stress. Not surprisingly, men generally feel more positive about themselves and their lives when they are home and not on constant call to take care of everybody and everything that needs doing.

But Women Are Responsible, Too

At this point in the chapter, if you are a woman you may be thinking that men are the problem because they don't carry a fair division of the work-load. If you are a man, you may be feeling defensive about what you per-ceive as criticism of men. But wait a minute—families are systems that both men and women design and sustain. If there are inequities in family life, then women, as well as men, must contribute to them.

Sure enough, when we consult the research we find that women often play a critical part in sustaining their roles as primary caregivers and homemakers. One way they do this is by accepting inequity as normal. For example, women reinforce inequity when they buffer men but don't ask their partners to buffer them when they need a reprieve from pressure. According to Hochschild's research, a number of women also justify men's lack of interest in housework, but they do not excuse themselves from doing the work. In other words, many women hold themselves to dif-ferent standards than those they apply to men for housework and caring. That's a fair choice if and only if women accept the consequences of the choice—namely, doing more household chores and spending more time with children and others who need care. It isn't fair, however, for women to take on extra responsibilities and then to blame men for not doing more.

Many men would be pleased to take over more of the responsibility for homemaking and child care if their partners asked or allowed them to do so. Yet for many women, self-concept is tied to being a good home-maker and mother, and that holds true even for a good portion of those who work full time outside the home. A colleague of mine offered an insight that is pertinent to our discussion. After he read an early draft of this chapter, he said to me, "My wife would be very upset with me if I tried to stop her from being the primary caregiver for our children. Her role as primary caregiver has nothing to do with my encouragement of that role or my desire that she do that role." As this man perceptively observed, his wife has her own self-definition and that involves being a primary caregiver.

Research by clinician Virginia Goldner and her colleagues supports this man's insights. Through their work in family therapy, Goldner's research team has concluded that homemaking and especially caregiving are central to many women's self-concepts. These women would feel inadequate if they were not heavily involved in taking care of homes and people, and they would resent anyone, including their husbands, who tried to usurp their roles. Because of this attitude, women often contribute to inequitable divisions of labor in families.

The Toll of Inequity

Regardless of why inequities exist in homemaking and caregiving responsibilities, they have serious consequences. A good deal of research shows a direct and strong connection between the amount of husbands' domestic contributions and wives' satisfaction with marriages. In addition, wives' physical and psychological health are affected by inequity. Hochschild reports that wives whose husbands don't contribute equally in the home suffer more minor and major physical problems than women whose husbands share the responsibilities. These overburdened wives endure emotional stress that ranges from disagreeable to debilitating. Finally, many wives resent inequity and don't perceive their contributions to the inequitable state of affairs. Over time, that resentment can poison a marriage.

Improving Communication

Like Lewis and Andrea, many couples want and try to achieve egalitarian unions. They intend to share equally in homemaking chores and child care. Too often, however, equal sharing isn't realized, and partners may have dramatically different perceptions of who is doing what and of what is happening in their relationship. Because the toll of inequity is substantial, couples need to develop mutual understandings about their work in the home. Research conducted in a variety of fields illuminates four steps a husband and wife may take to reduce inequity and its undesirable consequences in their relationships.

Notice and Communicate About "Invisible Labor"

A first step in increasing understanding is to make invisible labor visible. Psychological responsibility is a major and ongoing part of the work in any family, yet it is often unseen and unappreciated. None of us likes to do things for others that the others disregard. Such tasks are thankless and they generate resentment that is unhealthy for relationships.

Partners can develop more consistent perceptions of what each person does if they learn to notice and name the invisible labor of remembering, coordinating, planning, and following up. These responsibilities can be added to a partner's perceptions of tangible chores for running a home and caring for children. Also, partners can confirm each other by noticing and commenting on formerly invisible labor. It's a good idea to say, "Thanks for remembering Fido needed a rabies shot" or "I appreciate your following up on the insurance claim." When others notice what we do, we are more likely to feel good about the efforts we make.

Develop Shared Standards for Assessing Contributions

Agreeing on standards for assessment is a second way to generate shared understandings of how much each partner contributes to household chores and care for dependents. As we saw with Andrea and Lewis, a common practice is for husbands and wives to use different standards to assess how much each person does. As long as partners don't understand that they are relying on distinct standards of judgment, they are likely to continue to misunderstand each other.

Dual-worker couples can improve their understanding and their relationship by agreeing on a standard for evaluating each person's contributions. Andrea might say to Lewis, "The reason it seems to me that I do more than my share is that you don't do as much as I do." Lewis might explain to Andrea, "The reason I think I'm pulling my share is that I do so much more than my father did." Understanding each other's perspective is a first step in creating an equitable relationship, because couples can communicate to generate a shared perspective on how to assess each person's contributions.

Monitor the Self-Serving Bias

Psychologists and communication scholars have studied what they call the *self-serving bias*. As you might suspect, this is a tendency to explain things in ways that serve our self-interests. Based on her studies of self-serving bias, communication scholar Beverly Sypher notes that most of us don't see ourselves as others see us. We also don't tend to see others as they see themselves. Instead, most people tend to notice what they do more than they notice what others do. Two types of this behavior are especially common and both pertain directly to the issues we've discussed in this chapter.

The first form of self-serving bias is a tendency to be more aware of our contributions than those of others. This bias commonly surfaces in varied contexts, including the workplace, groups, personal relationships, and families. Thus, Lewis's perception that he does a lot may reflect his greater awareness of what he does than what Andrea does. Andrea's opinion that she does more than Lewis is probably influenced by her perceiving all her contributions and not noticing all the ways Lewis gives to the family.

A second form of self-serving bias involves giving ourselves credit for what we do well and excusing ourselves for what we do poorly or don't do at all. For example, Andrea may think she is a good wife and mother because she always makes time to prepare nutritious meals and spend time with her son. She may excuse herself for not being a thrifty shopper by reasoning that "I don't have time to clip coupons and figure out which store is having sales and I can't do anything about prices anyway." Notice that what Andrea credits in herself she attributes to stable factors (she *always* prepares good meals and spends time with her son) that are within her control (she *makes* time). On the other hand, she avoids full responsibility for not being a thrifty shopper by blaming external factors (time, store sales) and circumstances beyond her personal control ("I can't do anything about prices anyway").

When we flip the coin, however, we find that attributional tendencies also flip: We're more likely to attribute what we perceive as shortcomings in others to stable and internal factors (he's not a responsible parent) and to circumstances that others could control if they wanted to (all he needs to do is make time; he should leave work earlier). Thus, the self-serving bias can lead us to judge ourselves a bit too generously and to judge others a bit too harshly.

Give Authority When You Give Responsibility

Finally, partners should consider the value of linking authority with responsibility. Lewis once told me of the first time he wrapped holiday gifts. Andrea walked in and began to correct him: "No, you have to tuck the side of the wrapping paper over before you tape it." "Don't use that bow with that paper. This one is better." "You have to put that gift in a box before you wrap it." Finally, Lewis gave up on wrapping. No wonder: He volunteered to do a job, but she insisted that he do it her way. Other men have told me of being discouraged from cooking, feeding babies, and so forth by women's constant corrections and criticisms.

Whenever we give people responsibility for a task, we should also grant them the authority to do the task their own way. This may mean Lewis won't wrap packages and vacuum the way Andrea would and that Andrea won't keep records and shop the way Lewis would. They may need to adjust their individual standards for various tasks to allow both of them the authority to meet responsibilities on their own terms.

In this chapter, we've dealt with an issue that is critical to achieving satisfaction in enduring romantic relationships. Fairness in responsibility for home life is important for everyone involved—partners and children, if there are any. Equity in domestic responsibilities is not strictly a gender issue. Although research shows that women more often than men do the majority of housework and child care, this isn't always the case. Furthermore, it doesn't matter *who* does the majority, whether a woman or a man is burdened with more than a fair share. What *does* matter is that inequity is harmful; it interferes with physical and emotional health, with performance on the paid job, and with satisfaction in relationships. Inequity hurts whether someone is doing more or less than others. When we feel we're doing more than our share, we get resentful and angry (not to mention tired). When we think we're not carrying a fair share, we may feel guilty. The costs of unfairly distributed responsibilities are so great as to provide a strong motivation to work for equity in our relationships.

There is no single formula for ensuring that each partner has a fair share of the work involved in running a home and nurturing a family. Couples work out different arrangements to suit their circumstances, values, and unique relationships. That's fine as long as both people are satisfied that their arrangement is fair. In an era when most women and men hold a job for pay and also work inside the home, partners must talk openly and honestly about their expectations, standards for judgment, and feelings regarding household chores and responsibilities for caring for children and other family members. It's equally important for each person to be aware of and to guard against possible perceptual distortions, such as the self-serving bias. Developing shared understandings and perspectives on domestic responsibilities is possible if partners commit to frank and fair communication.

Key Words

- buffer zone
- dual-worker relationships
- inequity
- invisible work
- psychological responsibility
- second shift
- self-serving bias

Reflecting on This Chapter

1. Think about what you contribute in your marriage or romantic relationship (or past ones). What standard do you use to assess your contributions? Do you compare what you do (or did) to what your partner does (or did), or do you compare what you do (or did) to what your same-sex parent did when you were growing up?

2. Research shows a strong gender influence on psychological responsibility. Find out whether this gender influence affects men and women that you know. Ask five men and five women to tell you the birthdays of their parents (or stepparents), each of their siblings (or stepsiblings), and the date of their parents' (or stepparents') anniversary. Ask your parents or stepparents who remembers medical appointments, veterinarian care, and so forth. What do your findings tell you about the influence of gender on psychological responsibility within your circle of friends?

3. What do you think about Ellen Goodman's idea that grateful can become grating? Have you ever offered to "help out" other people? If so, did you assume that you were helping them with *their* jobs, not participating equally in jobs for which you and they had equal responsibility?

4. If you are in a committed relationship, how much of a buffer zone do you have when you come home after a stressful day in your paid job or at school? How much buffering is your partner granted when she or he

returns home after a stressful day at work? If you aren't in a committed relationship, think about how much of a buffer is extended to each partner in couples you know, including your family.

5. What do you think of the idea that responsibility should be accompanied by authority? Have you ever been assigned responsibility for doing something but not been given the authority to do it your way? Have you ever asked others to do something and then interfered with how they choose to do the task? Is this fair? Does it encourage taking responsibility in relationships?

6. Have you ever enacted the self-serving bias? Think about how you account for your own shortcomings and those of others and how you explain your own good deeds and theirs. Do you use the same kinds of explanations for yourself and other people? If not, experiment with making more generous assumptions about others. Does this change your perceptions of and feelings about them?

References

Bolger, N., DeLongis, A., Kessler, R. C., & Wethington, E. (1989). The contagion of stress across multiple roles. *Journal of Marriage and the Family, 51,* 175–183.

Bruess, C., & Pearson, J. (1996). Gendered patterns in family communication. In J. T. Wood (Ed.), *Gendered relationships* (pp. 59–78). Mountain View, CA: Mayfield.

Burley, K. A. (1991). Family-work spillover in dual-career couples: A comparison of two time perspectives. *Psychological Reports, 68,* 471–480.

Crosby, F. (1991). *Juggling: The unexpected advantages of balancing career and home for women and their families.* New York: Free Press.

Crouter, A. C., & Helms-Erikson, H. (1997). Work and family from a dyadic perspective: Variations in inequality. In S. Duck (Ed.), *Handbook of personal relationships* (2nd ed., pp. 487–503). West Sussex, England: Wiley.

The daughter track. (1990, July 16) *Newsweek,* pp. 48–54.

Fowers, B. J. (1991). His and her marriage: A multivariate study of gender and marital satisfaction. *Sex Roles, 24,* 209–221.

Goldner, V., Penn, P., Sheinberg, M., & Walker, G. (1990). Love and violence: Gender paradoxes in volatile attachments. *Family Process, 29,* 343–364.

Goodman, E. (1981). When grateful begins to grate. In E. Goodman, *At large* (pp. 92–93). New York: Summit.

Gottman, J. M., & Carrere, S. (1994). Why can't men and women get along? Developmental roots and marital inequities. In D. Canary & L. Stafford (Eds.), *Communication and relational maintenance* (pp. 203–229). New York: Academic Press.

Gottman, J. M., & Levenson, R. W. (1986). Assessing the role of emotion in marriage. *Behavioral Assessment, 8*, 31–48.

Gottman, J. M., & Levenson, R. W. (1988). The social psychophysiology of marriage. In P. Noller & M. A. Fitzpatrick (Eds.), *Perspectives on marital interaction* (pp. 182–200). Clevedon, UK: Multilingual Matters.

Gottman, J. M., & Levenson, R. W. (1992). Marital processes predictive of later dissolution: Behavior, physiology, and health. *Journal of Personality and Social Psychology, 63*, 221–233.

Hamchek, D. (1992). *Encounters with the self* (3rd ed.). Fort Worth, TX: Harcourt Brace Jovanovich.

Henry, T. (1995, January 1). For child care, mom is home alone. *USA Today*, p. D1.

Hochschild, A. (1997). *The time bind: When work becomes home and home becomes work*. New York: Metropolitan Books.

Hochschild, A., with Machung, A. (1989). *The second shift: Working parents and the revolution at home*. New York: Viking/Penguin.

Larson, R., & Richards, M. H. (1994). *Divergent realities: The emotional lives of mothers, fathers, and adolescents*. New York: Basic Books.

Nussbaum, M. (1992, October 18). Justice for women. *New York Review of Books*, pp. 43–48.

Okin, S. (1989). *Justice, gender and the family*. New York: Basic Books.

Pleck, J. (1987). American fathering in historical perspective. In M. S. Kimmel (Ed.), *Changing men: New directions in research on men and masculinity* (pp. 83–97). Newbury Park, CA: Sage.

Shellenbarger, S. (1997, 16 April). For many, work seems like a retreat compared with home. *Wall Street Journal*, p. B1.

Suitor, J. (1991). Marital quality and satisfaction with the division of household labor across the family life cycle. *Journal of Marriage and the Family, 53*, 221–230.

Sypher, B. (1984). Seeing ourselves as others see us. *Communication Research, 11*, 97–115.

Thompson, L., & Walker, A. (1989). Gender in families: Women and men in marriage, work, and parenthood. *Journal of Marriage and the Family, 51*, 845–871.

Wilkie, J. (1991). The decline in men's labor force participation and income and the changing structure of family economic support. *Journal of Marriage and the Family, 53*, 111–122.

Wood, J. T. (1994). *Who cares?: Women, care and culture*. Carbondale: Southern Illinois University Press.

Wood, J. T. (1994). Engendered identities: Shaping voice and mind through gender. In D. Vocate (Ed.), *Intrapersonal communication: Different voices, different minds* (pp. 145–167). Hillsdale, NJ: Lawrence Erlbaum.

Yougev, S. (1987). Marital satisfaction and sex role perceptions among dual-career couples. *Journal of Social and Personal Relationships, 4*, 35–46.

| 18 |

I CAN'T TALK ABOUT IT NOW

. . .

Understanding Different Orientations

to Conflict

Takisha and William are locked into a tense discussion, the latest in a series of arguments about whether they will move to Minnesota. Takisha has been offered the job of her dreams: vice president of a training and development firm located in Minneapolis. William has never lived outside of Virginia, and he has no desire to do so now.

"This job is an exceptional opportunity for me," Takisha says, repeating what she has told William before. "Can't you understand that?"

"I see that, but it's not an opportunity for me, and you don't see that," William replies. "You have a good job here. We both do. Why can't you let well enough alone?"

"Because it isn't good enough when I have such a big chance to advance."

"It is good enough, good enough for me, anyway!"

"But you can be a network technician anywhere. Your career doesn't depend on being here, so a move wouldn't damage your career. I can't go any farther in my job here. I can only advance if we move to Minneapolis. Not moving would damage my career."

"You have a fine career here. Why can't you just be satisfied and leave well enough alone?"

"You're not being reasonable."

"I am being reasonable. But life is about more than jobs. We can't live anywhere. This is our home." William paces as he speaks. "We don't belong in Minnesota."

"William, I know you're comfortable here. I know you love Virginia," Takisha says. "I can understand that. But can't you at least *try* living somewhere else? You might find you like it."

"I wouldn't like it. I don't need to try living there to know I won't like it. I hate snow and cold weather, and I don't like the hassles of a big city."

"So you're saying that a place means more to you than I do?" she demands.

"You said that. I didn't."

"That's the only conclusion I can draw if you refuse to move, knowing what this means to me." She moves closer to him. "Please work with me to make this happen."

"Stop trying to control me," he barks. "You're not going to roll over me just to get what you want."

"I'm not trying to roll over you. I'm trying to figure out how to come to some decision that works for both of us."

"I plan to stay here, with or without you." He clamps his jaw firmly and stares ahead at the wall.

"Sweetheart, you can't mean that," she says softly. "We can work this out if we really try."

William moves away and cradles his head in his hands. He doesn't speak.

"Don't go silent on me, William," she says. "The only way we can work this out is to keep talking."

"I'm talked out," he mumbles.

"But we haven't resolved the issue," she insists. "We have to keep talking until we work it out."

He shakes his head and doesn't speak.

"William, what would it take to persuade you to move to Minneapolis?" she asks. "What would make the move comfortable for you?"

"Nothing. I don't want to move." His voice is tense and tired.

"Well, that's not good enough. Come on, talk to me about what would make this move good for you."

"Nothing. I don't want to move, period."

"Please don't be so inflexible," she asks. "There have to be ways we can work out something that suits both of us. How about an experiment? We'll move to Minnesota and commit to staying there for one year. At the end of that time, if you're not happy, we can reassess our options. How does that sound?"

"Just let me be," he says, moving across the room.

"How can I do that when we aren't through with this discussion?"

"We are through. I'm talked out," he says, his voice strained and his jaw muscles flexing tensely.

"William, not talking doesn't solve anything," she insists. "Please talk to me."

"I can't talk about this now," he thunders and stomps to the door, opens it, walks out, and slams it behind him.

What is Takisha to think when William walks out on her and the argument? Often people in Takisha's position think the other person is refusing to deal with conflict. They feel that the other person (William in this case) doesn't care enough about the relationship to work through problems. Takisha may feel that when William stomps out he is dismissing the importance of her career and is disrespecting their relationship.

But Takisha's feelings are only half the picture. What is William feeling? He may feel pressured by Takisha's demands for talk. He may feel she is trying to control him by manipulating him to do what she wants. He may not share Takisha's view that she's inviting him to collaborate. Also, he may not be comfortable talking about deep feelings, such as his attachment to Virginia and his anxiety about moving to an unfamiliar place.

Why does he walk out instead of working with Takisha to resolve the issue? Takisha perceives his departure as a sign that he doesn't care about her or the issue, but that may not be what leaving means to William. Perhaps he leaves because he cares so strongly about Takisha and the relationship that the discord between them is tearing him up. Perhaps he feels so strongly about not moving he is afraid he'll become belligerent, or even violent, if he doesn't leave. Perhaps he sees leaving as the only way to avoid letting the conflict degenerate into open warfare. Perhaps he sees nothing to be gained by staying and talking more because he doesn't know what else to say.

If Takisha understands how William perceives conflict, she might realize that his leaving is not a sign that he doesn't care about her career or their relationship. If William figures out that Takisha sees talking as a way to make them closer, maybe he will feel less pressured by her requests to talk. And perhaps if each of them learns that people have different ways of responding to conflict, they can better understand how each views conflict and why they both respond as they do.

Understanding the Misunderstanding

Psychologist Caryl Rusbult and her colleagues have studied how people respond to interpersonal conflict. Rusbult's work shows four basic responses to conflict. These are habitual responses that we learned at some point and now repeat without much thought or contemplation of alternative ways we might respond when tension surfaces in relationships.

The Exit-Voice-Loyalty-Neglect Model

Rusbult graphs responses to conflict in terms of whether they are active (assertive) or passive (yielding) and whether they affect relationships in ways that are constructive (preserve the possibility of continuing the union) or destructive (undermine the relationship and its future).

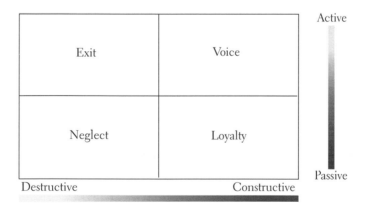

The *exit response* is to leave an argument or even end a relationship when conflict arises. William relied on the exit response when he stomped out on the conversation with Takisha. Another version of the exit response is what marriage counselor John Gottman calls "stonewalling." The person who stonewalls refuses to discuss problems and conflicts. The stonewaller may stick around, but he or she will not talk about problems. Exit, then, may be physical or psychological; either way, the person who

KUDZU. By permission of Doug Marlette and Creators Syndicate.

exits ceases to be involved in the conflict. Exit is an active response
because it is forceful. Because it doesn't allow people to resolve differences, however, it can damage relationships.

The *neglect response* occurs when a person denies or minimizes problems. When presented with a problem, the neglecter may say, "You're
making a mountain out of a molehill" or "You're blowing this all out of
proportion." William used the neglect response when he told Takisha that
her career advancement is less important than other things in life.
Neglecters often gloss over tensions and conflicts rather than deal with
them. Because neglect is not forceful, Rusbult labels it passive. Because it
doesn't address problems fully and with respect for each person's feelings,
neglect can be destructive for relationships.

Loyalty responses involve quietly staying loyal to a partner and a relationship. Someone who uses this response may silently hope things will
get better. Alternatively, she or he may think, "It could be worse" or "This
doesn't matter a whole lot in the big picture." Loyalty may also be
expressed by transferring anger or blame from the other person to oneself:
"I should have known better." "I expect too much." Because loyalty
doesn't assertively engage problems, it is passive. Because it assumes a
relationship is worth continuing, it can have a constructive impact on
relationships and people's feelings for each other.

The fourth response is *voice*, which is an active way to manage conflict. The voice response engages the conflict and invites the other person
to collaborate in resolving it. "Let's talk about our problem" is a voice
response. "I want to work this out with you" and "I'm willing to discuss the
issue" are also voice responses. Because voice actively works to resolve
problems, Rusbult considers it constructive for relationships.

In the example that opened this chapter, William used the neglect
and exit responses, and Takisha relied on voice. According to Rusbult,

their responses are typical of their respective sexes. Her research shows that men are more likely than women to respond with neglect or exit. Women, on the other hand, are more likely than men to choose voice and loyalty when conflicts arise.

The Influence of Gender

Some scholars think the different response tendencies of women and men reflect gender socialization. Psychologist Carol Gilligan maintains that women are socialized to value relationships and to use talk as a way of maintaining them. Masculine socialization typically places less emphasis on talk. As a result, many men have little or no training in how to talk about problems, especially problems that involve strong feelings. They may also feel frustrated if they can't fix a problem. Masculine socialization encourages men to fix things, to engage in instrumental activities that solve problems. If men feel they cannot do this when conflict erupts, they may communicate that the problem is unimportant or they may walk out on discussion or even the relationship.

Anne Campbell has studied links between aggression and gender. She reports that boys and girls typically are taught different meanings for conflict. She explains that girls are most often taught to respond to conflicts by talking (voice) and turning anger and disappointment inward (loyalty). Masculine socialization is more likely to encourage aggressive responses to conflict—asserting dominance to maintain control and self-esteem. Many boys are also taught not to harm girls, however, so they may not feel able to respond aggressively in conflicts with women. It's not surprising, then, that men might choose to minimize conflicts (neglect) or leave when arguments erupt (exit) rather than risk losing control or acting aggressively toward women.

Further insight into the link between gender and responses to conflict comes from psychologist Eleanor Maccoby, who has studied socialization patterns typically experienced by girls and boys. Maccoby informs us that, at early ages, many boys are taught to derail tense interaction by threatening, inhibiting, contradicting, or topping a partner. William contradicted several of Takisha's statements and he issued a veiled threat to break up their relationship if she insisted on moving. He also showed little empathy with Takisha's feelings and desires. When these measures don't work, boys (and later the men they become) may feel they can't get control, so they exit rather than suffer outright defeat.

Girls, more often than boys, are taught to enable others in conversations. Typically, they learn to try to understand what others need and feel and to support others, even while disagreeing with them. Takisha expressed understanding of William's love of Virginia and his reluctance to move, and she tried to get him to talk with her about what he would need to be comfortable moving to Minneapolis.

John Gottman adds to our understanding of differences in how women and men typically respond to conflict. He maintains that men and women have different physiological reactions to tension and confrontation. During such times, men's blood pressure rises more quickly and stays elevated for longer periods of time than does women's. In other words, many men have a more intense physiological response to conflict than do women. Thus, it may cost men more than women to engage in conflict.

Working with his colleague Sybil Carrère, Gottman studied men and women in marriages in which they were in conflict about responsibilities for homemaking and child care (see Chapter 19 for a fuller discussion of this topic). Husbands often felt flooded by their wives' complaints. The men felt overwhelmed by criticisms and complaints. They felt psychologically and physiologically deluged and this disabled them from responding constructively. The women were less likely to feel flooded when they encountered negative emotions and criticism, and were more likely to feel that they could continue dealing with conflict.

Why do men and women differ so often in initiating and responding to discussions of problems? Carol Tavris, a social psychologist, suggests that women are expected by others and themselves to be "relationship experts," so it is their job to notice problems and to work to address and resolve them. Girls and later women, says Tavris, have the role of identifying and bringing up problems in relationships. In childhood socialization, many girls learn how to talk about interpersonal tensions. Because they have experience in working through problems, dealing with conflict tends to be less uncomfortable for them psychologically and physiologically than it is for many men.

Psychologist Sharon Brehm extends Tavris's analysis by suggesting that women's socialization tends to make them sensitive to and aware of existing and potential problems in relationships. They may also see as problems events or conditions that men do not perceive or consider significant. In other words, women may feel a need to address issues that men don't perceive as difficulties, disappointments, and failed expectations. Brehm suggests that this difference may reflect women's higher expectations of relationships.

My own research confirms what we've discussed in this chapter. Several years ago I asked heterosexual women and men to describe how they responded to crises in their relationships. Although there weren't differences in the issues men and women cited as precipitating crises, there were clear differences in how they responded to the events. Men were more likely to deny that any difficulty existed (neglect) or to walk out (exit) when an acute problem erupted. Women consistently gave priority to voice as a means of responding to these extreme difficulties. If voice failed, many of the women in my studied relied on loyalty—quiet allegiance to the relationship despite its problems.

I later replicated my study with lesbians and gay men. Again, I found that men tended to respond to crises by neglecting problems and especially by walking out on relationships. Again, the women gave priority to talking about problems, to working collaboratively to resolve issues or at least to understand each other. Caryl Rusbult and her colleagues confirm my findings by reporting that gender is more important than sexual orientation in shaping people's responses to conflict in relationships.

Improving Communication

The first step in dealing effectively with conflicts is to understand that people differ in how they view and respond to problems, tensions, and crises. Someone who doesn't know how to talk about feelings and fears may not see voice as a useful or helpful response to conflict. A person who experiences substantial physiological discomfort when relationship tension arises may be less willing to engage in conflict than someone who is less physiologically taxed by it. A person who has been socialized to believe people should talk through differences may regard exit as a dismissive and counterproductive response to problems. On the other hand, someone who doesn't feel comfortable talking about problems may regard exit as a reasonable response to conflict.

Try to Understand Different Views of Conflict

William and Takisha might improve their communication if they realize they don't see conflict in the same way. To her, it's a call to engage, talk, and resolve problems. To him, it's a contest for control and he doesn't want to lose. In other words, they have different constitutive rules for what conflict is, or what it counts as.

The relationship would benefit if William understood that Takisha isn't trying to control him; that's not what arguments are about for her. The relationship would also be helped if Takisha understood that William feels pressured by her needs and her demands for talk and that he views conflict as a competition for power.

People who have different individual ways of responding to conflict can develop a variety of strategies for talking about tense topics without harming their relationships. I know of one couple much like William and Takisha. Like the men in John Gottman's studies, the man in this couple felt emotionally flooded when his wife brought up problems or complaints. He felt that she was trying to control him, to remake him into a person different from who he was. Early in their marriage, he would deny or minimize conflicts or he would stonewall. His wife relied on voice and was hurt continuously when he wouldn't talk with her. She interpreted his behavior as expressing a lack of caring about her and problems in their relationship.

When the couple's efforts to resolve their differences were unsuccessful, they sought therapy. After several months of counseling, each one began to understand how the other viewed conflict and why each of them responded in particular ways when tension arose in their relationship. Now when he feels emotionally flooded and unable to respond, he doesn't just leave. Instead, he says, "I can't talk about it now, but I promise I will later when I've thought it through." This signals his wife that he does care about the issues and will discuss them — but later, after he's calmed down and regained the sense of control he needs. His response gives her the assurance she needs that he will collaborate with her to resolve the problem. It also gives him the time and space he needs to regain his emotional equilibrium.

Evaluate Your Responses to Conflict

Because our responses to conflict tend to be habituated, we seldom reflect on them. If we think about our ways of dealing with conflict, however, we may discover that they don't always serve us well. Realizing this provides us with an incentive to change how we act and what consequences follow.

An acquaintance of mine realized she was hurting herself and her relationship by not giving voice to her dissatisfactions and frustrations. As she explained to me, "They don't go away. They fester in me." She relied on the loyalty response virtually any time she encountered conflict with friends or romantic partners. Because that response did not enhance her self-esteem or her relationships, she worked to learn to voice her concerns assertively but not aggressively. She now feels that her relationships are more honest and healthy and she has greater self-respect.

Enlarge Your Response Repertoire

Another way to improve communication during conflict is to broaden your ways of responding to relationship tensions. Most of us have one or two habitual ways of reacting when problems erupt—behaviors for dealing with interpersonal tension that are almost automatic. Some of us consistently respond by trying to talk about the problems; others of us unfailingly react by refusing to discuss the issues or even by walking out on relationships.

Yet habitual ways of reacting to conflict are neither permanent nor absolute, and they may not be the most constructive ways for us to use. With commitment and patience, we can change our usual patterns of dealing with relationship tensions. Takisha might adopt the loyalty response so that William has some time to mull over the issues before talking about them. William could commit to talking about his feelings about the move, difficult as that would be for him. The point is that we can choose to move out of the restrictive framework of our habitual responses to conflict. Doing so allows us to communicate in ways that are effective in a range of situations that invite diverse modes of response.

We don't change our habituated responses to conflict easily or immediately. To do so, we must make firm commitments to changing and we must develop patience. The first requirement for change is a serious commitment to learning new ways of viewing and responding to conflict. Unless you really want to change, you can't. You may find the motivation to do so, however, if you realize that your habitual ways of responding to conflict are not serving you or your relationships well.

The second requirement for change is patience. We need to be patient with ourselves and our partners. It's unrealistic to expect that the first few times we use an unfamiliar response style we will do it with maximum effectiveness. It's much more realistic to realize that the more we try a new style, the more comfortable and skillful we will be in using it. We also need to be patient with our partners. Like us, they have habituated responses to conflict and to our ways of dealing with it. When we change our approach to conflict, they may not immediately change how they respond to us. Given time and consistent effort to become proficient in new response styles, our partners and we will change the way we communicate about difficult issues.

Conflicts are part of relationships and human interaction. They're inevitable and they can be productive for us as individuals and for our relationships. Their productivity, however, depends on two conditions. First, we should recognize and respect different ways of responding to conflicts. Second, we should reflect on our own responses to conflicts and ask whether they are effective, honest, and respectful of ourselves and others. If not, we have the freedom to choose to become proficient in other modes of responding. We can change how we act and, if we do, we will influence changes in our partners and the relationships we collaboratively create and inhabit.

Key Words

- conflict
- exit response
- gender socialization
- loyalty response
- neglect response
- voice response

Reflecting on This Chapter

1. Psychologist John Gottman reports that there are physiological differences in how women and men respond to conflict. Do you think physiological differences are innate, or is it possible that socialization teaches men to respond to conflicts more intensely than women?

2. How does Caryl Rusbult's model of responses to conflict fit with your experience in relationships? Can you identify patterns in your responses to conflict? Can you identify patterns in your partners' responses to conflict? Can you see why you and others have sometimes not been able to agree on how to deal with tensions and problems?

3. In her model, Caryl Rusbult labels *exit* as destructive and *voice* as passive. Another perspective is that exit can sometimes be constructive —for instance, if the alternative is emotional and/or physical violence. Voice might be destructive if it forces confrontation or floods the other person. Should we temper Rusbult's labels for these responses?

4. In this chapter, you read about gender-related differences in responses to conflict. Which of the explanations do you find most credible? Do you think women are more sensitive than men to relationship problems, have higher expectations for relationships than men, or both?

5. Try out this chapter's advice to move beyond your habituated responses to conflict. If you typically have relied on neglect and exit responses, try using voice. If you routinely respond to conflict with voice, consider loyalty, exit, or neglect. How do you feel using unfamiliar responses to conflict? Do you notice differences in how your partner responds to your communication?

6. Return to the conversation between William and Takisha that opened this chapter. Using what you've learned about ways of responding to relationship conflict, can you rewrite the interaction so that it is more productive? Is it possible to rewrite the interaction by changing only one person's (William or Takisha) communication, or must both partners change to change what happens between them?

References

Brehm, S. (1992). *Intimate relationships*. New York: McGraw-Hill.

Campbell, A. (1993). *Men, women, and aggression*. New York: Basic Books.

Crouter, A., & Helms-Erikson, H. (1997). Work and family from a dyadic perspective: Variations in inequality. In S. Duck (Ed.), *Handbook of personal relationships* (2nd ed., pp. 487–503). West Sussex, England: Wiley.

Gilligan, C. (1982). *In a different voice: Psychological theory and women's development*. Cambridge: Harvard University Press.

Gottman, J. (1979). *Marital interaction*. New York: Academic Press.

Gottman, J., & Carrère, S. (1994). Why can't men and women get along? Developmental roots and marital inequities. In D. Canary & L. Stafford (Eds.), *Communication and relational maintenance* (pp. 203–229). San Diego, CA: Academic Press.

Gottman, J., & Levenson, R. W. (1986). Assessing the role of emotion in marriage. *Behavioral Assessment, 8*, 31–48.

Gottman, J., Markman, H., & Notarius, C. (1977). The topography of marital conflict: A sequential analysis of verbal and nonverbal behavior. *Journal of Marriage and the Family, 39*, 461–477.

Heavy, C., Layne, C., & Christensen, A. (1993). Gender and conflict structure in marital interaction: A replication and extension. *Journal of Consulting and Clinical Psychology, 61*, 16–27.

Jones, E., & Gallois, C. (1989). Spouses' impressions of rules for communication in public and private marital conflicts. *Journal of Marriage and the Family, 51*, 957–967.

Klein, R., & Johnson, M. P. (1997). Strategies of couple conflict. In S. Duck (Ed.), *Handbook of personal relationships* (2nd ed., pp. 469–486). West Sussex, England: Wiley.

Maccoby, E. (1990). Gender and relationships: A developmental account. *American Psychologist, 45,* 513–520.

Rusbult, C. (1987). Responses to dissatisfaction in close relationships: The exit-voice-loyalty-neglect model. In D. Perlman & S. Duck (Eds.), *Intimate relationships: Development, dynamics, and deterioration* (pp. 209–238). London: Sage.

Rusbult, C., Zembrodt, I., & Iwaniszek, J. (1986). The impact of gender and sex-role orientation on responses to dissatisfaction in close relationships. *Sex Roles, 15,* 1–20.

Tavris, C. (1992). *The mismeasure of woman: Why women are not the better sex, the inferior sex, or the opposite sex.* New York: Simon & Schuster.

Wood, J. T. (1986). Different voices in relationship crises: An extension of Gilligan's theory. *American Behavioral Scientist, 29,* 273–301.

Wood, J. T. (1994). Gender and relationship crises: Contrasting reasons, responses, and relational orientations. In J. Ringer (Ed.), *Queer words, queer images: The (re)construction of homosexuality* (pp. 238–264). Albany: New York University Press.

| 19 |

BUT I THOUGHT YOU SAID
YOU LOVED ME

. . .

Understanding the Difference Between

Love and Commitment

I had known Sherry for two years when she came to my office last autumn. We met when she enrolled in my course in interpersonal communication. Sherry discovered a subject that fascinated her, so she changed her major to communication and she asked me to be her adviser.

Over the two years that followed, Sherry and I became friendly enough to share parts of our personal lives with each other. I tell her about the mischief my kitten Sadie regularly gets into, and she tells me how her mother is recovering following back surgery. She knows I worry about my 15-year-old nephew's infatuation with what I consider morbid stories and films, and I know that she's debating whether to apply to graduate school or look for a job after graduation.

When Sherry came into my office that autumn day she was visibly upset. It didn't take long to discover why: Her boyfriend, Jason, had just broken up with her.

"I just don't understand," she told me, shaking her head. "He said he loved me, and I believed him."

"Maybe he did love you. Maybe he does," I said.

"If he loved me, he wouldn't have broken up."

"Not necessarily. We can love people with whom we don't want to spend our lives."

"But that doesn't make any sense. If you love someone, you *do* want it to be forever. That's totally what love is," she insisted. "Jason just lied to me about loving me."

"Maybe; maybe not. What led you to think he wanted to be with you forever?" I asked.

"Because he said how much fun I was, and he was always talking about how much he enjoyed being with me."

"Did he say anything else — anything else about how he felt about you and the relationship?"

Sherry thought for a moment before answering. "Well, he said he liked to talk with me because I helped him sort out his ideas." She reviewed the relationship, then added, "And he said he felt really close to me."

"Did he ever say he planned to be with you next year? Did he ever talk about the two of you long-term?"

"Well, not exactly, but I assumed that he felt we were long term," she said. "After all, he said he loved me."

"Love and commitment to a future don't necessarily go hand in hand," I said gently.

"That's pretty much what Jason said. He said he did love me, but that didn't mean he wanted to settle down now," Sherry said. "He said he never tried to mislead me into thinking that we were long term."

"Perhaps he didn't."

"But he said he loved me," Sherry returned to her refrain. "And now he says he feels terrible that I'm hurt and that I feel like he betrayed me."

"Loving someone doesn't necessarily mean you want to spend your life with the person."

"I don't understand what you mean."

An hour later when Sherry left my office, she had a better understanding of Jason and their relationship, even if she didn't have the relationship she wanted and had assumed existed between them. Like many people, Sherry assumed love and commitment go together or are even the same thing. Not so.

In this chapter, we discuss differences between love and commitment. As we'll see, the two aren't equivalent. They mean distinct things. Even more important, they imply distinct futures for a relationship. When people don't understand the difference between love and commitment, they may be in for some unpleasant surprises.

Understanding the Misunderstanding

Sherry's misunderstanding of Jason's feelings is not uncommon. That's because intimacy can involve a range of different features, not all of which are linked to endurance. Academics in a variety of fields have conducted considerable research that helps us figure out just what is involved in intimate relationships. It seems that intimacy can involve any or all of three distinct qualities: passion, love, and commitment.

Passion

When many people think about intimacy, passion is what first comes to mind. Passion is an intensely positive feeling. It's why we feel butterflies in our stomach and like we're falling head over heels. It's why we feel we can't get enough of another person. Passion can be fast and furious; it can be exciting and exhausting.

Passion often involves powerful physical attraction. With a romantic interest we may want to kiss and be kissed, look into each other's eyes, to hold hands or link arms, or to engage in sexual activities. With a friend, we may want to hug and touch and share confidences. Although passion frequently includes strong erotic, sensual, or sexual feelings, physical arousal isn't the only way we experience passion.

Intensity is the crux of passion, and intensity may be emotional, spiritual, intellectual, physical, or a combination of these. Two people may feel passion when they engage in vigorous discussion of social issues or politics. We may feel deeply attracted to a person with whom we share central spiritual values. We may feel passion for a friend or sibling who has been with us through pivotal life experiences. Passionate feelings can also be aroused when we are with someone we find physically attractive and exciting. Passion is all these things. In our lives, we may be drawn intensely to others in many different ways.

Love

Love is feelings of closeness and comfort in the present moment. We feel comfortable with someone; we feel warm when we are together. Like

Jason, when we love someone we may say "I have so much fun with you," "I really like talking with you," and "I love you." And we may mean each of those statements, just as Jason may have.

Beverly Fehr is a psychologist who teaches and conducts research at the University of Winnipeg in Manitoba, Canada. Over the years, she and her colleagues have conducted a series of studies to clarify what love is. They report that for most Westerners, the core of love is feelings of contented companionship. In six separate studies, Fehr and her associates found that people who are asked what love is say it involves trust, caring, friendship, and respect. Fehr's respondents placed priority on being comfortable with an intimate and feeling close.

Far less central in people's descriptions of love is passion. Fehr and her colleagues report that many people do mention passion as part of love, but it is more peripheral than close, comfortable companionship. Most people seem to regard the intensity and yearning that characterize passion as desirable, but distinct from love. When they describe love and loving, they talk about feeling safe, contented, valued, and warm in a relationship.

Another important feature of love is that it is oriented to the present. Love is a feeling that is fueled by rewards and gratifications we receive from a relationship. Jason's love was kindled by the fun he had with Sherry and the value he got from talking with her. These were rewards that sparked his feelings of love. Yet all these feelings are confined to the present moment. Jason didn't say he wanted to have fun with Sherry for the rest of his life. He didn't say he wanted to talk with her in the years ahead. Because it is present oriented, love alone isn't a guarantee that a relationship will continue.

Commitment

As enjoyable as passion and love can be, they aren't the cornerstone of long-lasting relationships. The real cement is commitment, which is an intention to remain with a relationship. It is the decision or intention to continue a relationship. It is the assumption that there will be a future, regardless of problems and hard times.

An important study conducted in 1985 sheds light on the difference between love and commitment. Mary Lund's experience as a family therapist in southern California led her to suspect that there is something beyond passion and love, something that is a key to whether a relationship endures or wanes over time. To find out whether her hunch was correct,

Lund found 129 people who were at periods in their lives when geographical moves were likely. She asked the people to respond to written surveys at two times — once before the life change occurred and once after it occurred. The surveys measured what Lund's respondents thought and felt about their current romantic relationships. In addition, Lund asked her respondents what they gave to and got from the relationship.

Lund's findings are clear and important. Two of her results merit special attention. First, she reports that commitment is far better than passionate love in predicting the continuation of a relationship. In other words, the intention to stay together is a more powerful bond than strongly positive feelings alone. Recalling what Jason said to Sherry, we can see that he didn't make statements of commitment. Nothing in how he described his feelings reflected an orientation toward the future.

Lund's second important finding is that investments generate commitment. Investments are what we put into a relationship that we could not get back if the relationship ended. We invest material things such as time, money, and gifts. We also invest emotionally when we give another person our trust, share our fears and hopes, and make efforts to understand and support him or her. In short, we invest ourselves. According to Lund, when we do that, our intention to remain in a relationship escalates.

Passion is	*Love is*	*Commitment is*
Intense feeling or attraction	Feeling safe and comfortable with another person	A decision to stay with someone for the foreseeable future
Something that happens to us	Something that happens to us	An act of will; a decision
Driven by needs and desires	Stoked by rewards provided by relationship	Cultivated by investments in a relationship
Tied to present	Present oriented	Linked to future
Unstable; subject to mercurial change	Subject to fading if disappointments, costs, or hard times come	Sturdy enough to weather bad times, periods of apathy, and boredom

We may be fortunate enough to have passion, love, and commitment in our intimate relationships—at least some of the time. Chances are good, however, that most of us will experience times in perfectly healthy relationships when we don't feel passionate and when we don't feel loving or loved. There are moments in any relationship, even the best of them, when partners don't feel strong passion or love for each other. They may be preoccupied with individual concerns. They may have serious financial, health, or family problems that stifle feelings of affection and attraction. They may be intensely involved with personal projects at work or in the community. They may just be bored temporarily with themselves, each other, or the relationship. Such moments are to be expected in any serious, sustained union. If love and passion are the only reasons people are together, they are likely to come apart when love and passion fluctuate. But if commitment is the cement of the relationship, many couples endure the normal periods of languor and disappointment.

In reflecting on years of relationship counseling, psychiatrist Aaron Beck remarked that passion usually ebbs, at least temporarily, over the course of a long-term relationship. When it does, he said, partners' dedication to each other and the relationship is what holds a relationship together. Agreeing with Beck, psychologist Sharon Brehm says commitment is the bottom line of enduring relationships.

Are love and commitment entirely unrelated? Not necessarily. Ideally, love and commitment go together. As Lund pointed out, "Although love usually accompanied commitment, commitment and investments alone told more about the likelihood of a relationship lasting over time" (pp. 17–18). Surely, most of us hope for an enduring romantic relationship that is enlivened by love and passion. We want the security of constancy and the zing of passion—yet it doesn't always work out that way.

Half a Loaf

In many relationships, either love or commitment is not present. In some cases there is love, and perhaps passion as well, but commitment doesn't exist for any number of reasons. My friend Elaine was deeply in love with Bob, a man she had dated for two years. He wanted to get married—he was committed to a future. Elaine, however, couldn't commit to a life with Bob because he was Christian and she was Jewish. Although Bob was willing to have an interfaith marriage, that wasn't acceptable to Elaine. She could imagine a life only with a Jewish partner. Another friend said

Keeping Up

This is such a dumb time, Jack, to start talking about whether or not something is written in stone.

he loved his partner "as much as I think I'm capable of ever loving anyone," but he didn't feel ready to settle down. The timing was not right for commitment.

When I was an undergraduate my roommate Laura fell passionately in love with Lloyd whom she dated throughout her college years. Everyone who knew Laura and Lloyd assumed they would marry. But they didn't. They were incompatible for the very reasons they were drawn to each other. They were both inclined to emotional extremes. When they were both ebullient, they were wonderful together. But when they were in negative, dark moods, they were terrible to and for each other. Their relationship was an emotional rollercoaster, which took a toll on both of them. Laura said she couldn't live a life of those extremes. Later she married a man whose calm, steady disposition provided the emotional anchor she needed.

It is also possible to have commitment without love. The most obvious example of such relationships is arranged marriages, a practice that was once widespread and is still followed in some societies. Early in a child's life (and sometimes even before birth), the child's parents make an agreement with another set of parents that their children will wed. The boy and girl may or may not meet prior to the wedding day. Arranged marriages don't assume love is necessary for a successful union. The marriages are used to link families together, not to provide love to the individual children. Arranged marriages generally endure, primarily because they take place within cultures that do not allow divorce and that value collective interests above individual pleasure. And love may develop in marriages that are arranged without respect for the partners' feelings.

In other relationships, both love and passion were present at one point but they have subsided or even stopped. Commitment remains, perhaps "because of the children" or religious principles that forbid divorce or because neither person has found a new partner. And in many cases people stay together for reasons of convenience and practical considerations. A couple may have a nice home, savings, and a comfortable lifestyle that neither could sustain alone. One or both partners' careers might be jeopardized by divorce, so they maintain their marriage, although love and passion are no longer part of it.

The assumption that love is the basis of marriage is not universal, nor is the assumption that love and commitment always go together. What we assume marriage or family is and includes varies from culture to culture and over time across any single culture.

Improving Communication

Because intimate relationships affect us deeply, we want to be careful in how we build them and in what we assume about them. We also want to make sure that we and those we care about share understandings about feelings and the future of relationships.

Distinguish Among Passion, Love, and Commitment

One way to increase shared understanding about relationships is to recognize distinctions among passion, love, and commitment. Even if we hope that all three will grace our intimate relationships, it's wise to understand differences among them. Had Sherry grasped the distinction, she might not have assumed something that Jason never promised. She might also have considered carefully whether Jason was making investments equal to hers in their relationship. Because investments build and sustain commitment, they are a good gauge of whether someone envisions a future.

There are also actions Jason might have taken to reduce the possibility of misunderstanding. Had he understood the distinction between love and commitment, he might have more clearly explained what he did—and did not—feel for Sherry and what he did—and did not—assume about their future. He might also have noticed how much Sherry was investing in the relationship and realized that she was more committed than he was and more committed than was justified, given his feelings. We should understand that love doesn't necessarily equal commitment and commitment doesn't necessarily require love.

Communicate Openly About Relationships

A second guideline for diminishing misunderstandings about relationships is to communicate clearly. Open, honest communication is critical to mutual understanding of what a relationship is and where it is, is not, and may be heading. Understand the difference. If Jason had read this chapter and if he had wanted to be honest with Sherry, he might have said to her, "I have a great time with you, and I love you, but I'm not sure I see a long-term future for us or for me and anybody at this point in my life." Had Sherry and I had our conversation earlier, she might have asked Jason, "What do you mean when you say you love me? Does it mean you want us to stay together or that you are enjoying the relationship right now?"

It's not easy to engage in candid discussions of a relationship, especially if you aren't sure whether you and the other person feel the same way about it. To ask what another person means when she or he says "I love you" can be awkward and difficult. Such uncomfortable conversations are less painful, however, than discovering, as Sherry did, that a future you assumed would come about is not to be. Difficult dialogue is also less upsetting than learning, as Jason did, that a person you care about feels you betrayed and misled her or him.

Communication won't resolve all the differences between intimate partners. It is, however, one important cornerstone for understanding and healthy relationships.

Key Words

- commitment
- companionship
- future
- intimacy

- investments
- love
- passion
- rewards

Reflecting on This Chapter

1. Have you ever been in a relationship in which only one person was committed? How could you tell the commitment wasn't mutual? What were the signs before the breakup?

2. Think about a relationship to which you and another person were strongly committed. It could be a friendship or a romantic relationship. Can you identify specific investments (not rewards) each of you made in the relationship? Can you evaluate their importance in sustaining the relationship?

3. Have you ever loved someone to whom you didn't feel committed (didn't envision a definite future)? Compare your feelings in that relationship with your feelings in a relationship to which you were committed. What are the differences?

4. Can you remember a relationship in which you moved into commitment? How would you describe the transition from not feeling committed to feeling committed? How did the change affect interaction, security, and other facets of the relationship?

5. In the United States, if commitment occurs, it tends to follow love. Do you think the reverse order is possible — that love can follow commitment? Consider arranged marriages that still take place in some societies. Can two people who don't know each other when they marry grow to love each other?

6. How important is love for marriage or enduring commitments? Can relationships be healthy without love? Do you know of any enduring relationships in which commitment exists but love does not seem present? If so, how would you describe the relationships and the partners' reasons for staying in them?

7. Think about a current or past relationship to which you are or were committed (not just in love). What did you invest? What did your partner invest? What would you (or did you) lose if the relationship ended?

References

Beck, A. (1988). *Love is never enough*. New York: Harper & Row.

Bellah, R., Madsen, R., Sullivan, W., Swindler, A., & Tipton, S. (1985). *Habits of the heart: Individualism and commitment in American life*. Berkeley: University of California Press.

Brehm, S. (1992). *Intimate relationships* (2nd ed). New York: McGraw-Hill.

Button, C. M., & Collier, C. R. (1991, June). *A comparison of people's concepts of love and romantic love*. Paper presented at the Canadian Psychological Association Conference, Calgary, Alberta.

Fehr, B. (1988). Prototype analysis of the concepts of love and commitment. *Journal of Personality and Social Psychology, 55*, 557–579.

Fehr, B. (1993). How do I love thee? Let me consult my prototype. In S. W. Duck (Ed.), *Understanding relationship processes, 1: Individuals in relationships* (pp. 87–122). Newbury Park, CA: Sage.

Fehr, B., & Russell, J. A. (1991). Concept of love viewed from a prototype perspective. *Journal of Personality and Social Psychology, 60*, 425–438.

Hendrick, C., & Hendrick, S. (1988). Lovers wear rose-colored glasses. *Journal of Social and Personal Relationships, 5*, 161–184.

Johnson, D. J., & Rusbult, C. (1989). Resisting temptation: Devaluation of alternative partners as a means of maintaining commitment in close relationships. *Journal of Personality and Social Psychology, 57*, 967–980.

Luby, V., & Aron, A. (1990, July). *A prototype structuring of love, like, and being in love*. Paper presented at the Fifth International Conference on Personal Relationships, Oxford, UK.

Lund, M. (1985). The development of investment and commitment scales for predicting continuity of personal relationships. *Journal of Social and Personal Relationships, 2*, 3–23.

Sternberg, R. J. (1986). A triangular theory of love. *Psychological Review, 93*, 119–135.

Sternberg, R. J. (1987). Liking versus loving: A comparative evaluation of theories. *Psychological Bulletin, 102*, 331–335.

| 20 |

DON'T YOU WANT TO SPEND TIME WITH ME ANY MORE?

. . .

Understanding the

Autonomy–Connection Dialectic

Kate and Ron fell in love and were inseparable for several months. Then one day Kate told Ron she needed some space—some time alone. Ron felt hurt and confused because he assumed this was the beginning of the end of their relationship. What else could it mean when she doesn't want to be with him any more?

Doug and Bill had been seeing each other for a year when they decided to go to Europe together. After two weeks of touring and seeing the sights, they returned home and neither called the other for a week. Doug felt guilty that he didn't want to call or be with Bill after such a fabulous vacation. Bill felt confused that he had no inclination to see Doug, whom he had assumed would be his partner for life. He'd felt so close to Doug on the trip, but right now he doesn't want to be with him.

Martha is uncomfortable in her friendship with Corina. In all her previous friendships, Martha has maintained a high degree of independence. In fact, she's been told more than once that she's too independent. But ever since she met Corina a few weeks ago, they've been together incessantly—shopping, talking, visiting, and often calling after get-togethers. Martha wants to continue this friendship, but she's afraid of losing herself.

One of the most common and most confusing dynamics in friendships and romantic relationships is the tension between desires for autonomy and desires for closeness. Most of us have experienced wanting to be close to someone who, like Kate, demanded some space. Probably you've also felt like Doug and Bill—temporarily uninterested in seeing someone for whom you care deeply. And you can empathize with Martha if you've ever felt you were losing yourself in a relationship.

Although conflict between wanting to be close to someone and wanting to preserve independence is common, it isn't well understood. In fact, many people, like Doug and Bill, think something is wrong if they don't want to be with someone they love. And like Ron, we may feel a relationship is spiraling downward if a friend or romantic partner asks for space or doesn't want to spend much time with us. Because the tension between desires for autonomy and connection is not well understood, problems can arise. We may misinterpret what it means when someone wants space or when someone wants more togetherness than we do.

In this chapter, we focus on the normal, if sometimes unwelcome, tension between our needs for independence and interdependence. We see why we need both and why we and people we care about sometimes misunderstand each other when our desires are not coordinated at a particular time.

Understanding the Misunderstanding

Leslie Baxter is a professor of communication at the University of Iowa. For more than a decade she has devoted her professional energies to understanding recurrent tensions in close relationships. The tensions that interest Baxter are called dialectics, or relational dialectics.

Relational Dialectics

Relational dialectics consist of two contradictory impulses, needs, or desires that are present in relationships. Because the needs in a relational dialectic are contradictory, they generate tension. The two impulses in a dialectic are interdependent because they affect each other and often fuel each other. For example, Bill and Doug fulfilled their desires for together-ness by spending two weeks in intense connection. They ate, slept, toured, and did everything else together for two weeks. Because they had such intense connection during their trip, their needs for independence were not nurtured and reasserted themselves when the pair returned home. Conversely, after long periods of isolation that satisfy our desires for inde-pendence, we often seek to reconnect with intimates. The interplay between contradictory needs is normal and productive.

The Autonomy–Connection Dialectic

Of the many dialectical tensions that can surface in relationships, the most common and most potentially difficult tends to be the friction between desires for autonomy and connection. According to Baxter and her colleagues, all of us desire connections with others. We want to be part of something larger than our individual selves. We crave involvement in relationships with certain people. We also want to be part of our com-munities. We long to participate in meaningful relationships with others and to blend our own lives with those of special others.

At the same time, says Baxter, we have desires for autonomy. We all desire to be separate from others — intimates, social groups, and the larger community. We want to be distinct, our own person who is unique from others. We enjoy individual pursuits and interests, and we may treasure time alone to read, think, dream, and just be with ourselves. We cherish our individuality and we want others to recognize and respect it.

Tensions from Dialectics

Tension arises for two reasons. First, our needs for autonomy and connec-tion may feel contradictory or at odds with each other. Consequently, we may worry that our feelings (and the actions that follow them) are incon-sistent. Are we fickle if we want to be with someone sometimes and don't want to see her or him at other times? This is what bothered Bill and Doug. Neither man could understand how they could be so close for two weeks and then not seek the other out.

Second, at times our contradictory needs aren't coordinated with those of our close friends and romantic partners. Misunderstandings can arise when one person in an intimate relationship needs independence at the same time the other person craves connection. The person who seeks autonomy may feel suffocated by the other person's desires for connec-tion. Meanwhile, the person who wants greater closeness may feel

"Look, instead of constantly grading one another, let's make this a simple pass/fail relationship."

Carole Cable

shunned by a friend or romantic partner's desire for distance or personal space. Kate's desire for time alone was at odds with Ron's hunger for more intimate togetherness.

Understanding Dialectical Tension

The first thing to understand about dialectics is that contradictory needs are normal and part of all relationships. Romantic partners and close friends want both intimacy and individuality. The same is true in parent-child relationships. Children need to assert their independence from parents to define their individual identities; at the same time, children need the assurance and foundation of connection with parents. Can you imagine not experiencing either of the impulses in the autonomy-connection dialectic? Would it be healthy not to strive for independence and individuality? Would it be wholesome not to seek communion with others? Of course not. Both needs serve us well. Working in complementary fashion, they allow us to enter into meaningful relationships without sacrificing our individuality. Conversely, in tandem they allow us to retain our personal uniqueness without having to deny ourselves intimate connections with others.

The second thing to understand about all dialectics, including the autonomy-connection dialectic, is that they are ongoing. We never resolve them once and for all. Instead, dialectics are continuous processes in our lives and our relationships. Kate and Ron may reach an understanding that allows them to deal satisfactorily with the current tension from her desire for time alone and his desire for togetherness; Doug and Bill may get their fill of distance and reconnect comfortably; Martha and Corina may be able to renegotiate the intensity of their friendship so that it may continue without engulfing Martha.

The tension between desires for independence and connection, however, will resurface every so often as long as Kate and Ron, Doug and Bill, and Corina and Martha stay together in a sound, dynamic relationship. In fact, tensions between dialectical needs are continuous—they are basic threads in the fabric of human relationships. Only occasionally and only temporarily are tensions not felt in relationships. *Dialectical moments* is the term Baxter uses to refer to intervals in relationships that aren't marked by dialectical tension. The times when we don't feel tension between contradictory needs are more rare than the times when we do.

Marriage counselor Maggie Scarf believes that the tension between being one's own self and also being part of an intimate relationship is the major dilemma in most marriages. She also notes that couples who maintain healthy relationships must address this tension again and again and again. It doesn't go away, because our needs for individuality and togetherness don't go away as long as we are whole, healthy human beings. The only way the tension can be squelched once and for all is to repress either the desire for autonomy or the yearning for union with another. Although that solution might allow us to escape the tension between these two natural impulses, we would be less healthy and whole human beings.

A final point about all dialectics is that they generate change in our relationships. When we experience the tension between competing needs for autonomy and connection, we do something to relieve our discomfort and to preserve our wholeness, which is nourished by both needs. Martha's discontent with what's beginning to feel like a stifling closeness with Corina may lead Martha to spend time alone or with other friends. For her to experience discomfort is a good sign; her desires for autonomy are feeling stifled and they are letting her know it so she can act to satisfy her need for independence.

The tensions we experience between conflicting needs for individuality and merger with others are like symptoms of physical problems: they let us know when something isn't right for us, when some of our needs are unsatisfied. We need to pay attention and do something when we experience dialectical tensions. Although they may be uncomfortable, even painful at times, the tensions are wholesome indicators that we need to do something if we are to stay whole.

Gendered Patterns

Years ago there was a television commercial in which a mother tried to do something for her child. Wanting to establish independence, the child resisted her efforts to help him and said, "Mother, please, I'd rather do it myself." In the commercial, the child was a boy. That's appropriate because boys tend to be encouraged to be more independent than girls.

From birth, children are channeled into gendered patterns. Most parents leave sons alone more often and for longer periods of time than they leave daughters alone. Also, parents allow and often encourage sons to go outside to play, to move beyond the home and yard on their own. To define their identity as males, boys must distinguish themselves from their mothers who are usually the primary caregivers. These facets of most boys' socialization foster independence as being central to masculine identity, encouraging boys to give it greater priority than forming and sustaining connections with others.

In contrast, parents tend to keep daughters closer to home and more tied into relationships. Parents usually talk more to daughters than to sons, and they encourage daughters more than sons to be empathic and oriented toward others. Also, girls do not have to separate from mothers to establish their feminine identity. Instead, they can define themselves within the mother-child bond. Nancy Chodorow, a distinguished psychoanalyst, summarizes the impact of feminine socialization when she notes that it leads many girls and women to place greater emphasis on relationships or connection than on independence.

It would be incorrect to think that males want only independence and females want only connection. The reality is that all of us need both. However, there are general differences between the degree of each that many women and men desire and find comfortable. In intimate relationships, men tend to want more independence than women want or find comfortable. It's equally common for women to want more connection, or togetherness, than their male partners seek or find comfortable. These, of course, are general patterns and individual women and men may depart from them.

The Demand-Withdraw Pattern

So common is the friction between partners' desires for different degrees of autonomy and connection that clinicians have given it a name: the *demand-withdraw pattern.* The demand-withdraw pattern is a cycle in which one partner's communication to enhance intimacy provokes countering withdrawal communication from the other partner. Research shows that women more often than men seek to create closeness and men more often than women withdraw from it.

One partner (usually, but not always a woman) seeks to deepen connection by talking intimately.

The other partner (usually, but not always a man) experiences this as a demand for more closeness than is wanted, so the second partner withdraws to preserve autonomy.

The more the first partner demands intimacy, the more the second one withdraws from it.

The more the second partner withdraws from closeness, the more the first one pursues.

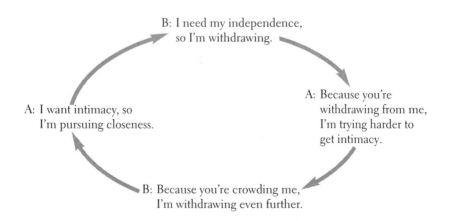

B: I need my independence, so I'm withdrawing.

A: I want intimacy, so I'm pursuing closeness.

A: Because you're withdrawing from me, I'm trying harder to get intimacy.

B: Because you're crowding me, I'm withdrawing even further.

In the demand-withdraw pattern, each person perceives the other as the instigator and himself or herself as reacting to the other's action. A thinks she is pursuing because B is withdrawing. B thinks he is withdrawing because A is pursuing. Both A and B are uncomfortable because their individual desires for autonomy and connection are not being satisfied.

In addition to the discomfort arising from unmet individual desires, there is another problem: two misunderstandings about what is happening. First, the communicators don't share an understanding of who is the initiator and who is the reactor in the demand-withdraw cycle. As long as A thinks B is the initiator and B thinks A is the initiator, the couple doesn't share meaning for what is happening between them. If each could perceive the cycle as one without a clear initiator or reactor, they might feel less defensive.

A second misunderstanding arises if partners interpret each other according to their own meanings, not those of their partner. If A values a lot of connection, she may interpret B's withdrawal as a rejection of her (notice the operation of constitutive rules here). In B's mind, however, he may be very committed to A even when he doesn't want interaction. And B's stronger desires for autonomy may lead him to interpret A's pursuit of connection as dependence. In A's mind, however, she feels her individuality is safe even when she is immersed in the relationship. In other words, desires for autonomy and connection may mean different things to different people.

Responding to Dialectical Tension

Baxter and her colleagues identify four ways that intimate partners deal with the tensions arising from contradictory needs. Some partners opt to satisfy one of the conflicting needs and to repress the other. Kate and Ron may decide to nourish togetherness and stifle their needs for independence. This type of response to dialectical tension denies one of the basic needs so it may not be healthy for individuals or relationships. Research shows that this method generally reduces satisfaction with relationships.

A second way to manage dialectical tension is to assign autonomy to one sphere of life (perhaps professional activities) and togetherness to a different sphere of life (perhaps family). This response addresses both needs, so it doesn't force a choice between the two. This method can be effective as long as intimates don't feel the need to nurture both needs in the same sphere of life.

A third response to dialectical tension is to compromise. Partners who choose this response try to meet each need enough to forestall debilitating discomfort, but they do not meet either need fully. Bill and

Doug might decide that on future vacations each of them will pursue independent schedules during the days and get together only in the evenings. This response doesn't allow Bill and Doug to vacation completely independently, nor does it allow them to immerse themselves in togetherness while on vacation. Instead, it opts for a compromise between the needs.

Finally, partners may choose to reframe dialectics so that they don't experience the different needs as contradictory. They communicate to redefine their needs as complementary. A good example of this comes from a study I did with several of my colleagues. In our investigation we asked people in established relationships to tell us how they perceived differences between them. A number of the couples told us that they perceived their differences as enriching their relationships. For these couples, differences were signs that each person's individuality was intact. In turn, that knowledge made them feel more comfortable in being deeply connected. At the same time, their awareness of the firm connection between them made individuality nonthreatening.

Improving Communication

Much of what we've already discussed provides clues as to how we might manage misunderstandings that often surround dialectical tensions in our relationships. Pulling together what we've covered, we can identify three guidelines for reducing misunderstanding and discomfort that arise when partners feel conflicting needs for autonomy and connection.

Recognize Dialectical Tensions as Normal

A first guideline is to realize that fluctuations in needs and the tensions that accompany them are normal. There is nothing unnatural or unhealthy about wanting closeness sometimes and independence at other times. This is normal for all of us. Consequently, we shouldn't criticize ourselves for being motivated by each need at different times. Also, we shouldn't reproach our friends and romantic partners for not always wanting the same amounts of closeness and independence that we may want. Sometimes partners' needs aren't synchronized. This can be unsettling, but it doesn't mean something is wrong with either person or with the relationship.

Express Your Feelings Clearly

A second guideline is to communicate clearly about your feelings regarding autonomy and closeness. It's foolish to assume that others understand what our needs mean to us. They may understand what the need for autonomy feels like to them, but that may not mirror what it means to us. Remember that Kate told Ron she needed some space without explaining to him what that implied about her commitment to the relationship. Ron might have been less hurt and more accepting of her need for independence had Kate said, "Right now I need some time alone. I'm still in love with you and I want us to continue, but I need some time with just myself." In the demand-withdraw pattern, B might have said to A, "Apparently we're not on the same wavelength right now. I'm feeling the need to be undisturbed for a while. Let me have some quiet time now and tomorrow we'll do something together."

Enlarge Your Ways of Responding to Dialectical Tensions

Finally, we might improve our relationships if we were to experiment with alternative ways of responding to dialectical tensions. Most of us respond in relatively habituated ways. Whatever we've done in the past is likely to be what we do in the present, often without asking if there are more constructive and satisfying ways we might behave. To avoid being stuck in your habituated ways of behaving, reflect on your usual responses to dialectical tensions and experiment with alternative responses.

In this chapter you've learned about different ways of managing dialectical tensions. This information provides you with the basis for experimenting with new responses to the friction between desires for autonomy and connection. Try out responses other than your usual ones. Talk with your intimates about how you manage dialectical tensions and how you might manage them better.

Contradictory needs within and between individuals are normal in all relationships. They are also healthy because they generate change that keeps relationships and individuals from becoming stagnant. Less healthy are the misunderstandings that arise when partners do not communicate about their needs. Partners can minimize the frequency and severity of these misunderstandings if they commit to talking honestly and sensitively about needs and how we can meet them.

Key Words

- autonomy-connection
- demand-withdraw pattern
- dialectical moment
- dialectical tension
- gendered patterns
- relational dialectics
- response to dialectical tensions

Reflecting on This Chapter

1. Think about a close friendship and a romantic relationship in your life. They may be either current or past relationships. Reflect on the ways in which you met your needs for independence and your needs for connection in each relationship. How satisfied are (or were) you with how you managed the tension between needs?

2. How much autonomy do you desire? How much connection is comfortable for you? Reflecting on your experiences in relationships, can you determine whether one of the needs is consistently stronger than the other? Are your needs for autonomy and connection consistent with gendered patterns discussed in this chapter?

3. If you wanted to encourage more autonomy in girls and more interdependence in boys, how would you do it? In what ways might you depart from conventional parenting practices in an effort to alter the typical outcomes of those practices?

4. Have you ever experienced the demand-withdraw pattern? If so, were you the pursuer or the withdrawer, or have you held both positions at different times? Think back on your experiences to recall how you felt. Did you feel rejected if you wanted intimacy when a partner wanted independence? Did you feel smothered if you wanted time away from a partner who was seeking intimacy? Did you talk with your partner(s) about your feelings?

5. Think about your needs for autonomy and connection during your life and in different relationships. Are your desires for both autonomy and

connection consistent, or do they vary at different times and in diverse relationships?

6. Can you trace the tension from the autonomy-connection dialectic in the relationship between you and your parents? How did/do you express and enact your desires for autonomy? How did/do your parents respond?

7. This chapter suggests that partners should communicate with each other to explain what needs for autonomy and connection mean to them. Try to articulate what those needs feel like when you experience them. What words can you use to help your intimates understand your feelings on your own terms?

References

Baxter, L. A. (1988). A dialectical perspective on communication strategies in relationship development. In S. Duck (Ed.), *Handbook of personal relationships* (pp. 257–273). New York: Wiley.

Baxter, L. A. (1990). Dialectical contradictions in relationship development. *Journal of Social and Personal Relationships, 7,* 69–88.

Baxter, L. A. (1993). The social side of personal relationships: A dialectical analysis. In S. Duck (Ed.), *Understanding relationship processes, 3: Social context and relationships* (pp. 13–165). Newbury, CA: Sage.

Baxter, L. A., & Montgomery, B. M. (1996). *Relating: Dialogues and dialectics.* New York: Guilford Press.

Baxter, L. A., & Simon, E. P. (1993). Relationship maintenance strategies and dialectical contradictions. *Journal of Social and Personal Relationships, 10,* 225–242.

Beck, A. (1988). *Love is never enough.* New York: Harper & Row.

Bergner, R. M., & Bergner, L. L. (1990). Sexual misunderstanding: A descriptive and pragmatic formulation. *Psychotherapy, 27,* 464–467.

Chodorow, N. (1978). *The reproduction of mothering: Psychoanalysis and the sociology of gender.* Berkeley: University of California Press.

Christensen, A., & Heavey, C. (1990). Gender and social structure in the demand/withdraw pattern in marital conflict. *Journal of Personality and Social Psychology, 59,* 73–81.

Crouter, A. C., & Helms-Erickson, H. (1997). In S. Duck (Ed.), *Handbook of personal relationships* (2nd ed., pp. 487–503). West Sussex, England: Wiley.

Goldsmith, D. (1990). A dialectical perspective on the expression of autonomy and connection in romantic relationships. *Western Journal of Speech Communication, 54,* 537–556.

Heavy, C., Layne, C., & Christensen, A. (1993). Gender and conflict structure in marital interaction: A replication and extension. *Journal of Consulting and Clinical Psychology, 61,* 16–27.

James, K. (1989). When twos are really threes: The triangular dance in couple conflict. *Australian and New Zealand Journal of Family Therapy, 10,* 179–186.

Montgomery, B. M. (1992). Communication as the interface between couples and culture. In S. A. Deetz (Ed.), *Communication yearbook* (Vol. 15, pp. 476–508). Newbury Park, CA: Sage.

Montgomery, B. M. (1993). Relationship maintenance versus relationship change: A dialectical dilemma. *Journal of Social and Personal Relationships, 10,* 205–224.

Rawlins, W. (1989). A dialectical analysis of the tensions, functions, and strategic challenges of communication in young adult friendships. In J. Anderson (Ed.), *Communication yearbook* (Vol. 12, pp. 157–189). Newbury Park, CA: Sage.

Rawlins, W. (1992). *Friendship matters: Communication, dialectics, and the life course.* New York: Walter de Gruyter.

Scarf, M. (1987). *Intimate partners: Patterns in love and marriage.* New York: Random House.

Wood, J. T., Dendy, L., Dordek, E., Germany, M., & Varallo, S. (1994). Dialectic of difference: A thematic analysis of intimates' meanings for differences. In K. Carter & M. Presnell (Eds.), *Interpretive approaches to interpersonal communication* (pp. 115–136). New York: SUNY Press.

| 21 |

PUTTING IT ALL TOGETHER

· · ·

W e've come a long way since the opening chapter in which we launched our study of misunderstandings in human communication. You've gained insight into some of the ways people differ in how they communicate and reasons for these differences. You've also discovered that differences in how we communicate can foster misunderstanding, tension, and ill will between people and social groups. Especially important, you've gleaned suggestions for ways to reduce misunderstandings that hurt individuals and jeopardize our collective well-being.

In these final pages we pull together key themes that weave through our discussions in this book. Our goal is to step back from the particularities of specific misunderstandings in order to see the big picture. Here we focus on three themes and one challenge that integrate and summarize the insights presented in the previous chapters.

Differences in Communication Arise from Personal and Social Experiences

One central theme of this book is that each of us reflects the range of personal and social experiences that make up our lives. Humans are not like the acorn, which can only become an oak tree. We are not born with an innate, unalterable genetic blueprint that preordains what we will become. Instead, we have the capacity to grow into many different things and develop an infinite variety of perspectives, skills, and interests.

Some of us grow into people who use chopsticks, speak Korean, and believe common concerns take priority over individuals' interests. Others of us grow into people who use knives and forks, speak English, and believe each person looks out for himself or herself first. We are exposed to and thus come to appreciate different kinds of music, language, and nonverbal behavior. We grow up in diverse families and friendship circles that teach us an array of ways to listen, engage in conflict, support others, and relate the events in our days. The experiences and relationships that frame our lives direct which of our many possibilities are brought to fruition and which never unfold.

We enter the world as potentials, and those potentials are shaped and reshaped throughout our lifetime. Some of our potentials are realized. Perhaps you learned to play an instrument, repair cars, and enjoy Greek food. As a communicator you may have learned to assert yourself, appreciate rap music, and enjoy talking about relationships. Other potentials are not realized. You may not have learned to play golf, enjoy opera, or eat sushi. As a communicator, you may not have learned to participate in call-response interaction, use ASL, appreciate country music, or express your feelings openly.

Both our realized and unrealized potentials reflect our life experiences. This is as true of our communication as it is of other aspects of ourselves. How we communicate is intimately related to the personal and social influences that have sculpted our personalities. Understanding this is a critical foundation of effective living, in general, and effective communication, in particular. Once we realize that how individuals communicate reflects their unique socialization and the contexts of their lives, we are able to see differences among humans for what they are — the product of life experience. Conversely, we are less likely to misinterpret differences for what they are not — inadequacies, oddities, deficiencies, inferiorities.

Effective Communicators Address Misunderstandings

A second theme is that differences in how we've learned to communicate often foster misunderstandings. This is natural, even inevitable. Yet it is neither natural nor inevitable to resign ourselves to misunderstandings and their fallout in personal and social life. There is a great deal that we can do to diminish misunderstandings in our interactions with others. In this book we've explored a number of ways to deal with differences and the misunderstandings they invite. We can summarize what we've learned about this theme in three guidelines that help us recognize, understand, and unravel many of the inevitable misunderstandings that arise when people communicate.

Recognize That People Communicate in Many Different Ways

First, effective communicators do not assume that everyone thinks, feels, and communicates as they do. To make that assumption would be ethnocentric (as well as egocentric). Our discussion in preceding chapters makes clear that what people think and feel, how they communicate, and the meanings they hold result from their personal and social experiences. We should also recognize that personal and social experiences vary widely among humans.

How we communicate seems natural and right and reasonable to us because we were socialized to see our style of communicating as normal. In spite of this perspective, our ways of communicating are actually arbitrary. They aren't "normal" or "right" in an absolute sense, nor are they necessarily more reasonable than other ways of interacting. Communication that differs from our own is equally arbitrary, equally learned, and equally reasonable, given the circumstances of others' lives.

Explain What You Mean, Want, Think, and Feel

Second, effective communicators do not presume that others do or should know what they feel, think, mean, and want. It's unrealistic to believe that someone without your unique experiences understands you perfectly. The most poisonous attitudes for relationships are expressed in phrases such as "If I have to ask, it's not worth having," "If Ann really loved me, she'd know what I mean," and "Chris should know what I want without my having to tell him."

Healthier attitudes for relationships are "Because I care about Ann, I'll tell her what I want and mean," and "Because Chris cares about me, he will want to learn what I think, feel, need, and want." These attitudes reflect the wisdom of knowing that others cannot be expected to know your mind, heart, and spirit. In addition, these attitudes motivate you to give others information they need—and have no reason to know on their own—to understand you.

Ask—Don't Assume—What Others Mean, Want, Think, and Feel

Extending the second guideline, a third principle for effective communication is to metacommunicate, or talk about how we communicate. Confirming, satisfying communication does not happen automatically. It is an accomplishment that results from skill, understanding, knowledge, and a commitment to understanding others. Couples have to talk through differences in constitutive rules to develop shared codes of meaning for their relationships. Friends and family members need to discuss their needs for autonomy and connection in order to generate ways of fulfilling each person's needs. People who identify with diverse social groups benefit by exploring not only differences in communication styles but also the cultural values that underlie those differences. Metacommunication is a key to individual growth through enlarged understanding between people.

These three guidelines provide a good foundation for addressing differences and the misunderstandings they can foster. Committing to these as principles will allow you to recognize and diminish many of the normal tensions that arise when people interact.

Respect for Diversity Is Critical for Personal Growth and the Health of Our World

A third prominent theme of this book is that effective communicators respect the range of lifestyles, values, and ways of communicating that make up our world. The emphasis on respecting diversity is not an effort to be politically correct. Rather, it stems from a deep conviction that positive regard for diversity is essential for us individually and collectively. When differences are not honored, we all lose. The national fragmentation and countless lives lost in former Yugoslavia are grim testimony to what happens when people cannot respect differences. We do not need more Yugoslavias.

Respecting differences among people and their communication styles docs not necessarily require us to incorporate others' ways into our own lives. We may choose to adopt some customs and communication practices of others because we find them valuable and enriching. For example, I've come to appreciate some of the grace and sensitivity to others that is typical of many Asian cultures, and I find it useful in tempering the assertive individuality that Western socialization encouraged in me.

We may also decide that we don't want to adopt some communication practices of others. I still am not a fan of gangsta rap and I don't appreciate interruptions when I am trying to speak, but I've learned to accept those communicative practices as legitimate, though different from the ones I learned and choose to embrace in my life. There is an important distinction between judging a specific kind of communication as wrong or bad and judging it as something you don't choose to practice personally. That is a distinction that shows respect for differences.

The Challenge of Our Era

Our era has been described as one of crisis. Many social commentators assert that we are confronting a social and moral crisis as we seek to accommodate differences in ways that neither oppress individuals nor rip the social fabric asunder. Perhaps we do face a crisis. If so, maybe that's a good thing. The Chinese word for crisis combines the symbols for danger and opportunity.

There are a number of serious dangers in the crisis we confront today as we struggle to participate in a pluralistic world. We may be tempted to succumb to ethnocentric thinking, which can only heighten divisiveness and ill will among people. Or we may settle for an uneasy, grudging tolerance of differences, which would not help us create a healthy, vibrant world in which everyone's heritage is respected. Another danger is that individuals may identify with particular social groups to the exclusion of seeing themselves as part of the larger whole. Any of these choices precludes the opportunities inherent in crisis.

And the opportunities are great. On the brink of a new millennium, we have the chance to create a richer, better world than has ever existed. We can build a world in which differences flourish, yet not at the cost of commonalities. Wholeness can grow from distinct parts that work together in harmony. In a speech to the World Future Society, Harlan Cleveland urged people around the world to learn how to be different together. Different. Together. Both.

My hope for you, and myself, and all of us is that we will work together to build a world that is respectful, equitable, generous, and compassionate for everyone. This is a world in which differences don't necessarily mean divisions. It is a world in which people respect their own and one another's heritage, values, and ways of communicating. It is a world in which individuals don't feel compelled to choose between loyalty to particular groups and identification with a larger culture. It is a world in which we recognize and celebrate both our similarities and our differences. That kind of world was what poet laureate Maya Angelou had in mind when she wrote *Human Family*:

> I note the obvious differences
> Between each sort and type
> But we are more alike, my friends,
> Than we are unalike.
> We are more alike, my friends,
> Than we are unalike.

The differences among us should not obscure our likenesses. Surely we all want personal growth, relationships that nurture us, and respect from ourselves and others. Surely we share a vision of a world in which both our differences and our similarities can flourish. Such a world is not beyond our reach. It is a way of living that we can collaboratively create. This is the remarkable, unprecedented opportunity of our era. We can

realize a better world for ourselves and one another if we only summon the commitment to do so.

We are more alike, my friends, than we are unalike.

Reflecting on This Chapter

1. Discuss one of this chapter's key points: Differences don't necessarily mean divisions. Reflect on your own experiences in dealing with differences among people. When was your awareness of differences accompanied by a sense of division? When was your awareness of differences not associated with division? What makes the difference between the two kinds of situations?

2. U.S. currency is imprinted with the Latin phrase "E pluribus unum," which means "from many, one." Is this a good motto for a country? Do you view it as consistent with the themes of this chapter and the book as a whole?

3. Elaborate the vision of society sketched in the final pages of this chapter. Imagine a world in which differences don't mean divisions and in

which individuals don't feel they have to choose between loyalty to particular groups and a larger culture. What would it take to realize that vision of society? What changes in education, media, and interpersonal communication would facilitate that vision?

4. Call to mind one or two crises that you've encountered in your life. Can you identify both dangers and opportunities that were present in the crises? Do you think that all crises harbor both dangers and opportunities?

5. In this and previous chapters, metacommunication has been recommended as a way to address misunderstandings. Researchers caution that when carried to extremes, metacommunication creates problems of its own. Marital counselors report that couples sometimes get locked into metacommunication and this diverts them from addressing whatever topic they were originally discussing. What guidelines might you suggest to reduce the likelihood that people will get locked into metacommunication?

References

Angelou, M. (1990). Human family. *I shall not be moved.* New York: Random House.

Boulding, K. (1990). *Building a global civic culture.* Syracuse, NY: Syracuse University Press.

Campbell, J., with Toms, M. (1990). *An open life.* New York: Harper & Row.

Cleveland, H. (1995, March–April). The limits to cultural diversity. *The Futurist,* pp. 23–26.

Erickson, E. (1968). *Identity, youth, and crisis.* New York: W. W. Norton.

Gudykunst, W. B., & Ting-Toomey, S. (1988). *Culture and interpersonal communication.* Newbury Park, CA: Sage.

Rosaldo, R. (1989). *Culture and truth: The remaking of social analysis.* Boston: Beacon.

Rothenburg, P. (Ed.). (1995). *Race, class and gender in the United States.* New York: St. Martin's Press.

GLOSSARY

Afrocentricity The set of beliefs, values, and cultural heritage of African Americans.

autonomy-connection dialectic The tension arising from contradictory yet normal needs to be independent of others and to be close to others.

braggadocio Extreme boasting used to demonstrate wit, humor, and verbal artistry; practiced primarily by African Americans. Also called *woofin'*.

brute facts Phenomena before humans attach meanings to them.

buffer zone The respite created by allowing someone who is stressed or tired not to meet his or her usual responsibilities.

call and response A communication pattern in which a speaker calls out to listeners and listeners respond by calling back. The call and response pattern is more often practiced by Africans and African Americans than by other groups.

censorship Silencing communication (verbal or nonverbal) because it is considered offensive.

classifying One function of communication; a way of organizing perceptions of phenomena.

cognitive schemata Mental structures that individuals use to organize perceptions. Four types of schemata are prototypes, personal constructs, stereotypes, and scripts.

commitment The decision to stay with a relationship; not synonymous with love. Commitment is fueled by investments in a relationship.

communication A dynamic process that occurs within systems, involving efforts to share meanings and thus create understanding.

communication rules Guidelines that shape how individuals communicate and interpret the communication of others. Communication rules include both constitutive and regulative rules.

constitutive rules Guidelines that define what counts as what in communication. Constitutive rules define such things as what kind of communication counts as showing respect, supporting others, and being rude.

content level of meaning The information in a message based on the literal or denotative meaning of the message.

contexts The environment within which communication occurs. Contexts for communication are multiple and include cultures, social groups, situations, settings, relationships, and times. All parts of communication are interconnected and affect one another.

culture   The interconnected system of institutions, structures, and practices that make up the way of life of a group of people.

Deaf   The cultural and linguistic group made up of persons who cannot hear.

deaf   The medical condition of being unable to hear.

defining   One function of communication; naming what exists and what it means.

demand-withdraw pattern   A progressive cycle in relationships, in which one partner demands increasing intimacy and the other partner progressively withdraws from intimacy.

dialectical moment   Intervals in personal relationships that are free of dialectical tensions. Dialectical moments cannot be sustained.

dialectical tension   The friction or unease that arises when people in a relationship feel contradictory needs.

dynamism   The quality of changing, evolving, moving ever forward. Human communication is dynamic.

Ebonics   A grammatically consistent and rule-governed form of language believed to have roots in West Africa. The word *Ebonics* is based on two root terms, *ebony* and *phonics*.

economic standing   Status based on current income and assets and the assumption of economic security or insecurity. Also called economic class, socioeconomic class, class, and social class.

essentialize   To make the assumption that a characteristic or set of characteristics is the essence—the essential nature—of all members of a group.

ethnocentrism   The use of one's own social and cultural groups as the standard for interpreting everyone.

evaluating   One function of communication; takes place when language or nonverbal behavior expresses the value, worth, or merit attached to phenomena.

exit   One of four responses to conflict. An active and generally destructive tendency to leave conflict, either by physically leaving or by psychologically removing oneself.

expressive   The view of communication as a means of sharing thoughts and feelings and building connections with others.

First Amendment   The amendment to the United States Constitution that guarantees all citizens of the United States the right to freedom of religion, speech, and the press.

gender   The set of social meanings attached to biological sex. Gender differs among cultures and social groups.

hate speech   Spoken communication that has the effect of demeaning others.

hearing   The physiological process that occurs when sound waves hit eardrums. Hearing is not the same as listening.

Horatio Alger myth   The belief that in the United States all individuals rise on the basis of their personal abilities, achievements, and merits.

implicit personality theory   The assumption that certain qualities go with other qualities in personalities.

incivility   Verbally or nonverbally expressed lack of courtesy and respect for others, including their identities and rights.

inequity The imbalance that exists when one individual in a relationship invests more and/or receives fewer benefits than the other individual in the relationship.

instrumental The view of communication as a tool to accomplish particular ends, such as resolving problems and giving advice.

investments What individuals put into a relationship that could not be recovered if the relationship were to end.

invisible work Unnoticed work; often housework or caring for children or other family members.

language Verbal communication that reflects and expresses the values of cultures and social groups and that shapes individuals' perceptions of phenomena.

levels of meaning The two distinct kinds of meaning that occur in communication. Meaning is expressed on both content and relationship levels.

liking One dimension of the relationship level of meaning. Liking (or disliking) concerns the degree of positive or negative feelings expressed between communicators.

listening A complex and active process that involves being mindful, physically receiving messages, selectively perceiving aspects of messages, organizing perceptions, interpreting others' communication, responding, and remembering.

listening noises Interjections that show interest in others' communication and encourage them to continue talking.

love Feelings of closeness in the present moment. Love is fueled by rewards and is not synonymous with commitment.

loyalty One of four responses to conflict; a passive, often constructive tendency to remain quietly loyal to another and to a relationship.

mainstreaming Attempts to integrate minority groups into the larger majority population.

male generic terms Language that literally refers only to males. *Chairman* and *policeman* are examples of male generic terms.

meaning The significance persons attach to communication based on the perceptions, interpretations, and values of their standpoints. Meanings of communication are multiple, having both content and relationship levels.

metacommunication Communication that is about other communication. Metacommunication allows people to comment on patterns of interaction and to alter them if desired.

mindfulness A decision to be fully present and attentive to others and to what is happening in a particular moment.

misunderstandings One result of failure to share meaning in communication. Misunderstandings often reflect personal differences and/or differences in communicators' social and cultural groups.

monitoring Noticing and regulating how we act and communicate.

muntu The African word for *mankind*.

neglect One of four responses to conflict; a passive, generally destructive tendency to minimize problems and tensions and to avoid discussing them.

nommo   The magical power that members of many traditional African societies believe inheres in words.

nonverbal communication   All communication that is not words themselves. Nonverbal communication includes a range of behaviors such as gestures, facial expressions, use of space, touch, accent, pronunciation, and inflection.

oralism   A movement that advocates teaching deaf children to communicate orally based on the assumption that learning to speak would help them participate effectively in societies where most people speak and hear.

paternalism   The effort to take care of others who are assumed to need guidance or special help.

personal constructs   One type of cognitive schemata used in the process of organizing perceptions. Personal constructs are bi-polar measuring sticks used to classify others; for example, selfish-unselfish and honest-dishonest.

personal differences   One source of misunderstandings in communication, arising from individuals' unique backgrounds, experiences, values, and beliefs.

persons with disabilities   Individuals who have some disability or disabilities. This term is preferable to "disabled person," because the former does not suggest that the individual's personhood is disabled.

playing the dozens   A ritualized exchange of insults in which each person tries to outdo the other with verbal artistry. Also called *joanin'*.

power   One dimension of the relationship level of meaning. Power reflects whether communicators see themselves as equals or as one person having greater power than another.

prototypes   One type of cognitive schemata used in the process of organizing perceptions. Prototypes are the models of a category of people. The person who is an ideal friend is the prototype for the category *friends*.

psychological responsibility   The obligation to remember, coordinate, and oversee matters relating to homes and taking care of children and other family members.

regulative rules   Guidelines for when and with whom it is appropriate to communicate about specific topics.

relational dialectics   Contradictory needs or impulses that operate in all relationships. Relational dialectics often create tensions and also move relationships forward.

relationship level of meaning   Expresses how communicators feel about each other and what relationship they have. The three dimensions of the relationship level of meaning are responsiveness (or lack of responsiveness), liking (or disliking), and power (or control).

residential schools   Educational institutions in which minority students live and learn together. Some deaf individuals attend residential schools.

responsiveness   One dimension of the relationship level of meaning; how aware of and involved with another one person appears to be.

retreat response   The refusal to comment on anyone or anything outside of personal experience and identity.

Sapir-Whorf hypothesis   The hypothesis advanced by Edwin Sapir and Benjamin Whorf that language shapes what we perceive and think.

scripts   One type of cognitive schemata used in the process of organizing perceptions. Scripts are guides to action that tell us what we and others should do and how our actions will unfold sequentially in particular situations.

second shift   The domestic work and caretaking responsibilities done after a full shift of work outside the home.

self-serving bias   The tendency of an individual to recognize what she or he does more than what others do; and/or the tendency to credit oneself for what we do well and attribute our failures or poor performance to others or to circumstances.

signifyin'   Speaking indirectly, rather than directly, to criticize another.

small talk   Communication that is about day-to-day matters and issues. Although called "small," research shows this kind of talk is central to healthy, enduring personal relationships.

social groups   Collections of individuals who share ways of perceiving, communicating, and interpreting actions.

social location   Individuals' places within particular social communities that influence how they think and act, as well as how they perceive others, situations, and events.

standpoint   The perspective shaped by and common to members of specific social groups that are defined by gender, race-ethnicity, sexual orientation, age, religion, economic class, and other factors.

standpoint theory   A commonsense explanation of differences which holds that members of discrete social groups differ in their perceptions, understandings, and communication styles.

stereotypes   One type of cognitive schemata used in the process of organizing perceptions; predictive generalizations of what others will do based on the groups into which we classify them.

stereotyping   The process of judging individuals on the basis of what is known or believed about groups to which they belong.

systems   The environment within which communication occurs. Systems for communication are multiple and include cultures, social groups, situations, settings, relationships, and times. All parts of communication are interconnected and affect one another.

totalizing   The practice of defining someone or something by a single quality, as if that one quality were the whole of the person or thing.

voice   One of four responses to conflict; an active, generally constructive effort to talk about tensions and problems.

TEXT CREDITS

Chapter 8

Page 104: Words and music by Ice T and Johnny (Sleepy John) Rivers. Copyright ©1990 Colgems-EMI Music and Rhyme Syndicate Music. All rights controlled and administered by Colgems-EMI Music Inc. and Rhyme Syndicate Music. All rights reserved. International copyright secured. Used by permission. Page 105: Words and music by Luther Campbell. Copyright ©1992 BMI. All rights reserved. Used by permission.

Chapter 10

Page 137: AXIS Center for Public Awareness of People with Disabilities. Used with permission. Page 140: Adapted from "Breaking Old Patterns, Weaving New Ties: Alliance Building," by Margo Adair and Sharon Howell, published by Tools for Change, P.O. Box 14141, San Francisco, CA 94114 ($7.00).

Chapter 21

Page 282: From *I Shall Not Be Moved* by Maya Angelou. Copyright ©1990 by Maya Angelou. Reprinted by permission of Random House, Inc.

INDEX